SHARI'A LAW IN COMMERCIAL AND BANKING ARBITRATION

AF763115

To my parents

Shari'a Law in Commercial and Banking Arbitration

Law and Practice in Saudi Arabia

ABDULRAHMAN YAHYA BAAMIR

Jeddah, Saudi Arabia

Routledge
Taylor & Francis Group
LONDON AND NEW YORK

First published 2010 by Ashgate Publishing

Published 2016 by Routledge
2 Park Square, Milton Park, Abingdon, Oxfordshire OX14 4RN
711 Third Avenue, New York, NY 10017, USA

First issued in paperback 2016

Routledge is an imprint of the Taylor & Francis Group, an informa business

Copyright © Abdulrahman Yahya Baamir 2010

Abdulrahman Yahya Baamir has asserted his right under the Copyright, Designs and Patents Act, 1988, to be identified as the author of this work.

All rights reserved. No part of this book may be reprinted or reproduced or utilised in any form or by any electronic, mechanical, or other means, now known or hereafter invented, including photocopying and recording, or in any information storage or retrieval system, without permission in writing from the publishers.

Notice:
Product or corporate names may be trademarks or registered trademarks, and are used only for identification and explanation without intent to infringe.

British Library Cataloguing in Publication Data
Baamir, Abdulrahman Yahya.
Shari'a law in commercial and banking arbitration : law and practice in Saudi Arabia.
1. Arbitration and award--Saudi Arabia. 2. Arbitration and award (Islamic law)--Saudi Arabia. 3. Banking law--Saudi Arabia. 4. Banking law (Islamic law)--Saudi Arabia.
5. Conflict of laws--Arbitration and award--Saudi Arabia.
I. Title
346.5'38082-dc22

Library of Congress Cataloging-in-Publication Data
Baamir, Abdulrahman Yahya.
Shari'a law in commercial and banking arbitration : law and practice in Saudi Arabia / by Abdulrahman Yahya Baamir.
p. cm.
Includes bibliographical references and index.
ISBN 978-1-4094-0377-7 (hardback) -- ISBN 978-1-4094-0378-4 (ebook) 1. Arbitration and award--Saudi Arabia. 2. Arbitration and award (Islamic law). I. Title.
KMT1829.B33 2010
347.538"09--dc22

2010014662

ISBN 13: 978-1-138-27706-9 (pbk)
ISBN 13: 978-1-4094-0377-7 (hbk)

Contents

List of Legislations, Treaties and Cases

Statutes and Conventions

Domestic Regulations of Saudi Arabia

Banking Control Law, '*Qanoon Moraqabat Albonok*' issued by Royal Decree No. M/5 dated 22/02/1386 H. (1966)

Foreign Investment Regulation, '*Nizam Alistithmar Alajnabi*' issued by Royal Decree No. M/1 dated 05/01/1421 H. (2000)

Foreign Investment Regulation, '*Nizam Alistithmar Alajnabi*' issued by Royal Decree No. M/4 dated 02/02/1399 H. (1979) (cancelled)

Mining Investment Law, '*Nizam Al Isithmar Al Ta'deni*' issued by Royal Decree No. M/47 dated 20/08/1425 H. (2005)

Oil Companies Law, '*Nizam Alsharikat Al Amilah Fe Haql Alpetrol*' issued by Royal Decree No. M/1 dated 09/01/1389 H. (1968)

The Arbitration Act of Saudi Arabia, '*Nizam Altahkeem Alsaudi*' issued by Royal Decree No. M/46 dated 02/07/1403 H. (1983)

The Basic Law of Saudi Arabia, '*Alnizam Alasasi Lil Hokm*' issued by Royal Decree No. A/90 dated 27/08/1412 H. (1992)

The Capital Market Law, '*Nizam Alsouq Almaliyah*' issued by Royal Decree No. M/3, dated 31/07/2003)

The Charter of the Saudi Arabian Monetary Agency 'SAMA', '*Nizam Mossasat Alnaqd Alarabi Alsaudi*' issued by Royal Decree No. 23 dated 23/05/1377 H. (1957)

The Code of Commercial Court, '*Nizam Almahkamah Altijaiyah*' issued by Royal Decree No. 32 dated 15/01/1350 H. (1931)

The Code of Law Practice, '*Nizam Almohamah*' issued by Royal Decree No. M/38 dated 28/06/1422 H. (2001)

The Company Law, '*Nizam Alsharikat*' issued by Royal Decree No. M/6 dated 22/03/1385 H. (1965)

The Competition Law of Saudi Arabia, '*Nizam Almonafasah Altijariyah*' issued by Royal Decree No. M/25 dated 04/05/1425 H. (2005)

The Implementing Rules of The Arbitration Act of Saudi Arabia, '*Al la'iha Altanfeziyah Le Nizam Altahkeem Alsaudi*' issued by the Prime Minister Order No. M/7/2021 dated 08/09/1405 H. (1985)

The Law of Commercial Mortgage, '*Nizam Alrahn Altijari*' issued by Royal Decree No. M/75 dated 21/11/1424 H. (2004)

The Law of Commercial Papers, '*Nizam Alawraq Altejariyah*' issued by Royal Decree No. 37 dated 11/10/1383 H. (1963)
The Law of Copyright, '*Nizam Hoqooq Almilkiyah Alfikriyah*' issued by Royal Decree No. M/41 dated 02/07/1424 H./30/08/2003
The Law of *Diwan Almazalim*, '*Nizam Diwan Almazalim*' issued by Royal Decree No. M/78 dated 19/09/1428 H. (2007)
The Law of Judiciary of 1975, '*Nizam Alqada'* issued by Royal Decree No. M/64 dated 14/07/1395 H. (1975) (cancelled)
The Law of Judiciary of 2007, '*Nizam Alqada'* issued by Royal Decree No. M/78 dated 09/09/1428 H. (2007)
The Law of Procedure before Shari'a Courts, '*Nizam Almorafa'at Ashar'iyah*' issued by Royal Decree No. M/21 dated 20/05/1421 H. (2001)
The Law of the Chambers of Commerce and Industry, '*Nizam Algoraf Altijaiyah Alsina iyah*' issued by Royal Decree No. M/6 dated 30/04/1400 H. (1980)
The Ownership of the Natural Resources of the Red Sea, '*Nizam Tamallouk Tharwat Albahr Alahmar*' issued by Royal Decree No. M/27 dated 09/07/1388 H. (1968)
The Regulation of the Committee for the Settlement of Banking Disputes, issued by Royal Order No. 8/729 dated 10/07/1407 H. (1987)

Other Official Documents

Diwan Almazalim's Circular No. 7 of 15/05/1405 H. (1985)
Royal Decree dated 23/10/1381(1962)
Royal Decree dated 5/9/1344 H. (1926)
Royal Decree No. (90/A) dated 28/06/1412 H. (1992)
Royal Decree No. (M/21) dated 20/05/1421 H. (2001)
Royal Decree No. (M/51) dated 1402 H. (1982)
Royal Decree No. (M/6) dated 24/02/1386 H. (1966)
Royal Decree No. (M/64) dated 1395 H. (1975)
Royal Decree No. (M/78) dated 19/09/1428 H. (2007)
Royal Decree No. (M/8) dated 22/02/1394 H. (1974)
Royal Decree No. 165 dated 7/5/1423 H. (2002)
Royal Decree No. 24836 dated 29/10/1386 H. (1967)
Royal Decree No. 37 dated 11/10/1383 H. (1963)
Royal Decree No. 5737 dated 9/04/1373 H. (1954)
Royal Decree No. 8759 dated 13/02/1374 H. (1955)
Royal Decree No. M/46, dated 12/07/1403 H. (1983)
Royal Order No. 4/110 dated 1409 H. (1989)
Royal Order No. 729/8 dated 10/07/1407 H. (1987)
Royal Order No. 8/729 dated 1407 H. (1987)
Saudi Arabian Monetary Agency Circular No. 333/BC/200 dated 22/08/1413 H. (1993)
The Circular of the Minster of Interior No. 10207 dated 07/02/1407 H. (1987)

The Council of Ministers Resolution No. 50 dated 25/12/1379 H. (1960)
The Council of Ministers Resolution No. 58 dated 1382 H. (1963)
The Minister of Justice Circular No. 107/2/T dated 25/08/1389 H. (1969)
The Ministry of Commerce Circular No. 31/1/331/91 of 1399 H. (1979)
The Ministry of Finance Circular No. 17/5583 dated 19/09/1409 H. (1989)

Bilateral Conventions

Agreement between the Government of the Kingdom of Saudi Arabia and the Government of Malaysia concerning the promotion and reciprocal protection of investment signed in Kuala Lumpur on 10 October 2000
Agreement between the Kingdom of Saudi Arabia and the Belo Luxembourg economic union (bleu) concerning the reciprocal promotion and protection of investments signed in Jeddah on 22 April 2001
Agreement between the Kingdom of Saudi Arabia and the Republic of Austria concerning the Encouragement and Reciprocal Protection of Investment signed in Riyadh on 30 June 2000
The Concession Agreement between the Government of Saudi Arabia and Standard Oil of California 'Aramco Concession', Jeddah, 29 May 1933
The Concession Agreement between the Government of Saudi Arabia and Lukoil Saudi Arabia Ltd, Riyadh, 4 May 2005

Non-Saudi Regulations

The Bid Regulation of 1957, Egypt
Arbitration Act 1996 (c. 23), UK
The Civil Code of 1949, Egypt
The Constitution of Kuwait of 1962, Kuwait
The Constitution of Yemen of 1994, Yemen
The Egyptian Constitutions; the 1980 amendment, Egypt
The Federal Constitution of the United Arab Emirates of 1971, United Arab Emirates
The UAE Federal No. 18 of 1993, 'Commercial Transactions Law', United Arab Emirates
The UAE Civil Procedure Code, Federal Law No. (11) of 1992, United Arab Emirates

International Conventions

Convention on the Settlement of Investment Disputes between States and Nationals of other States, 'ICSID Convention'. The International Centre for Settlement of Investment Disputes, 14 October 1966
Rules of Arbitration of the International Chamber of Commerce, 'ICC Rules'. The International Chamber of Commerce, 1 January 1998

The United Nations Convention on the Enforcement and Recognition of Foreign Arbitral Awards, 'The New York Convention'. The United Nations, 7 June 1958

UNCITRAL model law on International Commercial Arbitration. United Nations Document No. A/40/17, 21 June 1985

Cases and Decisions

Domestic Cases, Awards and Decisions

Domestic arbitral awards and decisions of Diwan Almazalim

Number	Year	Number	Year
19/28	1979	104/T/4	1998
50/1418	1988	73/T/4	1998
22/1409	1988	44/1419	1998
18/1409	1988	16/1420	1999
66/1409	1989	59/1419	1999
60/D/4	1989	369/2/Q	2001
135/1410	1990	992/2/Q	2001
12/1411	1991	34/1422	2001
28/1411	1991	102/1422	2001
194/1411	1991	90/1422	2001
185/1411	1991	34/1422	2002
54/1411	1992	95/1422	2002
115/1412	1992	91/1423	2002
1622/1412	1992	91/1423	2002
63/1413	1993	103/1423	2002
87/1413	1993	116/1423	2002
107/1413	1993	651/1/Q	2003
46/1413	1993	54/5/Q	2003
38/1415	1994	369/1424	2004
231/1415	1995	102/T/5	2004
39/1416	1995	87/1424	2004
44/T/3	1996	47/1424	2004
61/T/4	1996	66/T/4	2005
99/T/4	1996	111/T/3	2005
53/T/3	1996	96/T/3	2005
150/T/3	1996	150/T/4	2006
125/1417	1997	111/T/3	2006
11/D/F/2	1997	21/T/3	2007

Decisions of the Committee for the Settlement of Negotiable Instruments Disputes

The Committee for the Settlement of Negotiable Instruments Disputes, decision No. 67/1404 dated 11/04/1404 H. (1984)
The Committee for the Settlement of Negotiable Instruments Disputes decision No. 82/1405 dated 08/05/1405 H. (1985)
The Committee for the Settlement of Negotiable Instruments Disputes decision No. 23/1404 dated 14/02/1406 H. (1986)
The Committee for the Settlement of Negotiable Instruments Disputes decision No. 13/1403 dated 01/06/1403 H. (1983)
The Committee for the Settlement of Negotiable Instruments Disputes decision No. 147/1406 dated 12/11/1406 H. (1986)
The Committee for the Settlement of Negotiable Instruments Disputes decision No. 85/1406 dated 10/10/1406 H. (1986)
The Committee for the Settlement of Negotiable Instruments Disputes decision No. 151/1406 dated 16/11/1406 H. (1986)
The Committee for the Settlement of Negotiable Instruments Disputes decision No. 300/1411 dated 22/06/1411 H. (1991)

Fatawa and Court Decisions

Council of Senior Ulama decision concerning murder. No. 38 dated 11/08/1395 H. (1975)
Council of Senior Ulama of Saudi Arabia, decision No. 52 dated 29/10/1420 H. (2000) Riyadh, Saudi Arabia
Decision No. 167 of the Shari'a Supreme Court of Riyadh concerning divorce dated 14/06/1392 H. (1972)
Decision No. 167 of the Shari'a Supreme Court of Riyadh concerning divorce dated 14/06/1392 H. (1972)
Fatwa of '*Majma' Albohouth Al Islamiya Bil Azhar*' the Islamic Research Committee of Alazhar concerning banking interest dated 23/09/1423 H. 28/11/2002. Cairo, Egypt
Fatwa of Sheik Abdul-Aziz ben Baz concerning divorce. No. 2157 dated 09/11/1391 H. (1971)
Shari'a Supreme Court of Taif decision No. 51 dated 26/06/1421 H. (2001)
Supreme Judicial Council, decision No. 291 dated 25/10/1401 H. (1980)
The decision of '*Majma' Alfiqh Alislami*' the Islamic fiqh Council of the Muslim World League concerning some kinds of sale contracts No. 19 dated 22/10/1428 H. 3/11/2007. Makkah, Saudi Arabia

International Arbitral Awards

American Independent Oil Company Inc. v. the Government of the State of Kuwait 'Aminoil Arbitration', 21 ILM 976 (1982)
Ed. Züblin AG v. Kingdom of Saudi Arabia, ICSID case No. (ARB/03/1)
Petroleum Development (Trucial Coast) Ltd v. the Sheikh of Abu Dhabi 'Petroleum Development Arbitration', 1 ICL Q 247 (1952)
Saudi Arabia v. Arabian American Oil Co. 'Aramco Award', 27 ILR 117 (1963)
Southern Pacific Properties (Middle East) Limited (SPP 'ME') v. Arab Republic of Egypt, ICSID case No. ARB/84/3
Texas Overseas Petroleum Company and California Asiatic Oil Company v. the Government of the Libyan Arab Republic 'Texaco Arbitration', 17 ILM 3 (1978)
The Government of the United Kingdom acting on behalf of the ruler of Abu Dhabi and His Highness the Sultan Said bin Taimur v. the Government of Saudi Arabia, Jeddah, 30 July 1954 (HMSO Cmd 9272, 1954).

Non-Saudi Court Decisions

Arab National Bank v. El-Abdali [2004] APP LR 10/22 (UK)
AT&T Corp v. Saudi Cabkle Co. [2000] 2 All ER (Comm) 625 (CA) (UK)
Ayoub-Farid Michel Saab, Fadi Michel Saab v. Jones Day Reavis & Pogue, Mohamed Amersi [2002] EWHC 2616 (Ch) (UK)
Banque Saudi Fransi v. Lear Siegler Services Inc. [2005] EWHC 2395 (Comm) (UK)
Beximco Pharmaceuticals Ltd v. Shamil Bank of Bahrain EC [2004] APP LR 01/28 (UK)
Downing v. Al Tameer Establishment [2002] APP LR 05/22 (UK)
Dubai Court of Cassation Judgment No. 17/2001 dated 10/03/2001 (UAE)
Husain v. the Minister of Finance, the Supreme Constitutional Court of Egypt, decisions No. 26/16/8 dated 16/11/1996 (Egypt)
Hussman (Europe) Ltd v. Ahmad Pharaon [2002] APP LR 04/16 (UK)
Islamic Investment Company of the Gulf (Bahamas) Ltd v. Symphony Gems NV and others [2002] All ER (D) 171 (Feb) (UK)
Midland International Trade Services Ltd v. Al-Sudairy (QBD, 11 April 1990), The Financial Times, 2 May 1990 (UK)
Saudi Arabian Monetary Agency v. Dresnder Bank AG, 2003 WL 23145143 (UK)
Sharikat Alnasr Lil Ajhizah Alkahrabaiyah wa Alelectroniya v. the Prime Minister and others, the Supreme Constitutional Court of Egypt, decisions No. 93/6/7 dated 15/05/1996 (Egypt)
The Court of First Instance at the South of Cairo, decision No. 4615 of 1992 (Egypt)

Acknowledgements

I am greatly indebted to the following people:

To my parents and family.

To my friends, Professor Ben Chigara and Judge Essam Abdulaziz Al-Alsheikh.

List of Abbreviations

ADR	Alternative Dispute Resolution
Aramco	Arabian American Oil Company
BIT	Bilateral Investment Treaty
GCC	Gulf Cooperation Council
ICC	International Chamber of Commerce
ICSID	International Centre for Settlement of Investment Disputes
IPO	Initial Public Offering
KSA	Kingdom of Saudi Arabia
OPEC	Organization of the Petroleum Exporting Countries
SAGIA	Saudi Arabian General Investment Authority
SAMA	Saudi Arabian Monetary Agency
UAE	United Arab Emirates
UNCITRAL	United Nations Commission on International Trade Law
WTO	World Trade Organization

Introduction

Prior to the establishment of meaningful judicial systems, use of force was the primary means of settling disputes.[1] This notwithstanding, there is nonetheless some evidence that humans knew and practised some form of arbitration even before the creation of identifiable legal systems and litigation. In the Middle East, over time, these practices developed to form a body of customs and traditions, referred to in Arabic as *urf.* As part of this process, people started to refer their disputes to selected third parties. The custom of the ancient Arabs laid down some general criteria for the choice of arbitrators, namely that they should be known for their impartiality, fairness and wisdom, as well as their social standing. For instance, monks could be appointed, because their religious influence could be beneficial in enforcing a judgment. The same logic applied to tribal chiefs, whose social position could help to determine a dispute and enforce a judgment.[2] As a result, arbitration became the tool of individuals seeking peaceful and fair dispute settlement via a third party. Following the creation and development of judicial bodies, arbitration continued to exist as an auxiliary dispute settlement mechanism, working under the supervision of the judicial authorities.[3]

Islamic law, known as *Shari'a*, introduced a comprehensive set of arbitration rules, giving arbitration similar weight to that of official litigation. Shari'a regulated all the steps of arbitral practice, from the initial arbitration agreement to the enforcement of the final award. In Saudi Arabia, the first attempt to codify the Shari'a arbitration rules came with the provisions of the Code of Commercial Courts of 1931; however, the code was not really good enough, because Shari'a courts failed, at that time, to recognize arbitration clauses and because the enforcement of arbitration awards was voluntary.[4] The wrong interpretation of the law by Shari'a courts with regard to the recognition of arbitration clauses and the voluntary execution of arbitral awards had a negative effect on arbitration in Saudi Arabia. As a result arbitration existed only in theory for many decades. The

1 W. Ragib, 'Hal Altahkeem Nao' min Alqada'?' ['Is Arbitration a type of Litigation?'] *University of Kuwait Law Journal*, 17/1 (1993), pp. 131–72.

2 See, in general, N. Albejad, *Arbitration in Saudi Arabia* (1st edn., Institute of Public Administration, 1999).

3 A. Saiyed, *Arbitration Rules: A Comparative Study between Shari'a, Kuwaiti and Egyptian Law* (1st edn., Aleman Publishers, 2000), pp. 5–8.

4 See the Code of Commercial Courts ratified by Royal Decree No. 32 dated 15/01/1350 H. (1931) published in *Umm Alqura Gazette*, issue No. 374–76 dated 22/03/1350 H. (1931).

second attempt came when Saudi Arabia enacted the Arbitration Code of 1983, which overcame many of the problems of the first code, but did not produce clear solutions to the crucial issue of banking arbitration.

In Saudi Arabia a major problem relating to conventional banking disputes developed, as the principles of conventional banking contradict the principles of Shari'a, especially when it comes to particularly sensitive issues such as interest. As a general rule, Saudi courts are not competent to settle disputes that arise out of banking activities as defined by the Banking Control Law of 1966. The competence is spread between different semi-judicial committees in addition to arbitration. The new amendment of the Law of Judiciary (‘*Nizam Alqada*', issued by Royal Decree No. M/78 dated 09/09/1428 H. 2007) reduced the number to one committee; however, even resorting to that committee does not guarantee the full enforcement of interest provisions in any agreement. This is because the Committee for the Settlement of Banking Disputes does not have full power to enforce its judgments if it provides for the payment of interest, and because the judgments of the Committee are not really binding, as will be seen later. It has been argued by many foreign researchers and practitioners that arbitration would be the best remedy for cases involving disputed subject matter under Shari'a. This argument does have some merit.

Even though arbitration can be a possible remedy for a banking dispute, there are many obstacles that make disputes related to conventional banking amenable to arbitration in theory only. The Saudi law of 1983 did not even give a clear answer to the question of arbitrability of disputes in general and of banking disputes in particular, referring the whole issue to the law on conciliation. The law on conciliation itself carries a great deal of ambiguity and conflict among the different schools of jurisprudence. In addition, there are no codified rules on conciliation in Saudi Arabia. In accordance with Shari'a teachings on conciliation, banking interest disputes are arbitrable. However, whether this applies in real life is debatable. Furthermore, the question of the arbitrability of banking disputes is of more importance in the aftermath of the recent global financial crisis, which, owing to tight governmental control, did not hit the Saudi banking system. The rest of the private sector was less fortunate, however, and suffered its impact in varying degrees. The case of the Saad Group and Al-Gosaibi Co. is the largest case of loan default in Saudi Arabia to date. It remains to be seen whether this case represents the peak of the crisis in the GCC region, or whether it is only the tip of the iceberg. There can be no quick conclusions here, particularly given the size of the case, the systemic risk associated with syndicated loans given to holding companies and the difficult global atmosphere. In this case, the central banks of Oman and the UAE have warned of the exposure of the two family groups to banks in their jurisdiction. There has also been a lot of speculation about the companies' ability to repay billions of US dollars and about whether the companies will go bankrupt or the banks will agree to reschedule the debts. In any event, arbitration may play a key role in settling such disputes.

This book examines various issues in arbitration law and practice in relation to Islamic Shari'a law and the law of Saudi Arabia in general, and to arbitration in conventional banking disputes in particular. The book also compares available remedies for the settlement of banking disputes in Saudi Arabia in order to identify those most appropriate. The work further provides a simplified reference to the principles of Shari'a law and its theories, as well as Saudi law and practice in general.

The book is divided into six chapters. Chapter 1 provides a very general background to Saudi law and its sources, in addition to examining some other related general legal issues such as Wahhabism, the role of the official Mufti and his influence on the legal system, the role of women in the legal system, foreign influence on Saudi law, and some of the recent economic developments. The chapter shows how Muslim scholars introduced the methodologies of *usul alfiqh* to allow Muslims to keep their laws updated, by regulating the reasoning process and putting restrictions on law transplantation within the Muslim state, and by using the concept of urf, or local custom, as one of the sources of legislation to protect the special identity of the society. The evolution of usul alfiqh, or the legal theories, as an independent science led to the creation of four main schools of thought, each of which adopted a different set of rules for reasoning and application, and different subordinate sources of law. The chapter also distinguishes between the three confusing concepts of Islamic law, Shari'a and Islamic jurisprudence on the one hand, and Saudi law on the other. Moreover, the chapter gives an overview of the related Saudi acts and regulations, as well as the role of Saudi Arabia as one of the major capital-exporting countries.

Chapter 2 provides historical background to arbitration in this very specific geographical area. The rules of arbitration discussed in this chapter, both Islamic and pre-Islamic, are the raw materials forming arbitration rules in the four schools of jurisprudence, which are themselves the basis of modern arbitration law in Saudi Arabia. The chapter begins with the law and practice of arbitration in the pre-Islamic period, which ended around the time of Prophet Muhammad (AD 570–632), and goes up to the time of the establishment of the four schools of jurisprudence. The chapter also shows how Islam upheld some pre-Islamic practices with regard to arbitration.

Chapter 3 discusses the next stage of the development of arbitration law in Saudi Arabia, examining the law of arbitration under fully developed Islamic jurisprudence, known as *fiqh*. The arbitration laws discussed in this chapter form the basis of the Arbitration Act of 1983 in Saudi Arabia. The chapter starts by outlining the difference between arbitration and litigation under Shari'a. This is followed by discussion of the definitions of arbitration. The chapter covers the arbitration rules of Shari'a, from the arbitration agreement to enforcement of the final arbitral award, making comparisons among the four Islamic schools and paying particular attention to the *Hanbali* school as the official school in Saudi Arabia.

Chapter 4 examines the regulatory attitude toward international arbitration in Saudi Arabia. It is in chronological order and is divided into two main parts. The first part looks at the period from the creation of the Saudi state in the 1920s up to the first oil boom in the 1970s. This section discusses the arbitration cases the Saudi Government was party to, such as the *Wahat Alburaimi* case of 1955 and the well-known case of *Arabian American Oil Company v. Saudi Arabia* 'Aramco award' of 1958, and their impacts on the Saudi legal system. The second part covers the time between the 1970s and the present. This period experienced a shift in attitude in order to attract foreign investment. Many important steps were also taken toward the reactivation of arbitration as an effective dispute settlement mechanism, such as the enactment of the Arbitration Act of 1983 and its Implementing Rules in 1985, and the ratification of the New York Convention of 1958.

Chapter 5 is an evaluation of Saudi arbitration law and judicial practice. The chapter links the Arbitration Act with common practice, as well as other relevant regulations and Shari'a sources. The Arbitration Act was too brief to cover all the related issues, so the Implementing Rules became crucial in explaining the ambiguous aspects of the Act in more detail. The chapter also discusses the issues of enforcement of arbitral awards, both domestic and international, and the public policy of Saudi Arabia, its sources and applications.

The sixth and final chapter discusses whether a dispute related to conventional banking business can be settled through arbitration or not. Following on from the discussion in the previous chapter, this one looks at the issue of the arbitrability of banking disputes requiring a reference first to the Shari'a law on conciliation. The chapter also explores the Shari'a law on banking interest as both the main motive in the banking sector and the main contradiction in the public policy of Saudi Arabia. This chapter further compares the judicial treatment of banking interest in Saudi Arabia with the neighbouring countries of Egypt and the UAE. Suggestions are made regarding the most suitable alternative remedy in the case of disputes involving elements contradicting Shari'a.

Chapter 1
An Introduction to the Law and Economics of Saudi Arabia

Al-Saud has been in existence since the eighteenth century, although Saudi Arabia itself is relatively newly-formed, united only in 1932. At first, it was formed as an alliance between the religious figure Muhammad ben Abdulwahhab, who was more of a social reformer, and Muhammad ben Saud, who was a political leader in the town of Aldiri'yah. Since its establishment, Saudi Arabia adopted the Islamic Shari'a as its main source of legislation; therefore any law contradicting the main principles of Shari'a is considered null and void. This chapter is an introduction to Saudi law in general, including the sources and applications of Shari'a law in contemporary legal systems. The chapter also gives an overview of the development of Saudi commercial regulation and the importance of Saudi Arabia, both as the largest economy in the region and as a major oil and capital-exporting state.

The Distinction between Islamic Law, Shari'a and Islamic Jurisprudence (Fiqh) and Saudi Law

Many outsiders and even Saudi lawyers commit the mistake of confusing Shari'a and Saudi law on one hand, and Shari'a and fiqh, or Islamic jurisprudence, on the other. It is important to distinguish amongst these three important concepts, because of the different degrees of flexibility in their application. It should be noted that these concepts – Islamic law, Shari'a, and Islamic jurisprudence (fiqh) – are used interchangeably, especially by Western scholars and practitioners. The term 'Saudi law' can also be used to describe Islamic law, for the reason that it does not contradict the principles of Islam; however, the distinction should be emphasized, as Saudi Arabia applies Shari'a law specifically, in addition to some transplanted acts and codes. These borrowed acts and codes are Islamic in concept, as they do not contradict Islamic law, but a few of them do contradict some of the Shari'a principles, meaning that the distinction becomes important.

Many Muslim scholars distinguish between Shari'a and Islamic jurisprudence, or fiqh in Arabic, as follows: the concept of Shari'a is broader than jurisprudence – the jurisprudence, as well as other theories of Islam such as the Islamic creed, comes under the umbrella of Shari'a.[1]

1 I. Abd-Alhaqq, 'Islamic Law: An Overview of its Origin and Elements', *The Journal of Islamic Law*, 1/1 (1996), pp. 26–31.

Generally speaking, Shari'a, or *Ash-Shari'a*, means 'the pathway' – a way to be followed and the way that a Muslim has to tread. In its original usage, the term Shari'a referred to the road to a watering place or the path leading to water, i.e., the way to the source of life.[2] From this last point, Arab lexicographers developed Shari'a to mean 'the law of water', which, over time, was extended to cover all issues of life.[3]

In the Quranic context, the word Shari'a describes any religion or principle that is followed by someone: 'Then we put you on a Shari'a (a way of Religion); so follow that (way), and follow not the desires of those who know not.'[4] And again: 'To each among you have we prescribed a law and an open way.'[5] When the Quran mentions Shari'a, it is in its broader context as applied to any human being; whereas, when describing Shari'a in relation to Muslims, scholars tend to use its narrower definition as the religion of Islam.

Shari'a is not simply a religious teaching or divine order; its scope can be expanded to encompass the way of life Muslims should follow, which involves more than mere formal rites and legal provisions. The broader definition of Shari'a suits the nature of its rulings, as it is not restricted to laws, regulations, beliefs or rituals; it covers all aspects of the private and public life of Muslims, both as individuals and as groups, and it includes the totality of Allah's commandment.[6]

Islamic jurisprudence, or fiqh, developed later, when reasoning became necessary to allow the Islamic legal and social system to regulate new circumstances. The word fiqh literally means 'understanding' – Islamic jurisprudence is an understanding of Shari'a texts based on applied knowledge of the Quran and the *Sunna*.[7]

The concept of Islamic law was not in use at the time of the classical Muslim scholars; it started to develop as a reaction to the Western influence on Muslim scholars and philosophers, especially after the French occupation of Egypt. The French occupation influenced Egypt in various ways, but the creation of modern statutes represented in the import of the Napoleonic Code and the formation of the Constitution of Egypt were the most notable benefits in the areas of law development and the codification of Islamic law.[8] It can be said that after the

---

2 Ibid.

3 C. Mallat, 'From Islamic to Middle Eastern Law: A Restatement of the Field (Part 1)', *The American Journal of Comparative Law*, 51 (2003), pp. 699–719.

4 The Quran 45: 18. It should be noted that the reference to the Quran hereinafter is made to the translation of the meaning of the Quran from Arabic to English. The translation was taken from the website of the Ministry of Islamic Affairs of Saudi Arabia and it is available at <http://www.al-islam.com> [accessed 11 March 2009].

5 The Quran 5: 48.

6 Supra n. 1, Abd-Alhaqq.

7 H. Motki, *The Origins of Islamic Jurisprudence: Meccan Fiqh before the Classical Schools* (1st edn., Brill Publications, 2002), p. 4.

8 J. Harold, *Bonaparte in Egypt* (1st edn., Hamish Hamilton Publications, 1963), p. 374.

French occupation of Egypt many Muslim scholars began to modernize Shari'a, taking the Napoleonic Code as a model for Shari'a reform.

At the present time, Islamic law is recognized as the entire system of law and jurisprudence associated with the religion of Islam, including: the primary sources of law (Shari'a), i.e., the Quran and the Sunna; and the subordinate sources of law and the methodology used to deduce and apply them (Islamic jurisprudence, or fiqh).

It has been noted that many Western scholars refer to Shari'a and Islamic jurisprudence interchangeably, which can lead to confusion, because fiqh, or jurisprudence, changes, whereas Shari'a remains constant. The distinction between Shari'a and jurisprudence should be maintained, because Shari'a is the foundation of all doctrines formulated and developed under fiqh, whereas fiqh is simply the understanding of the sources of Shari'a.

The kingdom of Saudi Arabia was united officially in 1932 but Saudi law did not start to appear until the mid 1960s, when Saudi Arabia experienced comprehensive reforms through introducing a number of basic laws. Very few codes were issued before the 1960s; the law was totally dependent on the individual reasoning of judges, along with ministerial circulars and royal decrees concerning specific issues.[9]

Outsiders might see Saudi Arabia as a place in which Shari'a is the law of the country, which is partly true. But Saudi law is more comprehensive than either Islamic law or Shari'a, in the sense that Saudi law encompasses Islamic law and the codes and regulations adapted from other laws within the sphere of the Shari'a principles. Saudi legislators bear the duties of not violating Shari'a and of keeping up with economic, social and political interests. The main dilemma faced by Saudi legislators is regulating prohibited activities under Shari'a, especially when such activities are important in promoting economic growth, e.g., some banking activities. For instance, the Banking Control Law of 1966 shows the way in which Saudi legislators deal with prohibited activities under Shari'a. The Law says nothing about banking interest, because legalizing it clearly in the Act would be a violation of the Constitution of the country; nonetheless, the law does leave room for the practical regulation of such activities, as will be seen in the final chapter.

The Evolution of Islamic Jurisprudence (Fiqh)

Islamic jurisprudence (hereinafter fiqh) has been described by Schacht (1959) as the Canon Law of Islam and the 'common law' of the whole Islamic world. Under Shari'a, the monarch is bound by the same duties of respect and obedience as are his subjects. The interpretation of the rules of fiqh, their extension or limitation

9 Examples of laws issued in that period and still in effect: the Banking Control Law of 1966, the Companies Law of 1965 and the Law of Commercial Agency of 1962.

when confronted by new cases and judgment as to how they can be adapted to new social needs are matters to be decided by *ulama*.[10]

Fiqh literally means 'deep understanding'; terminologically, fiqh is the process of deducing and applying Shari'a principles and injunctions in real or hypothetical cases or situations. The same term is used to refer to the collective body of laws deduced from Shari'a through the use of usul alfiqh methodologies. The only fundamental difference between fiqh-based injunctions and Shari'a-based injunctions is that Shari'a injunctions are not amendable or even negotiable, whereas injunctions established under fiqh should be flexible and amendable in accordance with the different circumstances and customs that play an important role in the application of such injunctions, provided that such customs do not contradict Shari'a. This difference can be observed by tracing the history of issues in contemporary life, such as some banking transactions, that are controversial now, but that formerly had a different legal status in the past. For instance, hire purchase contracts are technically prohibited because they contain two agreements in one, referred to as '*bai'anfi bai'ah*' in fiqh treatises. However, the social need for such contracts and the desire to reduce dependence on bank loans have led some scholars to accommodate hire purchase within Shari'a legality requirements.

Owing to economic necessity, the legal status of banking interest has been modified and the prohibition relaxed in some Muslim countries, regardless of its validity under Shari'a. Even in Saudi Arabia, which is known for a degree of strict adherence to Shari'a rulings, banking interest has become more acceptable, at least in the business community. Islamic jurisprudence has an element of what can be called cautious or restricted flexibility, as shown in the above hire purchase example, whereby economic necessity can lead to the integration of commercial practice and religious standards but not to the modification of divine law. Social attitudes, or urf, may affect the legal status and legality of some controversial subject matters; nevertheless, the change in social attitudes toward banking interest, or *riba*,[11] will never lead to reconsideration of its legal status, because the injunction prohibiting riba came from the Quran, which is the main non-negotiable source of Islamic law.

The objective of fiqh is to demonstrate the practical application of Shari'a. The scope of the application of fiqh is very wide: it applies to all areas of law and life, including religious, political, civil, criminal, constitutional and procedural law; the administration of justice; and the conduct of war.[12] One of the main conditions that should be provided in a fatwa is conformity with the real life of the recipient of

---

10 J. Schacht, 'Islamic Law in Contemporary States', *American Journal of Comparative Law*, 8 (1959), pp. 133–36. Ulama are scholars in theology and law.

11 Riba is an Arabic term that describes a set of strictly prohibited commercial transactions. It can refer to banking interest or usury; it can also refer to the credit sale of identical objects. For more details please see Chapter 6.

12 S. Ramadan, *Islamic Law, its Scope and Equity* (1st edn., Macmillan, 1960), p. 64.

that specific ruling, meaning that the spirit of the law should prevail over the strict wording of the text.[13]

Classical scholars during the eighth and ninth centuries divided fiqh as a science into two broad categories. The first is called usul alfiqh (the roots of fiqh) and refers to the systemized methodology and principles of interpretation used in ascertaining the law. The second is *foru' alfiqh* (the branches of fiqh) and is similar to the actual practice of law, dealing with rendering decisions that derive from the application of usul alfiqh.

Usul alfiqh

There is an independent field of study of Islamic law called usul alfiqh, or the science of source methodology in Islamic jurisprudence. Although Alshafi'e, the founder of the *Shafi'e* school, was the first scholar to introduce usul alfiqh as an independent science, Usul alfiqh needed a few decades to develop.[14] There are many definitions for this term. Alghazali, a classical scholar, defined it as the fundamental sources or roots from which Islamic jurisprudence (fiqh) can be derived.[15] Another scholar, Alrazi, defined it as the aggregate, considered per se, of legal proofs and evidence that, when studied properly, will lead either to certain knowledge of a Shari'a ruling or to at least a reasonable assumption concerning the same; the manner by which such proofs are adduced; and the status of the adducer.[16]

There is an ongoing debate among Muslim scholars regarding the actual number of fiqh sources. However, they do agree on these five sources: the Quran; the Sunna; al ijtihad; al ijma'; and al qiyas.[17]

Al ijtihad Ijtihad can be translated from Arabic as a 'human activity', and refers in legal usage to the endeavour of a scholar to derive law on the basis of evidence found in Shari'a texts. The result of ijtihad, or the discovery or formulation of a new legal rule, is to be reached through interpreting Shari'a texts and applying the *qiyas*. By interpreting Shari'a texts, a Muslim scholar can discover the reason behind an expressed legal rule; and from there, through analogical deduction, he

13 Fatwa is an Arabic term to describe a legal opinion of a Muslim Scholar concerning issues of religion, law or legal interpretation.

14 See generally M. Alshafi'e, *Alrisalah* (1st edn., Dar Alkotoub Al Ilmiyah, 2001).

15 F. Mitha, *Algazali and the Ismailis: A Debate on Reasoning and Authority in Medieval Islam* (1st edn., Institute of Ismaili Studies, 2001), p. 10.

16 F. Al Razi, *Al Mahsul Fi 'Ilm Usul al* Fiqh, ed. Dr. Taha Jabir al 'Alwani (1st edn., Imam Muhammad ibn Saud Islamic University, 1979), Vol. 1, p. 94. Cited from T. Alwani, *Source Methodology in Islamic Jurisprudence* (3rd edn., The International Institute of Islamic Thought, 2003), p. 1.

17 H. Khan, 'Nothing is Written: Fundamentalism, Revivalism, Reformism and the Fate of Islamic Law', *Michigan Journal of International Law*, 24 (2002/2003), p. 273.

can extend a given rule to cases of a similar nature.[18] There is a general impression that the use of ijtihad was blocked around the eleventh century when some scholars declared the gate of ijtihad closed, but actually Muslim scholars have continued to use it in various legal and religious issues.[19] Nowadays, there is a preference for so-called 'ijtihad jama'e' or 'group ijtihad', which is a form of limited ijma'. In group ijtihad, a group of scholars meet to decide on new matters, instead of resorting to the individual ijtihad of the time of the great scholars who created the four schools. Some may argue that group ijtihad is similar to the concept of ijma'; however, they differ in that group ijtihad needs the agreement of only a group of scholars, whereas ijma' needs the agreement of most of the scholars of the time. The decisions issued by committees such as the Council of Senior Ulama of Saudi Arabia, the Islamic Fiqh Academy of Makkah and the Fiqh Council of Alazhar can be considered a sort of group ijtihad.[20]

Al ijma' Al ijma' refers to the consensus of qualified Islamic scholars of a given generation on particular points of Islamic law. On points where the Quran and the Sunna do not give particular guidance, the scholars as a community reach an agreement.[21] This methodology has its reference in the Quran in the following verse:

> O ye who believe! Obey God, and obey the Prophet, and those charged with authority among you. If you differ in anything among yourselves, refer it to God and His Prophet, if you do believe in God and the Last Day: That is best and most suitable for final determination.[22]

The qualifications necessary to participate in ijma' are set out in the fiqh textbooks; however, each one of the participants should also practise individual reasoning in his own right. Some groups of scholars require judges to be able to participate in such a process, as will be seen when talking about arbitrators qualifications. Theoretically, some scholars describe ijma' as the most important legal notion in Islam; through it, they believe, Islamic societies should be able to establish

---

18 B. Al-Muhairi, 'Islamisation and Modernisation within the UAE Penal Law: Shari'a in the Pre-modern Period', *Arab Law Quarterly*, 10 (1995), pp. 287–309.

19 W. Hallaq, 'On the Origins of the Controversy about the Existence of Mujtahids and the Gate of Ijtihad', *Studia Islamica*, 63 (1986), pp. 129–44.

20 The Islamic Fiqh Academy, resolution No. 8 dated 18/01/1985. Makkah, Saudi Arabia. See also B. Schabler, L. Stenberg and R. Mottahereh, *Globalization and the Muslim World,* (1st edn., Syracuse University Press, 2004), pp. 99–100.

21 Butti, Al-Muhairi, 'The Position of Shari'a within the UAE Constitution and the Federal Supreme Court's Application of the Constitutional Clause concerning Shari'a', *Arab Law Quarterly*, 11 (1996), pp. 219–44.

22 The Quran 4: 59.

permanent legislative institutions.[23] In practice, there has not been any successful ijma' since the time of the companions of Prophet Muhammad, owing to political divisions and cultural differences.[24] Despite the fact that absolute ijma' cannot be reached, scholars can usually attain ijma' in a certain geographic area or within a certain *mathhab*.

Al qiyas Al qiyas can be considered as the source of continuity of the fiqh. Al qiyas, or qiyas, is defined as the process of analogical reasoning from a known injunction to a new injunction. Qiyas involves analogical reasoning based on the primary sources of Shari'a, the Quran and the Sunna. According to this method, the ruling of the Quran and the Sunna may be extended to new problems provided that the precedent (*asl*) and the new problems (*far'*) share the same operative or effective cause (*illah*).[25] An example of this would be when the established prohibition of alcohol (from the Quran) is used to prohibit the use of drugs that produce similar effects to the intoxication of alcohol, even though there is no mention of drugs in the Shari'a texts.[26] As mentioned above, the Quran is not a collection of laws and codes; the first impression reading the Quran gives is that everything is lawful unless prohibitive injunctions exist, either in the Quran or in the Sunna.

Ijma' is ranked higher than qiyas in the order of fiqh methodology. To participate in ijma' over a disputed matter, the scholars, or *fuqaha'*, must have a deep knowledge of the Quran and the Sunna and their related sciences, most notably the Arabic language. The Arabic language requirement is very important in order to enable scholars to grasp the intentions of the Shari'a texts.[27] Qiyas was originally a fluid concept of reasoning from prior sources, through argument by analogy, argument *a fortiori*, argument *a majore ad minus*, argument *a minore ad majus* or argument *a contrario*. Reasoning through qiyas was broad enough to provide for flexible development in the law; its techniques permitted limitations and extensions of pre-existing rules. Over time, qiyas has become restricted, owing to a misunderstanding of its real sense, to a strict or literal interpretation of the law. This, in turn, has led to the development of the *istihsan*, which seeks to remedy this restriction by promoting the spirit and essentially social purpose of the law, i.e., to assure the satisfaction of human interests.

The above five sources of fiqh are agreed on by all the schools of fiqh; the disputed sources will be discussed below.

---

23 I. Abd-Alhaqq, 'Islamic Law: An Overview of its Origin and Elements', *Journal of Islamic Law and Culture*, 7/1 (2002), pp. 27–54.

24 Ibid.

25 J. Makdisi, 'Legal Logic and Equity in Islamic Law', *American Journal of Comparative Law*, 33 (1985), pp. 63–78.

26 Ibid.

27 N. Aghndies, *Islamic Theories of Finance: With an Introduction to Islamic Law and Bibliography* (1st edn., Gorgias Press, 2005), p. 71.

Istihsan The term istihsan can be translated as 'juristic preference' or as 'public interest'.[28] It is the process of selecting one particular acceptable solution over another because the former appears to be more suitable for the situation in hand, even though the selected solution may be technically weaker than the rejected one. Istihsan has also been defined as a process of selecting the best solution for the general public interest in the form of *ijtihad.* Istihsan does allow judges and scholars some flexibility in interpreting the law if it will be useful. In other words, istihsan is permission to allow the spirit of the law to prevail over the precise wording of the law.[29] Scholars of different schools give this concept different names; the Hanbali scholars call it istislah, which translates as 'equity' or 'public interest'; meanwhile, the *Maliki* scholars call it almasaleh almursalah, which is more like a departure from strict adherence to the texts in favour of public welfare.[30] Istihsan is sometimes called 'the hidden qiyas', as opposed to 'the apparent qiyas', which requires a strict application of the law.

Istihab, or istis'hab Istihab, or istis'hab, is best defined as 'the presumption of continuity'. This concept is well-known in Western laws, which provide that things or situations continue to exist until the contrary is proven. This principle was introduced by Alshafi'e, founder of the Shafi'e mathhab, and it is considered to be a limited principle. It applies only to cases where there is no evidence available and, at best, establishes the continuance of a fact in existence that has already been proven to exist.[31] Examples of when istis'hab might be used are: presuming that a missing person is still alive until his or her death is confirmed; continuing a marriage unless dissolution is proved; and adhering to the fundamental Islamic law principle stating that a person is innocent until proven guilty.

Urf – 'Local Custom'

Islamic jurisprudence recognizes local custom as an important source of law only when such practice does not breach Islamic principles. This applies even if the custom relates to a non-Muslim society. Custom can be defined as that which is practised more often by people in a particular geographic area than by others. Islam considers custom to be unwritten law formed by the practice of people throughout generations. Custom is incorporated into the law through the procedure of judges, court judgments and ijma'. When a judge is unable to find an applicable text from the Quran or the Sunna, or cannot find an ijma' or an accurate qiyas, he will turn

28 H. Fadel, 'The Islamic Viewpoint on New Assisted Reproductive Technology', *Fordham Urban Law Journal*, 30 (2002), pp. 148–50.

29 Ibid., p. 150.

30 Supra n. 25; Makdisi, p. 73.

31 Supra n. 27; Aghndies, p. 104.

to the custom of the community to determine the issue.[32] As a simple example, if an agreement does not determine the commission in a sale contract, the judge will turn to the usual practice of the place of the conclusion of the contract and issue his judgment on that basis. Custom can serve as persuasive evidence or as the basis for legal presumption; however, even when the case requires reference to local custom, judges still rely on experts and notaries to indicate the acceptable form of the local customary practice.[33]

As a final remark about usul alfiqh, it is appropriate to add this quote from Professor Hallaq, who concluded that:

> [U]sul alfiqh as a mixed product of human reasoning was articulated in a double-edged manner as it was both descriptive and prescriptive. It expounded not only the method of modus operandi of juristic construction of the law as the later scholars carried them out, but also the proper and sound ways of dealing with the law. Moreover, usul alfiqh provided the jurists with a methodology that allowed them not only to find solutions for a new case, but also to articulate and maintain the existing law. Even old solutions to old problems were constantly rehabilitated and reasoned anew.[34]

Codification of Shari'a Law

The call to codify the rules of Shari'a in a similar way to modern Western codes and acts has met with some success in different Muslim countries. Issued in 1882, *Majallat Alahkam Al Adliyah*, the so-called 'Majalla', was the first-known attempt to codify the Shari'a. The Majalla did not work in practice, because it was drafted for a non-Muslim authority and because it forced the society to follow the *Hanafi* school to the exclusion of the others. The popular belief that the Majalla was drafted as a civil code for the Ottoman Empire is partly incorrect. The Majalla was initially drafted under a reciprocal agreement between the Ottoman Empire and the Russian Orthodox Church; it was only later that the Majalla was adopted as the Ottoman civil code. In the aftermath of the Crimean War (1853–1856), a Muslim population was living within the Russian Empire; there was also a number of Orthodox Christians living within the Ottoman Empire. The original agreement resulted in the Majalla being adopted as a Muslim code in exchange for a Christian code.

---

32 S. Heynman, *Islam and Social Policy* (1st edn., Vanderbilt University Press, 2004), p. 102.

33 L. Rosen, *The Justice of Islam: Comparative Perspectives on Islamic Law and Society* (1st edn., Oxford University Press, 2000), p. 16.

34 W. Hallaq, *The Origins and Evolution of Islamic Law* (4th edn., Cambridge University Press, 2007), p. 148.

As a general rule, Shari'a judges decide on each case individually without giving any consideration to precedents. Moreover, the judge is not bound by the rules of any school of jurisprudence and he can choose to apply whichever rules are the most convenient for the given case. This leaves the judge free directly to apply the principles and spirit of the Shari'a texts under his own reasoning.

In Saudi Arabia, where the Quran and the Sunna form the substantive law, codification of the teachings of the Quran and the Sunna might impair the Shari'a and take away some of its flexibility. It could be said that codification might disable all the mechanisms of usul alfiqh that would enhance the culture of single school jurisprudence. In addition, codification might make the teachings of one school prevail over the rest of the schools' teachings – such strict adherence to one opinion might achieve equality, but not equity. For laymen, codification might become a tool for emphasizing the differences among the Islamic schools; rather than encouraging the accommodation of different opinions and practices, codification would become, instead, in that case, a tool of segregation. However, codification is needed in those areas of practice that emerged as a result of changing circumstances. Moreover, any prospective codification should concentrate on the procedural issues, which are the only parts that really need to be reformed.

Foru' alfiqh – 'Branches of Fiqh'

The result of applying the methodologies of usul alfiqh to Shari'a texts is known as *foru' alfiqh* in Arabic, which translates literally as 'branches of fiqh'. Foru' alfiqh are the actual laws or legal interpretations of Shari'a texts, as can be found in the fiqh textbooks, referred to as fiqh. Scholars have categorized foru' alfiqh according to subject matter; however, there is disagreement over these classifications, as each group of scholars has divided the branches in different ways. Classical scholars divided foru' alfiqh into the two broad categories of *ibadat* and *muamalat*.[35] Ibadat is the part of the teachings concerned with the relationship between human beings and Allah; whereas muamalat regulates the relationships among people. The most common classifications for *fiqh al muamalat* are:

- family
- food
- wills, trusts, estates and inheritance
- contracts, trade and commerce
- property
- criminal
- evidence
- administrative procedure
- administration of justice (*al qada*)

35 The term ibadat can be translated as rituals, whereas the term muamalat can refer to different meanings such as transactions, dealings, conducts, etc.

- zakat[36]
- domestic relations
- relations with non-muslims
- war
- ethics.

The Emergence of the Islamic Schools of Thought (Mathahib)

Differences of background, circumstance, personal understanding of Shari'a texts and application of usul alfiqh have a great influence on legal interpretation in real life. Some Muslim scholars stop at the clear wording of the Quran and the Sunna, while others go further, attempting to achieve a deeper understanding using analogies, reasoning or even personal opinion. When talking about Sunni Islam, there are four main developed schools of thought, or *mathahib*, in Arabic.[37] The differences between these schools are noticeable only in very minor practical divergences, which are owing to differences in the interpretation of Shari'a texts; otherwise, the four schools are basically one, for the reason that Sunni Muslims do not identify themselves according to their mathhabs.

The four main schools in existence nowadays are Hanafi, Maliki, Shafi'e and Hanbali. These schools exist because their teachings have been maintained and developed by their followers, giving them the potential to spread around the Muslim world and allowing them to keep up with changes in daily life. In pre-Islamic times, Arabs used to rely on their memories to store events, stories and poetry. The same concept was applied to the Quran, the Sunna and the teachings of religious scholars, especially in the early stages of Islam's development. During the first two centuries of Islam, the Quran and the Sunna were transferred between generations by narration, using the same methodology as the Arabs before Islam. By the ninth century, a few attempts were made to collect the Sunna, the teachings of the scholars and other intellectual works. Those efforts resulted in the spread of some scholars' works over others. These ways of scholarly thought were followed by other scholars and, as a result, people started to refer to the followers of a particular school of thought by the name of the founder.

Hanafi School

The Hanafi school is the oldest of the four schools of Islamic law; it was named after its founder, Abo Hanifa, Annu'man Ben Thabit (699–767), also known as

36 Zakat is one of the five pillars of Islam. Zakat is the giving of a certain percentage of one's wealth to certain beneficiaries after the fulfilment of some conditions.

37 For a deeper understanding of the emergence of mathhabs, please see, generally, P. Bearman, R. Peters and F. Vogel, *The Islamic School of Law: Evolution, Development and Progress* (1st edn., Harvard University Press, 2005).

Alimam Ala'azam, 'the greatest imam in Iraq'. Although this school is the oldest, it is also considered to be the most open to modern ideas and the most liberal in certain matters. The Hanafi school is characterized by the use of subjective opinions (*ra'i*), which partly gave it its name, ahl ar ra'i. The teachings of this school give priority always to the Quran, then to the Sunna and finally to Abo Hanifa's opinion. New problems are examined and often anticipated by the use of qiyas. Urf, or local custom, is not a source of law, but it can be a dependable reference in the case of a lack of other sources.[38] The Hanafi school is also known for giving legal opinions or fatwa in proposed, or sometimes imaginative, cases that did not exist at the time of discussing the matter. The Hanafi school was the official school of the Ottoman Empire and a selected part of the Hanafi teachings was embodied in the Majalla as an attempt to codify the financial provisions of the Hanafi teachings.[39] The followers of this school spread to Iraq, the region of the Caucasus and South Asian countries such as Pakistan, India and Bangladesh.

Maliki School

The Maliki school was founded in Medina, Saudi Arabia, by Malik Ben Anas (713–795). His major work, *Almuwatt'a,* was the first comprehensive work in Islamic history; it includes a collection of the Sunna, in addition to a selection of the Medina scholars' ijma' in his time. This ijma' is mainly based on the Quran, the Sunna and qiyas. Along with the main sources of Shari'a, Malik added the practices of the people of Medina at the time of the Prophet Muhammad's companions as a source of legislation.[40] A draft code in French, based on Maliki teachings, was prepared by M. Morand in Algeria in 1916, but this work has remained in draft form.[41] The Maliki school is widespread in North and West Africa.

Shafi'e School

The Shafi'e school was founded by Muhammad ben Idri's Alshafi'e (769–819). Alshafi'e was a student of Malik ben Anas, founder of the Maliki school, and was also influenced by the Hanafi scholar Muhammad ibn Alhasan Alshaibani, but he soon founded his own school. The Shafi'e teachings are mainly eclectic, borrowing from both Maliki and Hanafi schools, because Alshafi'e himself was inspired by both schools. Alshafi'e was the first scholar to address the concept of

38 A. Aljaziri, *Ketab Al* Fiqh *Ala Almathahib Al Arba'a* (1st edn., Dar Alkutob Alilmiyah, 2003), p. 28.

39 See, generally, M. Alatasi, *Sharh Almjallah* (1st edn., Maktabah Haqqaniyah, 1949).

40 M. ben Anas, *Almuwatt'a,* ed. Muhammad Fouad Abdulbaqi (1st edn., Dar Alkotoub Alilmiyah, 2000), p. 3.

41 S. Saleh, *Commercial Arbitration in the Arab Middle East: Shari'a, Syria, Lebanon and Egypt* (2nd edn., Hear Publishing, 2006), p. 5.

usul alfiqh (legal theories) in his book *Alresalah.* The Shafi'es do not recognize the concept of istihsan but they do emphasize the concept of istislah. The Shafi'e school is the official school in Indonesia, Malaysia and Brunei Darussalam, and it is widespread among the Kurds (Turkey, Syria, Iran and Iraq), Egypt, Yemen and the whole of East Asia.

Hanbali School

The Hanbali school is the official school in Saudi Arabia, which makes it the most relevant school for this study. The Hanbali school was founded by Ahmad ben Muhammad ben Hanbal (780–855), who was a narrator of the Sunna and a Shafi'e student. The teachings of Ibn Hanbal are quite conservative because they are strongly based on the Quran and the Sunna, with a little room for qiyas and other methods of reasoning. Although the Hanbalies are relatively strict in religious ritual, they are the most tolerant and flexible in commercial and financial transactions.[42] As mentioned above, the Hanbali is the official school in Saudi Arabia; it is also widespread in some parts of Syria and in some of the Gulf States. In 1927 King Abdul-Aziz Al Saud (1876–1953) declared his intention to draft a code embodying the teachings of Hanbali scholar Ibn Taymiyyah. Although this plan was opposed by traditional religious scholars and was eventually given up, Ibn Taymiyyah's teachings are still one of the main pillars of the Saudi legal system. Despite the fact that cancelling the codification plan was heavily criticized, it did favour the legal system as a whole in terms of allowing more flexibility in deciding controversial subject matter in disputes, concerns with family and criminal law. Non-Saudis in general use the term Wahhabism, or Wahhabiya, when describing the Saudi legal system or the official religious school in Saudi Arabia, which is actually a misunderstanding of the political history of that country, as will be seen below.

The Establishment of the Legal System in Saudi Arabia

The Foundation (1920s–1960s)

The modern state of Al Saud was established in 1932, when the King of Hejaz and Sultan of Najd, Abdul-Aziz ibn Saud, established the kingdom of Saudi Arabia with himself as absolute monarch. Since his first days as King of Hejaz, Abdul-Aziz was concerned with establishing a modern independent legal system based on the principles of the Islamic Shari'a. In issue No. 64 of Umm Alqura, the official gazette, dated 5/9/1344 H. (18/03/1926), King Abdul-Aziz issued the first provisional regulation for the judiciary; according to that royal decree, the act had

---

42 See, generally, S. ben Hanbal, *Sirat Alimam Ahmad ben Hanbal*, ed. Muhammad Alzali (1st edn., Almaktab Alislami Lel Tiba'a wa Annashr, 1997).

the title of Provisional Act to Reform the Shari'a Courts. The act consisted of 15 articles, with very simple wording; it gave general guidance and established the framework of the Shari'a courts. In his speech at Majlis Alshura,[43] King Abdul-Aziz held the Shari'a principles as the main source of legislation in the kingdom. He added that all legislation should be approved by the Shura Council before becoming effective in order to enhance transparency and public participation in the process of decision-making.[44]

In the following year, another royal decree called for the establishment of two summary courts in Mecca, in addition to the Shari'a Supreme Court Almahkamah Alshar'iyah Alkobra. The decree also called for establishing summary courts and Shari'a courts in Jeddah and Medina.[45] The same royal decree established a committee, to be in charge of appeals and judicial supervision, and named it Hay'at Almuragaba Alqada'iyah; the name of the committee later changed to Hay'at Altadqeqat Alshar'iyah. The committee used to serve as a court of appeal and as a regulator and supervisor for all the judicial bodies in the kingdom at that time.[46] A few weeks later, the King gave his order to establish ketabat alad'l, 'the notary public'.[47]

The provisional law of 1926 was replaced in 1931 by nizam sair almuhakamat Alshar'iyah, which was more comprehensive than the previous one and more concerned with the procedural issues of judicial proceedings. The new act came with only 36 articles at first; it was amended in 1936, and increased to 142 articles, under the title of nizam almurafa'at. In 1938, another act established the competence of judges and their responsibilities. The latter two acts were redrafted in 1952, under the titles of nizam tarkeez almasoliyat Alshar'iyah, and nizam tanzeem al a'amal al idariyah fee aldawa'er Alshar'iyah. By Royal Decree dated 23/10/1381 (1962) the old committee for judicial supervision or Hay'at Altadqeqat Alshar'iyah was replaced by Mahkamat Altamyeez, or the court of appeal, which opened in Mecca in the same year. The court of appeal worked under a provisional regulation till the approval of its law by Royal Decree No. 24836 dated 29/10/1386 H. (1967); the new regulation gave Mahkamat Altamyeez an exclusive duty to serve as a superior court instead of executing the load of duties of the old committee, which included revision of the regulations, legal consultation and a commercial court in some situations, in addition to its duty as a court of appeal.[48] The above regulations established the foundation of the Saudi judicial system, which was

43 It is a consultative body equivalent to parliament; it was founded in 1924 under the name of Almajlis Alahli (the National Council).

44 The speech dated 9/03/1349 H. (1930).

45 *Umm Alqura Gazette*, issue No. 140 dated 21/02/1346 H. (1927).

46 Ibid.

47 *Umm Alqura Gazette*, issue No. 143 dated 13/03/1346 (1927) and issue No. 144 dated 20/03/1346 (1927).

48 The Ministry of Justice of Saudi Arabia, *Litigation in Saudi Arabia: History, Institutions and Principles* (1st edn., The Ministry of Justice of Saudi Arabia, 1999), p. 89.

followed not only by many royal decrees and ministerial decisions, but also by administrative circulations in many fields of activity, such as commerce, banking, labour, social security, arbitration, etc. Such legislations intend to complement Shari'a, not to replace it, and they can also be considered as updates to existing Shari'a principles.

Judicial Bodies in Saudi Arabia

Competence for the settlement of disputes is generally divided, in Saudi Arabia, between different judicial and semi-judicial bodies. These bodies are supervised by different ministries in accordance with the dispute subject matter. According to the 2007 amendments to the law of judiciary, the judicial bodies in Saudi Arabia are:

- the judicial bodies under the Ministry of Justice, courts of first instance, courts of appeal and the High Court;
- the independent judicial authorities – the Board of Grievances, Diwan Almazalim; and
- the semi-judicial committees that work under the supervision of the competent ministry, such as the Committee for the Settlement of Banking Disputes of SAMA, the Committee for the Settlement of Customs Disputes, which belongs to the Ministry of Finance, etc.

The Ministry of Justice

In 1962 King Faisal gave his order for establishing the Ministry of Justice; however, it was another eight years before the ministry started its activities. The first judiciary law was issued by Royal Decree No. (M/64) of 1395 H. (1975); this law experienced a major amendment in 2007. The recent amendments will change the face of the Saudi judicial system considerably, as for the first time there will be specialized courts for each branch of legal practice in Saudi Arabia. Prior to these amendments, a judge deciding a criminal case one minute might settle an inheritance dispute 30 minutes later. The Ministry of Justice was allowed a transition period of two years before the new law became effective; however, the transition has been taking place very slowly. As with the previous law, the new law covers various issues related to the judicial system, such as: provisions securing the independence and impartiality of the courts; types of court and their jurisdictions; judges, their appointments and promotions; and the role of the Ministry of Justice, etc. Interestingly, the law comprises 85 articles on only eight A4 pages.

In the foreseeable future, there will be three main divisions for Shari'a courts in Saudi Arabia. According to article 9 of the 2007 judiciary law, Shari'a courts shall consist of:

- the High Council of the Judiciary, Almajlis Al'ali Lilqada'
- the High Court, Almahkama Al'olia
- the Court of Appeal, Mahkamat Alisti'naaf
- the courts of first instance, Mahakim Aldaraja Al'oula. This class of court is subdivided into:

    - general courts
    - courts of personal status
    - commercial courts
    - labour courts.[49]

The High Council of the Judiciary – Almajlis Al'ali Lilqada'

The new amendments of the Law of Judiciary split the competence of the supreme judicial council, or Majlis Alqada' Ala'ala, between two newly-formed bodies. The duty of being the highest court in the kingdom was assigned to the High Court. The rest of the duties, including supervising judicial affairs in the country and establishing new courts, appointing judges, etc. are among the duties of this council.[50]

The High Court – Almahkama Al'olia

The High Court in Riyadh was constituted partly to replace the Supreme Judicial Council, or Majlis Alqada' Al A'ala, which, in its current structure, is the result of many decades of development from the committee of judicial supervision in the 1920s to the enactment of the previous law of judiciary of 1975. The new High Courts will have legislative, administrative and judicial powers. The High Court as a successor to the Supreme Judicial Council will be the highest judicial authority in the kingdom, which makes it the final court of appeal. The duties of the High Court in accordance with article 11 of the Law of Judiciary of 2007 are:

- giving legal opinions with regard to issues related to the judiciary upon the request of the Minister of Justice;
- examining questions referred to said court by the King, with a view to issuing relevant Shari'a guidance;
- reviewing death, amputation or stoning sentences;
- reviewing cases in which one of the parties is not satisfied with the decision of the Court of Appeal, in case the decision of the Court contradicts Shari'a or the decision was issued by a court lacking the competence to decide such a matter; and

49 The Law of the Judiciary of Saudi Arabia, Royal Decree No. (M/78) dated 19/09/1428 H. *Umm Alqura Gazette*, issue No. 4170 dated 30/09/1428 H. (12/10/2007).

50 See article 5 of the Saudi Law of Judiciary of 2007.

- examining Shari'a questions that, in the opinion of the Minister of Justice, require a statement of general Shari'a principles.

Just like the Supreme Judicial Council, the High Court's decisions on cases referred to it from the Court of Appeal are binding upon all other courts, including the Court of Appeal. As a result, the High Courts have a powerful influence on the development of law in the country.

The previous law of judiciary of 1975 provided for the regular publication of a selection of judicial decisions; however, the first volume of the judicial decisions report of the Saudi courts was not issued until 32 years later, in 2007, under the title of *Modawanat Alahkam Alqada'iyah*. It contained a small selection consisting of 39 court decisions and nine of the Supreme Judicial Council's resolutions.[51]

The Court of Appeal

The Court of Appeal was established in 1927, under the name of Hay'at Altadqeqat Alshar'iyah. After the enactment of the law of judiciary of 1975, the same committee functioned under the name of Mahkamat Altameez. The new law added a new division to this court and divided it into five departments: the Civil Division, the Criminal Division, the Personal Status Division, the Commercial Division and the Labour Division.[52]

Courts of First Instance

The general courts were established by the same royal order that established the Court of Appeal in 1927. The judge in these courts sits alone except in cases of executions, stoning, amputation, kidnapping, armed robbery and other serious criminal offences specified in the judiciary act, which must be decided by three judges.[53] These courts have civil and criminal jurisdiction as they deal with more cases than other judicial bodies in the kingdom. Saudi courts in general assume jurisdiction over all cases brought before them except in cases *in rem* involving real estate located outside the kingdom.[54] The general courts have the authority to deal with all civil and criminal cases, regardless of their nature and financial value, unless cases fall under the competence of other judicial bodies that have been given exclusive jurisdiction, such as the Saudi Arabian Monetary Agency, the Ministry

51 See, generally, The Ministry of Justice of Saudi Arabia, *Modawanat Alahkam Alqada'iyah* (1st and 2nd edn., Ministry of Justice of Saudi Arabia, 2007).

52 See the 2007 Law of Judiciary, article 16.

53 Article 10.4, 2007 Law of Judiciary.

54 See the law of procedure before Shari'a Courts, Royal Decree No. (M/21) dated 20/05/1421 (19/08/200). *Umm Alqura Gazette*, issue No. 3811 dated 17/06/1421 (15/09/200).

of Commerce, Diwan Almazalimm, the Ministry of Culture and Information, etc.[55] The new law of judiciary provides that such courts should also be divided into the same five departments – Civil, Criminal, Personal Status, Commercial and Labour – as the Court of Appeal.[56] The law joined most of the semi-judicial committees in the new courts, with the exception of issues over which Shari'a courts might dispute legality, such as banking disputes, insurance, media and information.

Independent Judicial Bodies

Shari'a courts have general jurisdiction over civil disputes; however, judicial regulation takes into account the constitution of specialized courts. The word 'independent' means that there is a dichotomy between these bodies and the authority of the Ministry of Justice. The jurisdiction of these bodies is defined in terms of both subject matter of and parties to the dispute.[57] The rule is that these commissions do not usually have the jurisdiction to adjudicate cases to which the Saudi Government or any of its entities is party, because such disputes should fall under the competence of the Board of Grievances, hereinafter Diwan Almazalim. The next few paragraphs will give a brief overview of the authority most connected with arbitration in Saudi Arabia in general and with banking disputes in particular. It should be noted that, with a few exceptions such as the Committee of the Settlement of Banking Disputes and the Committee for the Settlement of Insurance Disputes, some of these committees will be incorporated under the competence of the newly formed courts of first instance.

Committee for the Settlement of Negotiable Instruments Disputes

The Committee for the Settlement of Negotiable Instruments Disputes is also known as the Negotiable Instruments Office. The Committee falls under the jurisdiction of the Ministry of Commerce and Industry. Established by the Law of Negotiable Instruments, the Commercial Paper Committee, also known as the Office for the Settlement of Commercial Papers Disputes, has the jurisdiction to hear claims concerning bills of exchange, promissory notes and cheques. The Negotiable Instruments Law provides the substantive legal provisions applied by the Commercial Paper Committee.[58] The law largely reproduces the provisions of the Geneva Convention Providing a Uniform Law for Bills of Exchange and

55 Ibid.

56 Article 20 of the Saudi Law of Judiciary of 2007.

57 A. Lerrick and Q. Mian, *Saudi Business and Labour Law* (2nd edn., Graham &Trotman, 1987), p. 222.

58 The Law of Commercial Papers, Nizam Alawraq Altejariyah. Issued by Royal Decree No. 37 dated 11/10/1383 H. (1963). *Umm Alqura Gazette*, issue No. 2010 dated 15/10/1383 H. (1963).

Promissory Notes of 7 June 1930 and for Cheques of 9 March 1931, even though Saudi Arabia has not become party to the conventions themselves. As Shari'a forbids the payment and charging of interest, provisions within the Conventions relating to interest were omitted from the Negotiable Instruments Law. In practice, this position has been applied by offsetting interest payments made voluntarily by the debtor against the principle of the debt. The procedure before the Committee is subject to the provisions of the Code of Commercial Courts of 1931. Decisions may be appealed to the Minister of Commerce.[59] The competence of settling negotiable instruments disputes will move to the Commercial Courts by 2010/11 and as a result, this Committee will disappear.

Committee for the Settlement of Banking Disputes of the Saudi Arabian Monetary Agency (SAMA)

The Committee for the Settlement of Banking Disputes was established under the Saudi Arabian Monetary Authority (SAMA) for the purpose of settling disputes between banks and their clients arising from contracts and transactions that do not concern commercial papers such as bills of exchange, which should be settled through a different Committee. In exercising its powers, the Committee may decide to freeze a party's assets or restrict parties from travelling outside of Saudi Arabia.

The Committee consists of three members who are appointed by the Ministry of Finance upon the recommendation of the Saudi Arabian Monetary Agency governor. There is only one Committee for the Settlement of Banking Disputes in the kingdom, which is located in Riyadh. The Committee is under the umbrella of SAMA and all its members are SAMA employees. All members are equal. The working mechanisms of the Committee will be examined in detail in the last chapter.

Board of Grievances – Diwan Almazalim

The Board of Grievances, hereinafter Diwan Almazalim, was created in 1955 as a department of the Council of Ministers, Majlis Al wuzara'.[60] The Board was later reconstituted as an independent entity.[61] At first the Board served as a general clearing house for complaints in the public domain; it has since evolved into the most important administrative and judicial body outside the Shari'a courts.[62] Some authors argued that Diwan Almazalim is a sort of Conseil d'État that has been borrowed by the Egyptians from the Napoleonic Code; however, the principle of

59 Ibid.

60 See the Royal Decree No. 02/13/8759 of 1374 H. (1955).

61 See the Royal Decree No. (M/51) of 1402 H. (1982).

62 G. Sfeir, 'The Saudi Approach to Law Reform', *American Journal of Comparative Law*, 36 (1988), pp. 729–44.

Qadi Almazalim was well known in Shari'a treatises many centuries prior to the foundation of the Napoleonic laws.[63]

Upon its establishment, Diwan Almazalim's competence was limited to receiving and investigating complaints to which the government or a governmental entity was party.[64] Owing to rapid economic growth following the oil boom in the 1970s and the trend of reducing the caseload in Shari'a courts, as well as founding a specialized legal body for settling commercial matters where the application of strict Shari'a rules may be seen as an impediment to the flow of foreign investment, the settlement of commercial and investment disputes has been added to the competence of the Diwan.[65] Another important step in that direction came when the Diwan was given the power to entertain applications for the execution of foreign judgments when questions of public policy arise.[66] The Diwan remained a commercial and administrative court until the issuance of the new Law of Diwan Almazalim, which changed the structure of the Diwan considerably.[67] The Diwan was restricted by the new law, which transferred the competence of settling commercial disputes from the Diwan to the new courts of first instance. With regard to arbitration, the Diwan is still the competent authority for the supervision of arbitration proceedings in Saudi Arabia. The Diwan is also competent for the enforcement of arbitral awards, both foreign and domestic, in addition to the enforcement of foreign judgments subject to the Riyadh Convention of 1983.[68] It is foreseeable that a procedural law for Diwan Almazalim, similar to that applicable before Shari'a courts, will be one day enacted.

The Diwan published some of its decisions and rulings at different stages in the 1980s and 1990s. In 2009, it announced the publication of more than 5,000 decisions, which were, according to the daily newspapers, printed in five volumes and given to judges and 'people who are interested in legal affairs!' Whatever the truth of that, the five volumes are not yet available either for sale or in academic libraries.

63 See, generally, M. Hanson, 'The Influence of French Law on the Legal Development of Saudi Arabia', *Arab Law Quarterly*, 2 (1987), p. 272.

64 Ibid.

65 Ibid. See also Royal Decree No. (M/51) of 1402 H. (1982). This opinion proved to be inaccurate for the reason that the Board of Grievances functions in the same way as Shari'a courts.

66 K. Roy, 'The New York Convention and Saudi Arabia: Can a Country Use the Public Policy Defence to Refuse Enforcement of Non-Domestic Arbitral Awards?', *Fordham International Law Journal*, 18 (1994–1995), p. 922.

67 The Law of Diwan Almazalim of Saudi Arabia, Royal Decree No. (M/78) dated 19/09/1428 H. *Umm Alqura Gazette*, issue No. 4170 dated 30/09/1428 H. (12/10/2007).

68 The Arab League Convention for Judicial Co-operation (Riyadh Convention). Signed in Riyadh, Saudi Arabia on 4 April 1983.

Wahhabism and Saudi Law

Foundation and Origin

Unfortunately, media forms such as televisions, radio and newspapers are the only sources of global information for many people, regardless of the fact that these media are largely biased and controlled by those who finance them. After September 2001, the Western world started to talk about something called Wahhabism when describing the state, law and religious institution of Saudi Arabia. Part of the Western media took an aggressive position against the Saudis, forgetting that they were talking about a different country with a totally different culture. It is likely that the majority of those media activists had never been to Saudi Arabia or even met a Saudi person.

The term Wahhabism, or Wahhabiya, has been used to describe the Islamic revival and reform movement that took place in the eighteenth century in the centre of Arabia. The movement mainly concentrated on restoring the correct Islamic rituals and beliefs, as polytheism had spread widely as a result of ignorance of Shari'a, especially among the Bedouins and people from remote villages and oases. Unlike some other reform movements of that era, the movement of Muhammad ben Abdulwahhab (1702–1791) did not start as a response to an external factor, such as European imperialism, hostility against the Turkish or the desire for political independence. The Wahhabi movement arose in response to internal conditions, notably the perceived deterioration in Muslim beliefs and practices.[69] What is called Wahhabism was no more than a socio-religious reform movement without any major contribution to the Islamic fiqh, because Muhammad ben Abdulwahhab was following the teachings of the late Hanbali scholars, especially Ibn Taymiyyah and Ibn Alqayem.[70] The name Wahhabiya was given to the movement of Sheikh Muhammad ben Abdulwahhab by its opponents, as the followers of Ibn Abdulwahhab called themselves Almuwahhideen (the Unitarians).[71]

The movement of Muhammad ben Abdulwahhab, or 'the Sheikh' as his followers called him, was described outside Najd as 'Islamic Orthodoxy'. The opponents of the movement inside Najd and within the Islamic world tried to stop it by attacking the movement and the Sheikh himself. For instance, they alleged that the Wahhabi school displayed an extreme hostility to intellectualism, spirituality and all sectarian divisions within Islam. Previous allegations were the main topics in a long debate between the Ulama of Najd and Hejaz during the eighteenth and nineteenth centuries. The Wahhabi movement also faced military attacks from outside the Arabian Peninsula. Starting in 1811, the military attacks led to the

69 See, generally, M. Kurdi, *Altareekh Alqaweem Le Mecca Wa Bait Allah Alkareem* (1st edn., Albaz Publications, 1962), Vol. 5.

70 Ibid.

71 N. Delong-Bas, *Wahhabi Islam from Revival and Reform to Global Jihad* (1st edn., Oxford University Press), p. 8.

collapse of the first Saudi state in 1818. The war between the Egyptian force of Muhammad Ali by the command of his son Ibrahim Pasha succeeded in stopping the 'political' Wahhabism, but it failed in defeating the faith of its followers. Some scholars of that time adopted an extreme position against the Sheikh to the extent that they described him and his students as apostates.[72] Meanwhile, the Western world came to see Wahhabism as a 'new Islamic sect' that encouraged intolerance and extremism.[73] Nowadays, Wahhabism in the Western context refers to the form of Sunni Islam practised in Saudi Arabia, which bears the characteristics of extremism and intolerance, and supports terrorism.[74]

The true main objectives of the Wahhabi movement are summarized in the following quotations:

> Muhammad ben Abdulwahhab perceived the religious, social and political problems of his society and the critical conditions through which the Najdi people were passing. Thus he dedicated his life and enthusiastic energy to bringing about a comprehensive solution to the various problems of the Najdi society through the establishment of a strong central government that would enforce the Shari'a and impose peace and order in the land. Ibn Abdulwahhab was prepared for the great task by his own education and training, and was assisted by the particular religious and political conditions of Najd in his time.[75]

> Ibn Abdulwahhab aimed at renewing and reforming the faith and the practice of his people and both concepts are fundamental components of Islam's worldview, embedded in the Quran and the Sunna of the Prophet and both concepts, renewal and reform involve a call for the return to the fundamentals of Islam, the Quran and the Sunna.[76]

Wahhabism and Politics

Sheikh Muhammad ben Abdulwahhab was initially persecuted by local religious scholars and political leaders who viewed his teachings as a threat to their power and influence. The Sheikh, who had been expelled from his home town Al O'yainah, looked for protection in many neighbouring towns but could not find any, either because the governors opposed him and his movement or because they

---

72 Ibid.

73 See, generally, supra n. 71, Delong-Bas and supra n. 62, Sfeir, p. 731.

74 C. Blanchard, *The Islamic Tradition of Wahhabism and Salafiyya* (Congressional Research Service Report for Congress, submitted on 17/01/2007).

75 U. Aljuhany, *Najd before the Salafi Reform Movement: Social, Political and Religious Conditions during the Three Centuries Preceding the Rise of the Saudi State* (1st edn., Ithaca Press in association with the King Abdul-Aziz Foundation for Research and Archives, 2002), p. 156.

76 J. Esposito, *Islam: The Straight Path* (1st edn., Oxford University Press, 1988), pp. 114–18.

feared his opponents. Eventually the Sheikh received a warm welcome in the town of Diriyah, which was ruled by Muhammad ben Saud.

Muhammad ben Abdulwahhab and Muhammad ben Saud formed an agreement to dedicate their lives to restoring the pure teachings of Islam to the Muslim community. The agreement was the Constitution of the first Saudi state; Muhammad ben Saud, 'the Imam', was required under this agreement to give political and military protection to 'the Sheikh'. Muhammad ben Abdulwahhab, in his turn,[77] gave spiritual guidance to the newly formed state under the political rule of Muhammad ben Saud. By 1788, the Saudi state ruled over the entire central province of Saudi Arabia. Since that time, the term Wahhabiya was used outside Najd to describe the Saudi state. The fame and success of the Sheikh's movement and the newly formed state stimulated the hostility as well as the panic of the Ottoman Empire, which was the dominant power in the Middle East and North Africa at the time. The Ottoman Empire and its allies in the region tried, as mentioned above, to break the Sheikh and the Saudi state in various ways. From then on, the term Wahhabiya started to be used for people of that particular geographic area, i.e., the central region of Saudi Arabia; and after that, for people who followed the teachings of Muhammad ben Abdulwahhab anywhere else, but especially for Saudis.[78]

Wahhabism and Saudi Law

The Saudi legal system is based totally on the Shari'a, the Quran and the Sunna. There is no reference to the word Wahhabiya in any of the codes, royal decrees or court decisions, or even in the curriculum of the Shari'a colleges in Saudi Arabia. The term Wahhabiya has been given by outsiders to Saudi Arabia, its law and its people; it is in use only outside the country. Article 1 of the Saudi Basic Law states that the kingdom of Saudi Arabia is a sovereign Arab Islamic state; and that its constitution is made up of the Quran and the Sunna.[79] Article 1 of the Law of Judiciary states clearly that Shari'a rules are the only source of legislation in Saudi Arabia; it does not mention Wahhabiya or Sheikh Muhammad ben Abdulwahhab. It can be said that Wahhabiya exists only in the minds of the opponents of Saudi Arabia, who transferred their inaccurate understanding to the world in a way that represents the movement of Muhammad ben Abdulwahhab as a new Islamic school or Mathhab.

---

77 The agreement affected the Saudi religious institution, as the Sheik's descendants are still in its top positions, e.g., the Minister of Justice, the Minister of Islamic Affairs and the Grand Mufti.

78 See, generally, A. Sa'ied, *The History of the Saudi State* (1st edn., Darat Almalik Abdul-Aziz, 1973).

79 The Basic Law of Saudi Arabia, *Alnezam Alasasi Lelhokm*, Royal Decree No. (90/A) dated 28/06/1412 H. (1992).

The Role of Women in the Saudi Legal System

Owing to some cultural controversies, women's participation in the Saudi legal system is very limited. In accordance with Shari'a ruling, women cannot be appointed as judges or arbitrators. This is not a matter for discussion in Saudi Arabia, as Shari'a requires arbitrators to be men. According to the vast majority of Shari'a scholars, the appointment of a woman as a judge/arbitrator is null and void, even if she gives a correct judgment.[80] Scholars have evidenced this opinion with the following Hadeeth:

> When the Prophet heard the news that the people of Persia had made the daughter of Khosrau their Queen, he said, "Never will succeed such a nation as makes a woman their ruler."[81]

The vast majority of Muslim scholars do not recognize the appointment of women arbitrators because women are not qualified to be judges.[82]

Scholars support their argument with the fact that a man's witness is equal to that of two women. The legal basis for this practice is the following Quranic verse:

> Two men shall serve as witnesses; if not two men, then a man and two women whose testimony is acceptable to all. Thus, if one woman becomes biased, the other will remind her.[83]

As stated, appointing women as judges is not a negotiable matter, however, in the near future, women will be allowed to practise law as licensed lawyers, and this issue is still under consideration by the Ministry of Justice. At the moment women are allowed to work as in-house legal advisers.

The Influence of the Mufti on the Application of Shari'a in the Saudi Judiciary

The role played by the official Mufti is very important because the Mufti is the highest religious authority in the Islamic state, occupying an intermediate position between the law, religion and real life. The main duty of the official Mufti is to give opinions concerning matters of Shari'a law and social affairs; in other words, the

80 M. Ibn Qodamah, *Almoghni* (1st edn., Hajar Publications, 1992), Vol. 11, p. 380.

81 A. Albukhari, *Aljame' Alsaheeh (Saheeh Albukhari)* (1st edn., Dar Aljeel, 2005), Vol. 9, Chapter 88, Hadeeth No. 219.

82 A. Al-Kenain, *Altahkeem fe AlShari'a Alislamiyah: Altahkeem Al'am, wa Altahkeem fe Alshiqaq Alzaouji* (1st edn., Dar Alasimah, 2000), pp. 77–79.

83 The Quran 1: 282.

Mufti is the authority which gives guidance on practical ways of applying Shari'a rules in legal and social matters.[84] It cannot be denied that the Saudi judiciary falls under the influence of the General Mufti, or Almufti Al'am, who works side by side with the monarch as a final resort after the Committee of the Senior Scholars, known as Hay'at Kibar Al Ulama'. The Grand Mufti belongs to the Hanbali school, and so the influence of the Hanbali school both on the reasoning of judges and on the application of Shari'a in Shari'a courts is very clear. The late General Mufti Sheikh Abdul-Aziz ben Baz (1910–1999), who served as a judge for many years, rejected the idea of basing legal opinions solely on the teachings of one school. Sheikh ben Baz instructed judges and scholars to liberalize their thinking and to develop a mechanism for allowing judges to decide on cases not on the basis of a particular school of thought, but on the basis of equity and mercy. It has been noted from his fatwa that Sheikh ben Baz always tried to find the simplest solution to any problem; in other words, he wanted to make life easier, and his judgments in the areas of family and criminal law are clear evidence of this approach.[85] Nowadays, it can be argued that the fatwa of Sheikh Abdul-Aziz ben Baz is one of the strongest legal sources before any Saudi court.[86] With the exception of Sheikh ben Baz, however, General Muftis of Saudi Arabia are known for their strict observance of the Hanbali teachings in accordance with the teachings of the scholar Ibn Taymiyyah.

The reasons behind the General Muftis' strict adherence to the Hanbali school under the teachings of Ibn Taymiyyah are firstly that the Hanbali school has been followed by the Saudi Arabian royal family since the time of the agreement between Muhammad Ibn Saud and Muhammad Ibn Abdulwahhab in the eighteenth century. Secondly, the vast majority of judges and senior scholars follow the Hanbali school because of either education or family background, especially the Mufti and the former minister of Justice (1993–2009), who are direct descendents of Sheikh Muhammad ben Abdulwahhab. The descendents of Sheikh Muhammad ben Abdulwahhab are known today as 'Al-Ash-Sheikh' and they occupy most of the highest religious and legal positions in the Government of Saudi Arabia.[87]

---

84 J. Skovgaard-Petersen, *Defining Islam for the Egyptian State: Mufti and Fatwas of the Dar al-Ifta* (1st edn., Brill Publishers, 1997), pp. 5–9.

85 For more details, see Sheik Abdul-Aziz ben Baz's fatwa concerning divorce No. 2157 dated 09/11/1391 H. (1971); see also the Council of Senior Ulama decision concerning murder No. 38 dated 11/08/1395 H. (1975); see decision No. 167 of the Shari'a Supreme Court of Riyadh concerning divorce dated 14/06/1392 H. (1972).

86 The supremacy of the fatwa over some codes and regulations can be seen by looking at decisions of the Shari'a court in disputed matters such as the sale of tobacco.

87 The General Mufti of Saudi Arabia is Sheik Abdul-Aziz ben Abdullah Al-Ash-Sheikh; the ex-Minster of Justice and chairman of the parliament Dr Abdullah ben Muhammad Al-Ash-Sheikh 1993–2009, a member of the same family, was appointed as the first Minister of Justice between 1975 and 1990; the Minister of Islamic Affairs since 1996, Sheik Saleh ben Abdul-Aziz Al-Ash-Sheikh, also a member of the same family, was appointed as the first official Mufti in 1954.

The importance of the General Mufti's role with regard to the judiciary is evident when the Ministry of Justice refers a question to him, asking for legal or religious guidance on a specific issue. The Mufti's answer is considered to be a sort of binding precedent before any court in Saudi Arabia. With regard to arbitration, the guidance of the General Mufti is very important in determining the rules of public policy and the application of Shari'a in Saudi Arabia.

The Influence of Foreign Laws on Saudi Law

Owing to the lack of legal experience at the time of Saudi Arabia's formation, King Abdul-Aziz had to use the existing Ottoman Codes as a base for the legal system and a supplement to Shari'a rules. The newly formed state had to work further to develop a suitable body of legislation, which depended on the available bodies of law and on foreign expertise. That trend was established by his order to the attorney general of Hejaz to adhere to the Ottoman regulations until further notice.[88] The Code of Commercial Courts of 1931 was extensively inspired by the Ottoman Code of 1850. With many amendments since that time, the Code is still in existence today; it includes a lot of Turkish terms and can be considered as a direct translation from the Turkish Code.[89] Moreover, King Abdul-Aziz attempted to codify the teachings of the four Islamic schools in a similar way to the Majalla's codification of the Hanafi fiqh; however, this step was strongly opposed by radical scholars and never saw the light of day. In conjunction with that attempt, the King ordered Shari'a judges not to be bound by the rules of one school of fiqh in a way that would lead to one school's ruling abrogating another's.[90] Yet some Ulama had their own agenda; they opposed the King's reform plans and tried to put pressure on all the judges in the kingdom to apply the Hanbali fiqh under the teachings of the late scholar Ibn Taymiyyah. The main reason for their opposition was fear that the expansion of civil jurisdiction might come at the expense of Shari'a and might lead, in the end, to the application of laws unrelated to Shari'a.[91]

Later, Saudi law became indirectly inspired by the French system. French law influenced Saudi law deeply because of the influx of foreign experts from other Arab countries, especially Egypt, which was under French occupation during the eighteenth and nineteenth centuries, as well as the young Saudi legal scholars who graduated from law schools in Egypt, Lebanon and France at a later stage. Moreover, many of the consultants of the Saudi kings were Egyptians or Syrians, either by birth, origin or education – these are also countries highly influenced

88 See the Royal Decree No. 1166 dated 27/12/1345 H. (1927).

89 See, in general, the Code of Commercial Courts of Saudi Arabia, Nizam Almahkamah Altijariyah, issued by Royal Decree No. 32 dated 15/01/1350 H. (1931).

90 Supra n. 62, Sfeir, p. 732.

91 Ibid., p. 733.

by the French legal system.[92] Those consultants imported Egyptian laws, which are direct translations of French laws, although, of course, in order to be adopted in Saudi Arabia, such regulations all had to comply with Shari'a principles. For instance, in 1966, Saudi Arabia enacted Royal Decree No. (M/6) dated 24/02/1386 H. entitled Regulation Governing Bids for Government Procurement, Sales and Leases. This was a copy of the Egyptian Bid Regulation of 1957, which was a textual translation of the French regulation of 1953. Another example of the French influence is the Saudi Companies Law enacted by Royal Decree No. (M/6) dated 22/03/1385 H. (1965). The law was copied from the Egyptian code, which was directly patterned after French company law.[93] The French influence can even be seen in the case of government representatives in the Aramco arbitration citing French administrative laws to support their arguments. The list of borrowed regulations is long and it applies to most aspects of Saudi law, such as the Banking Control Law of 1966, the Labour and Workers Regulation of 1969 and the Law of Procedure before Shari'a Courts of 2000. Although these laws have been borrowed from foreign sources, they are still Islamic in the sense that they do not contradict any Shari'a principles.

The Scope of Application of Shari'a Law in Muslim Countries

Since the time of the Cold War, the application of Shari'a law has been a matter of controversy in many Muslim countries. In Egypt, for instance, the regime of the late presidents Jamal Abdul Nasser and Anwar Al-Sadat battled against the application of the Muslim brother's version of Shari'a law. The application of Shari'a law in Egypt at that time was against the socialist ideas of President Nassir. In the 1970s, President Al-Sadat felt under pressure from Muslim activists, leading to the 1980 amendment, which implies that Shari'a rulings should prevail over all man-made regulations. According to article 2 of the 2007 Constitution, 'Islam is the Religion of the State. Arabic is its official language, and the Islamic Jurisprudence (Shari'a) is a principal source of legislation.'[94]

During that time, the application of Shari'a in other Arab countries was faced with obstacles such as foreign occupation in countries like Algeria and Tunisia, multi-faith societies like Lebanon, and Communist ruling regimes like the one that existed in South Yemen until 1990. Yet the application of Shari'a remained an important social element in GCC states and was the main basis for the establishment of the state of Saudi Arabia, as will be seen in the course of this book.

---

92 See, generally, D. Holden and R. Johns, *The House of Saud* (1st edn., Sedgwick and Jackson, 1981).

93 Supra n. 63, Hanson, p. 289

94 Article 2 of the Constitution of Egypt, ratified on 5 April 2007.

Nowadays the influence of Islamic Shari'a on modern legislations varies widely, owing to the degree of social pressure or to the public policy of the ruling regime.[95] The position of Shari'a within the constitution and legal system of Arab countries can be classified into two main categories. First, countries where the Quran and the Sunna are themselves the law and the only sources of legislation. Saudi Arabia stands alone in this category, as the only country to have the Quran and the Sunna as the substantive law and the main sources of public policy.[96] Furthermore, Saudi Arabia has some Shari'a-based codified acts, such as the Arbitration Act of 1983, and also some borrowed acts from other countries such as Egypt that fall within this category, because any law or practice that contradicts the principles of the Quran and the Sunna violates public policy. Second, states where Shari'a is either the main source or one of the sources of legislation. Most Arab countries fall within this category, as their constitutions state.[97]

In some Arab countries, Islam is only the religion; the influence of Shari'a is not as great as in other countries. However, the laws of personal status, such as the Moroccan family law, are based mainly on the principles of Shari'a.[98]

Saudi Codes

After the unification of Saudi Arabia, King Abdul-Aziz started working on building the foundation for a legal system. As mentioned above, the King of Hejaz ratified the laws establishing Shari'a courts and the Shura Council, issuing the first regulation concerned with commerce in 1926. The founding body was a committee to settle disputes between traders, under the name of Majlis Altojjar, or the traders' council. Other than the memories of some elders, no evidence has survived from that period. However, its name suggests that the council was little more than a conciliation committee, which might well have been sufficient for the then relatively primitive economy, which depended on only a handful of sources. The establishment of Majlis Altojjar was followed by the establishment of what is known as Mosajjil Alsharikat, or the companies registry, which became the foundation stone of the Ministry of Commerce and the first step towards regulating

95 For more details please see N. Abiad, *Shari'a, Muslim States and International Human Rights Treaty Obligations: A Comparative Study* (1st edn., British Institute of International and Comparative Law, 2008).

96 See articles 1 and 7 of the Basic Law of Saudi Arabia, *Alnizam Alasasi Lil Hokm,* issued by Royal Decree No. A/90 dated 27/08/1412 H. (1992).

97 Article 2 of the Egyptian Constitution states that Islamic Jurisprudence is the principal source of legislation. Article 2 of the Constitution of Bahrain states that Islamic Shari'a shall be a main source of legislation. Article 3 of the Constitution of the Republic of Yemen of 1994 states that Islamic Shari'a is the source of all legislations.

98 See the preamble of the Moroccan Family Code (Moudawana) of 5 February 2004.

commerce in what came to be known as Saudi Arabia.[99] The long-lasting Code of Commercial Courts of 1931 was inspired extensively by the Ottoman Code of 1850. With many amendments since that time, the Code is still in existence today and still includes a lot of Turkish terms. The Code might even be a direct translation from the Turkish Code, bearing in mind that the Turkish had just left the country after many centuries of occupation. In 1946 the regulation of the Jeddah Chamber of Commerce was issued, but it was not until 1953 that Royal Decree No. 10/22/5/5703 provided for founding a Ministry of Commerce in Saudi Arabia. The Ministry was competent for the settlement of commercial disputes until 1987, when this competence was transferred to Diwan Almazalim and remained there for 20 years. The following section will give an overview of the codes that are mostly connected with commercial disputes in Saudi Arabia.

The Law of Trademarks

In accordance with international standards, the Law of Trademarks provides protection to the owner of the trademark by ensuring the exclusive right to use it to identify goods or services, or to authorize another to use it in return for payment. It can be said that the long-awaited reform provides relatively poor protection, mainly for two reasons. One may argue that the weakness is owing to the vast scope of public policy restrictions, but, in reality, it is owing to the great degree of misconduct in different public entities, including the customs authorities, the Ministry of Commerce and the local municipal authorities, or so-called Baladiyah. The Law came into effect to replace the Trademarks Law issued by Royal Decree No. M/5, dated 4/5/1404 H. (1984), which was ineffective. The Act excludes different kinds of signs, flags and emblems from being registered or considered as trademarks because that would violate public policy.[100]

Although the same law provides for some fairly strict disciplinary actions, the enforcement mechanism is weak. The Ministry of Commerce usually argues that it lacks manpower and the technical infrastructure needed to enforce the law. Questions may arise here about how counterfeit goods enter into the country in the first place and then how they are marketed publicly on such a huge scale. It has been reported in one of the daily newspapers that the competent department in the Ministry of Commerce has only seven members of staff who are responsible for inspecting hundreds of thousands of shops, warehouses and factories in the kingdom.[101] This enabled the counterfeit brands market in Saudi Arabia to reach several billion US dollars in 2008. With the exception of articles 2 b, c, d and e, the

99 Ministry of Commerce of Saudi Arabia <http://www.commerce.gov.sa/aboutus/history.asp> [accessed 5 March 2009].

100 Please see article 2 of the Law of Trademarks of Saudi Arabia, issued by Royal Decree No. M/21 dated 28/05/1423 H./07/08/2002.

101 *Okaz Saudi Newspaper*, issue No. 2881 dated 07/05/2009.

Ministry is not doing all it could to counter a violation costing the world economy, including the Saudi economy itself, billions of dollars every year.

The Law of Copyright

The Saudi Law of Copyright of 2003 came into effect to protect intellectual works and meet Saudi obligations towards the WTO. However, there is a big issue with the enforcement of this law. People are regularly offered copies of Hollywood movies yet to be shown in US cinemas, or unlicensed, normally expensive computer software for less than £3. In fact, most small computer shops will offer an illegal copy to their customers as a first choice. The lack of enforcement of the Law of Copyright has led to the black market spilling into high street stores. According to article 24 of the Act, officers at the Ministry shall investigate all violations, visiting media and commercial facilities, warehouses, public institutions and private establishments that use intellectual works in their activities. They shall have the power of judicial investigation and protection of proofs.[102] However, in real life the picture is totally different, as illegal copies of movies, software in particular and books to a lesser degree are sold in public. For instance, the printing shops around King Abdul-Aziz University in Jeddah offer ready photocopies of a wide variety of academic books, without any respect for copyright law. Moreover, the printing shop inside the central library of the same University also photocopies whole books, completely ignoring the copyright law notice posted on its door, which states clearly the limits for photocopying books for academic use.

In the context of Islamic law, such practice violates many principles of Shari'a, notably the following Quranic verse:

> O you who believe! Obey Allah and obey the Messenger, and those of you who are in authority.[103]

Violation of copyright is a prohibited practice under Shari'a because it breaches the law imposed by the authorities and can be considered an unlawful acquisition of other peoples' property. This also violates the teachings of another Quranic verse:

> O you who believe! Eat not up your property among yourselves unjustly except it be a trade amongst you, by mutual consent.[104]

The issue of enforcing the Law of Copyright is complicated, because the Ministry of Culture and Media, which has jurisdiction, blames the weakness of enforcement

102 The Law of Copyright of Saudi Arabia, issued by Royal Decree No. M/41 dated 02/07/1424 H./30/08/2003.

103 The Quran 3: 59.

104 The Quran 4: 29.

on lack of available facilities and manpower. One of the main causes of the problem is the limited working hours of the supervisory department responsible for performing the duties quoted in article 24, which are only from 8 a.m. to 2 p.m., Saturday to Wednesday.

Initially, the law provides for five stages of penalty for infringing copyright. Article 22 puts the penalties in the following order:

- a warning;
- a fine not exceeding 250,000 riyals;
- closing the violating establishment or the one participating in the violation of copyright, for a period not exceeding two months;
- confiscating all copies of the work along with the materials used or intended for use for the infringement of the copyright;
- imprisonment for a period not exceeding six months.[105]

It should be noted that the Ministry of Culture and Media is the competent authority for the execution of this law, through a committee that has among its competence the settlement of copyright disputes. The decisions of the committee can be appealed to Diwan Almazalim within 60 days from the date of the notification of the decision.[106]

Competition Law

The unlawfulness of anti-competitive practice is a known concept within the four schools of Islamic jurisprudence. The legal basis of the prohibition of anti-competitive practice comes from the principle established by the Hadeeth of Prophet Muhammad, which reads: 'La Dharar wa La Dhirar.' This translates as 'There shall be neither unfair loss nor the causing of such loss.' It also means that a person should not harm others, either directly or indirectly, and should not be harmed by others in return. In order to implement the principle of 'La Dharar wa La Dhirar', the Quran prohibits riba and any practice entailing harmful effects on others, including all sorts of anti-competitive behaviour. The Quran clearly states: '[D]o not undervalue properties and goods that belong to others.'[107] The Sunna also prohibits many types of sale contract and unethical practice. In addition, Prophet Muhammad was the first person ever to talk about the idea of 'fair trade'. Such rules include the prohibition of prejudicing the original producers and sellers, as the Prophet said: 'You should not try to cancel the purchases of one another and do not go ahead to meet the caravan but wait till it reaches the market.' However, the Hadeeth does allow for a margin not exceeding 33 per cent of the market value

105 Supra n. 102, article 22.

106 Ibid., article 23.

107 See, generally, S. Alsadlan, *Alqawaid Alfiqhiyah Alkubra wa Matafarra' Minha* (1st edn., Dar Balancia, 1997), especially Chapter 5. See also the Quran 7: 85.

– if it exceeds that, the affected party have the right to claim either compensation or the annulment of the contract.

In recent years, Saudi markets have suffered severely, particularly from the absence of the application of these laws and principles. In 2008 there were two main supply crises: the first one increased the price of reinforced steel; and the second resulted in a shortage of wheat flour supply. In the case of the reinforced steel, the producers all had their own fixed price, which they agreed to increase, in many instances with different percentages. The producers took advantage of the construction boom in GCC countries and channelled most of their production towards neighbouring countries such as Qatar and the UAE, blaming the condition of the global markets for the increase in prices and absence of products. Before the Saudi Government imposed measures to reduce prices, like allowing the import and banning the export of reinforced steel, the prices reached a high peak of something like SR 5,000 per ton, up from an average of SR 1,830 per ton in 2006.[108] The reinforced steel situation was identically repeated with wheat flour, where some distributors hid the subsidized wheat and others illegally exported it to neighbouring countries.[109] These practices are contrary to parts of article 4 of the Competition Law, which does not allow controlling the price of commodities and services meant for sale by increasing, decreasing or fixing their price or acting in any other manner detrimental to lawful competition. The law also prohibits restricting the free flow of commodities and services within markets, or removing them, wholly or partially by hiding, unlawfully storing or refraining from dealing in them. Under the Competition Law, the Ministry of Commerce established a Council of Competition Protection to supervise enforcement. The decisions of the council can be appealed before Diwan Almazalim.[110] Yet a brief glance at the Saudi market shows that, as with other regulations, this law has little notable effect in real life, with many people not even aware that such a law exists.

Company Law

The first Company Law of Saudi Arabia was issued by Royal Decree No. M/6, dated 20/07/1965 and has undergone many amendments throughout its life. The Act might be subject to more slight amendments in the coming years, to cope with the expected expansion of the Saudi economy. The following section will examine the main aspects of the existing company regulations in Saudi Arabia, with reference to Shari'a law as it prevails over all laws and man-made regulations. The Act deals generally with the organization of companies created by mutual agreement, where one or more partners agree to conduct business for profit with a view to sharing profits and losses as agreed. Compared to the company regulations

108 *Alriyadh Saudi Newspaper*. Issue No. 14686 dated 8 September 2008.

109 *Okaz Saudi Newspaper*. Issue No. 2447 dated 28 February 2008.

110 See, generally, the Competition Law of Saudi Arabia, issued by Royal Decree No. M/25 dated 04/05/1425 H. (2005).

of other countries, the Saudi Act is brief, even seen against the Egyptian law that was taken as its source.

When talking about companies in their general contexts, Shari'a treatises do not really distinguish between commercial partnership and partnership formed for any other purpose. However, Shari'a sources do distinguish between different kinds of commercial partnership according to capital ratio, type of business activities, partners' contributions and management of the company.

The law defines a company as a contract under which two or more persons undertake to participate in an enterprise for profit, with each contributing a share in the form of money or services, with a view to dividing any profits (realized) or losses (incurred) as a result of such enterprise.[111] The definition of the Act is more precise than that quoted in the classical Shari'a texts, which merely describes a company as a partnership in liability and management.

The types of company permissible under Shari'a vary in accordance with the different schools of jurisprudence. Generally speaking, companies under Shari'a can be classified into two main categories according to their main purpose: Sharikat Amlak and Sharikat Oqoud.

Sharikat Amlak is the result of joint ownership of a property, through purchase, gift, inheritance or other source. Sharikat Oqoud is the result of a contract wherein two or more parties stipulate on sharing the liabilities and management of their property, labour and/or expertise for commercial purposes.

Sharikat Oqoud is the one concerned with commercial activities and it can take one of the following forms:

- Sharikat Inan applies when partners provide money or assets for trading, and share gains and liabilities in accordance with the portion of capital provided by each of them. All the parties usually contribute to the effort of managing the company.
- Sharikat Mofawadah applies when all the partners are jointly liable for each other's actions. As a commercial partnership it is recognized only by the Hanafi sSchool; the other three schools rejected it owing to its high degree of gharar, or risk – the Mofawadah contract contains two major elements in one, i.e., partnership and a guarantee.
- Sharikat Wojouh has its roots in the word Wajh, which means 'face'. In this type of company, parties use their liabilities or creditworthiness to buy goods or acquire services in order to make a profit. The division of profits is subject to an agreement between the parties and, if losses occur, they are measured by the percentage of ownership or liability.
- Sharikat Abdan is the simplest sort of partnership and the most primitive one. The word Abdan means 'bodies', and, in this type of company, parties

111 Article 1 of the Company Law of Saudi Arabia Royal Decree No. M/6 dated 20/07/1965.

share the gains of their physical effort, such as a group of labourers sharing both the work and gains in accordance with the agreement.
- The form of company most commonly used by big corporations is Sharikat Modarabah. Here, some partners provide capital or assets while others provide management, i.e., some contribute assets while others contribute knowledge and expertise. Profits are shared according to the agreement of the parties.

The types of company available under Saudi Company Law are exactly those available under Egyptian law, which is a translation of the French Company Code. According to article 2 of the Company Law of Saudi Arabia, without prejudice to the types of companies available under Shari'a law, companies should take one of the following eight forms:

1. general partnerships – Sharikah Tadamoniyah
2. limited partnerships – Sharikat Tawsiyah Basitah
3. joint ventures – Sharikat Mohassah
4. corporations – Sharikat Mosahamah
5. partnerships limited by shares – Sharikat Altaosiyah Belas'hom
6. limited liability partnerships – Sharikah That Mas'oliyah Mahdodah
7. companies with variable capital – Sharikah That Ra'as Maal Qabil Liltagier
8. cooperative companies – Sharikah Tawouniah.[112]

Article 2 adds that, in the case of setting up a company that does not take one of the above eight forms or one of the recognized forms under Shari'a, the contract will be considered null and void and the persons who have made contracts in its name shall be personally and jointly liable for the obligations arising from such contracts.

Islamic law is flexible when it comes to partner contributions to a company. A partner's contribution may consist of a certain sum of money, i.e., a contribution in cash, or a capital asset, i.e., a contribution in kind. The contribution may also take the form of manpower or skills and expertise; however, it may not consist solely of the partner's reputation or influence.[113]

There are only a few events upon which a company may dissolve where the Company Law shares Shari'a teachings. A company may dissolve upon the expiration of the term fixed for the company. A company may dissolve when realizing the objective of its establishment, as in the case of a company formed to serve a particular purpose or upon finding it impossible to perform its objectives. In the latter case, Shari'a rules relating to the frustration of a contract apply. Article 15 of the Law adds that the company may dissolve all assets and transfer interests to one partner. The transfer will change the legal character of the company from a

112 Royal Decree No. M/23 dated 28/06/1402 H. (1982).
113 The Company Law of Saudi Arabia, article 3.

company, or Sharika, to a sole trader, or Moassasa Fardiyah. Such a change means a lot, especially with regard to issues such as corporate governance and zakat. A company may dissolve if all the company assets are lost and the remaining assets cannot be utilized effectively. A company can also dissolve if it merges with another company or if the partners agree to dissolve it before the expiry of its term, except when the memorandum of association does not enable them to do so. Finally, a company may dissolve by legal injunction from a Shari'a court or by order from the Minister of Commerce.

The Law of Procedure before Shari'a Courts

As another form of codification, the Law of Procedure before Shari'a Courts can be described as a codification of the daily practice on which Shari'a might have some kind of influence; however, the reality is different. The committee who drafted this law merely summarized the equivalent Egyptian law, reducing it from more than a thousand articles to just 266.[114] However, it does combine hundreds of ministerial decisions and internal circulars in one piece of regulation that, in its simplicity, covers most of the issues related to the procedural rules. This law is of vital importance to arbitration proceedings in Saudi Arabia, as it fills the gaps in the Arbitration Act and in cases where the law of arbitration is silent, as will be demonstrated later in this book. It is proposed to redraft the Law of Procedure, possibly by 2010/11.

The Capital Market Law

Although Saudi Arabia issued its first Capital Market Law in 2003, the stock market had existed for more than 70 years prior to that. The first IPO in Saudi Arabia took place in 1935, when the Arab Automobile Company was established as the first joint stock company in Saudi Arabia, trading in shares that remained unregulated until 1984. By 1973 there were 14 share companies in the kingdom and shares, as with government bonds nowadays, were traded mainly by major banks and wealthy individuals. Thus there were very few disclosure requirements regarding companies' financial position. After 1973 and the first oil boom, known in the West as the oil crisis, Saudi Arabia and other members of the GCC accumulated a relatively large cash reserve in a very short period of time.

This wealth had to be channelled and invested in various economic and social sectors; however, the small population of some countries and overall lack of opportunities led the oil wealth to be either invested in real estate and construction or reinvested in US Treasury securities, a process dubbed 'petrodollar recycling'. In this way a secondary market started to develop, not as a tool for enhancing

114 See the Law of Procedure before Shari'a Courts issued by Royal Decree No. M/21 dated 15/09/2000.

economic activities, but as a wealth-recycling mechanism, adding no real value to the economy.

The stock market continued to develop under a strange supervisory structure consisting of the Saudi Arabian Monetary Agency, the Ministry of Finance and the Ministry of Commerce and Industry. Royal Decree No. M/3 dated 31/07/2003 enacted the long-awaited Capital Market Law. The law established the Capital Market Authority and a few implementing rules of issues, such as listing rules, corporate governance rules, merger and acquisition rules, market conduct regulations, etc. Moreover, the Capital Market Authority established the Committee for the Settlement of Securities Disputes, which functions in a similar way to the Committee for the Settlement of Banking Disputes of the Saudi Arabian Monetary Agency.

The Commercial Mortgage Law

The Commercial Mortgage Law of Saudi Arabia can be considered as a codification of Shari'a teachings on mortgages. Issued by Royal Decree No. M/75 dated 13/01/2004, the Law and its implementing rules require a security pledged to a debt of a commercial nature to be tradable, i.e., it should be legal under the law of Saudi Arabia, requiring that the amount of the debt be fixed in the contract, and thus excluding the possibility of recovering interest. Apart from that, the recovery of interest is not foreseeable, because the law names Diwan Almazalim as the competent authority for the implementation of this Law, which functions in the same way as the Shari'a courts.

The Economy of Saudi Arabia

The development of the Saudi economy is tightly linked to the development of the oil industry and the increase of oil prices in global markets. Prior to the discovery of oil and the flow of hard currencies, the Saudi economy was fairly primitive. With the exception of the Hejaz province, the rest of the country was either self-sustained or starved. By the time of the collapse of the Ottoman Empire and the ruling regime of the Sharif of Mecca or the Sharif of Hejaz in 1924, the country was entering a new economic era. When Ibn Saud assumed power over Hejaz, he started a comprehensive reform movement with the purpose of modernizing his people's lifestyles in general. All the measures adopted by the King at that time in all aspects of life concerned with improving the economy. The King started by improving education, security and health care, before paying a great deal of attention to the judiciary and justice. Most importantly, King Abdul-Aziz built a good relationship with his neighbours and with the important economic and political superpowers, notably the United States. This proved to be the right decision, as adopting socialist ideas contradicts the teachings of Islam and would have gone against the public interest of the new kingdom. Since the 1930s, the

Saudi economy has experienced many ups and downs, which were coupled mostly with political events in the region affecting the prices of oil and petrochemicals.

The economies of Saudi Arabia and other GCC countries can be described as 'oil rentier' economies, because they are economies that depend on the revenue generated from non-renewable natural resources, in this case, oil and gas. Almost no taxes are paid by the public to help the economy to sustain itself. The main disadvantage of this type of economy is the slow and even declining level of economic growth, which is owing primarily to the relatively stable levels of oil production and flat oil revenues, combined with an unanticipated rapid increase in population.[115]

In the financial crisis of 2008/09, the world looked at Saudi Arabia, already a member of the G20, as a major capital-exporter, along with other GCC countries, Russia, China, etc. However, Saudi Arabia had its own agenda for diversifying its economy – to reduce the short-term risks associated with oil dependence and to meet the needs of its growing population.[116]

The Saudi economy is going through a phase of reform and diversification to reduce the dependence on oil exports and to build a service-based economy in the coming years, with the idea of moving towards a high-tech economy at a later stage. This book is not concerned with economic theories and predictions; however, to give the reader a general idea, the next few paragraphs will give an overview of some important economic opportunities in Saudi Arabia.

Saudi Arabia accumulated great cash reserves from what can be called the second oil boom of 2005–2008. Compared to the 1970s, the Saudis are now using their cash more wisely, reducing dependence on oil exports and investing in new technologies, tourism, financial services and education. There were some speculations that the Saudi Government would follow the other GCC governments and increase the portfolio of its Sovereign Fund, although this can now be seen as investing for someone else's future!

It can be said that Saudi Arabia is among the very few countries in the world where the credit crisis of 2008/09 did not have significant impact either on private or public sectors. During the crisis, the Saudi Government continued its ambitious development plans, with new economic cities rising in almost every region in the kingdom and daily announcements of new projects and developments. The Government is also financing some advanced academic research projects, sending thousands of postgraduate students to universities in the West and the Far East, and the banking sector is considerably strong. This is all thanks to tight governmental supervision over almost all economic activities, although the inherent increase in the levels of bureaucracy and misconduct could be criticized. The Saudis will

115 R. Looney, 'Development Strategies for Saudi Arabia: Escaping the Rentier State Syndrome', *Strategic Insights*, 3/3 (March 2004). Available online at <http://www.ccc.nps.navy.mil/si/2004/mar/looneyMar04.pdf> [accessed 10 May 2009].

116 Saudi Arabia has one of the fastest growing rates for population in the world, as more than half of all Saudis are younger than 20 years old.

need decades to reach the stage of having a stable economy not based purely on the export of crude oil.

Privatization and Restructure

The word 'privatization' is an elastic term that has many definitions and interpretations, which vary according to place and circumstances. The definition mostly closely describing Saudi practice is 'the partial transfer of state-owned enterprises to the private sector first and then to the public through the IPO'.[117]

The Saudi public sector has been in need of a major restructure in order to be able to function properly in this rapidly changing world. In pursuance of the kingdom's efforts, aimed at reducing the burden on the government sector and providing public utilities to citizens through appropriate economic means in the private sector, the Council of Ministers issued Resolution No. (219) dated 6/9/1423 H. (11/11/2002), approving a list of utilities targeted for restructuring and privatization. The reform of such public bodies not only covers the economic side, but includes even some political issues that are not otherwise attracting much public attention. The list of targeted public entities is huge in terms of size and number, entailing a great opportunity for almost everyone, because the accomplishment of these plans will reduce the burden of subsidizing and funding such services by the Government, increase the participation of the private sector in the GDP, create jobs and provide higher quality services to normal people. The plans include privatizing and restructuring the following public entities:

- Allegiance Authority
- Department of Zakat and Income Tax
- Saline Water Conversion Corporation
- Saudi Electricity Company
- Saudi Arabian Airlines
- Saudi Railways Organization
- General Authority of Civil Aviation
- Grain Silos and Flour Mills Organization
- Centennial Fund
- roads
- agricultural services
- water and sewage
- General Ports Authority
- health services
- Saudi Arabian Mining Company
- sports clubs
- social services

117 B. El-Dean, *Privatisation and the Creation of a Market-Based Legal System: The Case of Egypt* (1st edn., Brill, 2002), p. 2.

- industrial cities
- mail service.

Economic Cities

The General Investment Authority supervises a number of economic cities that aim at achieving balanced economic development throughout the regions of the kingdom and at creating job opportunities for citizens. The development of these cities will take place throughout a period of more than two decades, which should guarantee better results than building everything at once and struggling to attract investors and maintain growth. These cities are discussed below.

King Abdullah Economic City King Abdullah Economic City is located 150 kilometres to the north of the city of Jeddah, near a small town call Rabigh on the western coast of the kingdom, and it has an area of 168 square kilometres. This economic city, to be established by the Emirate Emaar Company, is one of the private sector's biggest projects in the GCC region. The city is expected to create one million job opportunities and provide two million housing units. The city consists of several major facilities including the industrial port, the business centre, the industrial zone and the resorts area, as well as the supporting areas, such as education facilities, hospitals and residences for workers in the city.

Prince Abdul-Aziz Ben Mosaed Economic City Prince Abdul-Aziz Ben Mosaed Economic City is located in Ha'il and has an area of 156 square kilometres. The city is expected to be one of the most important economic cities in the Middle East in terms of logistic supplies and services, owing to its distinguished geographical location. The city has a dry port with a capacity of 1.5 million tons a year for shipping goods. The city also has an industrial zone and an area for supporting services.

Economic Knowledge City Economic Knowledge City is located in the Medina region and has an area of 48 square kilometres. The city is expected to attract investments of SR 25 billion and to create about 20,000 job opportunities. The city consists of several facilities, including the Taibah Complex for Sciences and Knowledge, the College of Administration and Technology, an Islamic centre and a business centre.

Jazan Economic City Jazan Economic City is located on the western coast of the kingdom and has an area of 100 square kilometres. It is expected to draw investments of SR 100 billion and to create 50,000 job opportunities. The city consists of several facilities, including the sea port, the energy and desalination plant, the industrial zone, the business centre, logistic services and facilities to support services and training.

The openness of Saudi Arabia to the rest of the world through new foreign investment laws and facilities is starting to produce promising results. Many giant corporations have been attracted to the irresistible incentives and have started to invest in the kingdom, as permanent owners and operators of business and industrial facilities.[118] It should be noted, however, that the same law is harming small and medium-sized local businesses and banks, by allowing small foreign 'investors' to enter the market, create jobs for their unemployed relatives, get loans and then disappear, leaving the bank with a bad debt.

A few missing links can be seen in the different enforcement mechanisms of many commercial regulations, which require better coordination among the different governmental bodies.[119] The attraction of foreign direct investments, especially small and medium-sized businesses, without prompt legal reform and strict application of the law, especially relating to tax regulations, is likely to turn Saudi Arabia into a centre for money laundering and commercial fraud. It will also increase the spread of socio-economic problems associated with unemployment and fraud, as most of the small foreign investors bring their own employees with them, do not pay any taxes and, above all, lack business ethics.

The economic importance of Saudi Arabia is far more than being just an investment host country, a member of the G20, or a capital-exporting power. If the Saudis succeed in implementing their ambitious development plans, coming generations of Saudis might be able to enjoy sustainable growth, provided that legislators and decision-makers address existing problems and social needs. The economy of Saudi Arabia has been going through a reform phase. More regulatory change is needed to cope with the transition period, which started with the privatization of the Saudi Telecom Company in 1998 and will last right up until the new development plans and economic cities pay back their cost. Slow reaction to changing circumstances appears to be a feature of the Saudi legal and economic systems, as was shown clearly by the collapse of the Saudi Stock Market in 2006. If, for instance, proper stock market regulations and corporate governance rules had existed and had been enforced before that time, the price bubble might not have been created and, consequently, the collapse might not have taken place. A few months after the collapse, at the end of 2006, the Capital Market Authority issued the Corporate Governance Regulations. Yet, despite their similarity to other regulations, do the Capital Market Regulations apply to everyone?

---

118 Saudi Arabian General Investment Authority. Available online at <www.sagia.gov.sa> [accessed 2 May 2009].

119 A. Baamir, 'Issues of Disclosure and Transparency in the Saudi Stock Market', *Arab Law Quarterly*, 22 (2008), pp. 63–87.

Chapter 2

The Law and Practice of Arbitration in Arabia from the Pre-Islamic Era to the Emergence of the Four Schools of Jurisprudence

Traditionally, there has been a cultural preference in the Arabic mentality for resolving disputes privately through negotiation, mediation and conciliation rather than through public litigation. As well as being linked to the structure of the society and the tribal or family traditions, this trend has historical roots that go back to the pre-Islamic era, or the period known in Arabic as al-jaheliyah. During that era, different tribal ruling systems controlled Arabia, amid the total absence of regulations and regulatory bodies. Even tribal chiefs did not have absolute power to regulate and settle disputes between individuals. As a result, revenge and war were common means of settling disputes. It has been reported that individuals and tribes referred to arbitration and other dispute resolution mechanisms, but this was mostly after their resources had been exhausted by war. According to Al-Ya'qoubi, a well-known Arab historian who lived in the tenth century:

> As a result of not having religions or laws to govern their lives, pagan Arabs used to have arbitrators to settle their disputes. So when they have a conflict regarding blood, water, grazing or inheritance they used to appoint an arbitrator who carries the characters of honour, honesty, older age and wisdom.

Furthermore, many people were known for being arbitrators at that time such as Aktham ben Saifi, Hajjeb ben Zurarah, Al-akra'a ben Habis and Abdulmuttalib ben Hashim, the grandfather of Prophet Muhammad; even Prophet Muhammad himself acted as an arbitrator in many incidents. Despite the great deal of discrimination practised against women, the appointment of female arbitrators was a notable feature of arbitration in that era. Historians have pointed to the important roles played by women arbitrators at that time and have quoted the names of many, such as Hind bint Alkhas, Jam'a bint Habis and Sahar bint Loukman.[1]

Prior to Islam, recourse to arbitration was voluntary, as was the enforcement of the final judgment. The attendance of the parties in the dispute at hearings was

1 J. Ali, *History of Arab before Islam* (3rd edn., Dar Al Elm Lelmalayeen, 1970), Vol. 5, p. 65.

an important condition for the validity of the arbitral award. With regard to the procedure, arbitrators were not bound by any certain rules apart from a number of customs, such as the obligation to hear the disputing parties on an equal basis and to bear in mind the customary rules of the tribe when examining proofs presented by the parties.[2] The procedural rules of arbitration under Islamic law were inspired by some of the pre-Islamic procedural practices that went on to form the basis of the laws of procedure in all Muslim countries today. One example is the rule providing that the plaintiff bear the burden of proof – if the defendant denies, the only thing that can be taken from him is the oath.[3] At that time, the oath was taken in front of one of the sacred idols of the tribe or village, or, in some cases, in front of one of the main Arab idols. If the defendant did not admit or defend himself and refused to take the oath, the arbitrator issued his decision in favour of the plaintiff.[4] Such rules were the result of the accumulated experience and practice of the ancient Arabs, based on the common sense of elders that continued to be followed by later generations and was partly adopted by Islam. The question arising now relates to the reasons Islam has upheld such pre-Islamic practices. It will be seen below that Islamic law adopts the concept of local custom (urf) as a source of regulation as long as it does not contradict the main principles of Shari'a. It is not necessary for these customs to be specific to Muslim society, provided they are not concerned with rituals and belief. This issue will be dealt with in detail when discussing the sources of Islamic law.

Lack of enforceability was one of the features of arbitration before Islam; however, in many cases, the losing parties voluntarily execute the arbitral award, either for moral reasons or because of social influence, especially when refusing the enforcement of the judgment is considered to be a violation or a disrespect of the tribal rules, which might lead the society to abandon them. In the worst case scenario, the voluntary execution of the judgment could prevent the sparking of wars and revenge, as such conflicts at that time started for the most minor reasons and lasted for years or even decades.[5]

Most of the pre-Islam disputes were related to issues of honour, leadership, blood and aversion. One of the most well-known disputes of that era was that between Amir ibn Altufail and his brother Alqam'a ben Altufail after the death of their father, who was chief of the Bani Amir tribe. The two brothers argued over the leadership of the tribe, so they agreed to refer the dispute to the chief of another

2 See, in general, Z. Alqurashi, 'Arbitration under the Islamic Shari'a', *Oil, Gas and Energy Intelligence*, Vol. 1, No. 2 (March 2003), pp. 30–44.

3 This principle was among the pre-Islamic principles developed and adopted by Shari'a.

4 A. Alahdab, *Altahkeem Ahkamouh wa Masaderouh* (1st edn., Naoufal Publications, 1990), Vol. 1, p. 37.

5 P. Hitti, *History of the Arabs* (10th edn., Macmillan, 2002), pp. 87–90. It was reported that a war between two tribes lasted for more than 40 years because of a dispute over the result of a camel race.

tribe to arbitrate between them. The other chief proposed that they should fight a duel with swords in front of him and others, suggesting that the winner would be declared leader of the tribe. However, an entire year passed without an end to the fight. As a final award, the chief of the other tribe decided that both should share the leadership of the tribe, which they did.[6]

The story of the reconstruction of the *Ka'bah* in Makkah, around the year AD 605, is another example of a typical arbitration procedure of that time. The story has been narrated by many historians and Hadeeth narrators:

> Once the walls of the *Ka'bah* were rebuilt, it was time to place the Black Stone (*Alhajar al Aswad*) on its south-eastern corner. Arguments went off about who would have the honour of putting the Black Stone in its place. A fight was about to break out over this issue, then Abu Umayyah, Mecca's oldest man, proposed that the first man to enter the gate of the mosque the following morning would decide the matter. That man was Muhammad. The people were delighted "This is Muhammad". "We accepted him as arbitrator", Muhammad came to them and they asked him to decide on the matter. He agreed. Prophet Muhammad proposed a solution that all agreed to place the Black Stone on a cloak; the elders of each of the parties to the dispute held on to one edge of the cloak and carried the stone to its place. The Prophet then picked up the stone and placed it on the wall of the *Ka'bah.*[7]

The above incident shows the main features of arbitration in that era, which are: that arbitration agreements were simple and spontaneous; that the agreement was not in writing; and that arbitration was similar to conciliation because the purpose behind the whole process was to reach an agreement and settle the dispute by any amiable solution, not to give a binding judgment.

In principle, the arbitration agreements of the old Arabs include all the essential elements of modern arbitration agreements. As seen above, the parties to the dispute stipulate to submit the dispute to arbitration; also the parties to the dispute identify the issue at the time of the dispute, agree on the time and the seat of the arbitration and nominate the arbitrators.[8] In its early stages Islam adopted the concept of arbitration and emphasized its validity on the basis of local customs and practices, which were considered to be a source of law under Shari'a.

---

6 E. Aljuhani, 'The New Saudi Arbitration Act', *Riyadh Chamber of Commerce and Industry Magazine*, 1 (1985), p. 22.

7 I. Hisham, *Seerat Ibn Hisham* (Ministry of Islamic Affairs, Saudi Arabia). Available online at <http://www.al-islam.com> [accessed 21 May 2009].

8 N. Albejad, *Arbitration in Saudi Arabia* (1st edn., Institute of Public Administration, 1999), p. 23.

Arbitration in the Early Stages of the Development of Islamic Law

Arbitration in the Quran

The Quran is the sacred book of Islam, believed by Muslims to be the infallible words of God dictated to Prophet Muhammad. It should be noted that the essential nature of the Quran is that it is not a code of law; nonetheless, it gives general guidance and sets up broad concepts.[9] The following Quranic verse supports this view and indicates that Muslims should follow the guidance of the Quran to regulate their lives, even if there is no Quranic ruling on specific issues: 'Now there has come to you a clear sign from your Lord, guidance and mercy.'[10] There are fewer than 500 verses referring to legal issues in the Quran.[11] Even in these verses there are gaps, as well as doubts as to whether the legal injunctions included in these verses are mandatory or permissive and as to whether it is subject to public or private sanctions.[12] The existence of these gaps can be regarded as an advantage that makes the Quranic injunctions flexible and suitable for every time and every situation, as demonstrated in the conflicts between scholars that occurred as a result of the differences in the understanding of Shari'a texts.

Many of the usual pre-Islamic practices such as revenge, female infanticide, robbery, etc. were abolished by Islam. However, the pre-Islamic methods of dispute settlement were recognized, confirmed and regulated. The validity of arbitration has been confirmed by the main sources of Shari'a at that time, as the other sources developed some decades or even centuries later.[13] The Quranic view regarding arbitration has two main lines. One says that, according to some verses of the Quran, arbitration is a form of conciliation, similar to 'amiable composition', which is not binding on the parties. According to these texts, the arbitrator's decision is neither binding nor final, unless it is accepted by the parties. Thus, arbitration does not have any judicial nature;[14] it is no more than conciliation.[15] The second group of texts recognizes arbitration as a binding dispute settlement mechanism that is similar to the modern arbitration.[16] The Quranic verses regarding arbitration use the word hokm, which means 'judgment' or 'arbitral award', and the word hakam, which means 'arbitrator'. 'Surely, we have revealed to you the Book with the truth, so that you may judge between people according to what Allah has shown

---

9 D. Pearl, *A Text Book on Muslim Law* (1st edn., Croom Helm, 1979), p. 1.

10 The Quran 6: 175.

11 The exact number is disputed; however, the number ranges between 80 and 500. For a partial list of the verses and the related topics, see, in general, I. Abd-Alhaqq, 'Legal Injunctions of the Quran', *Journal of Islamic Law*, 2 (Spring/Summer 1997).

12 Supra n. 5, Hitti, p. 95.

13 The recognized sources of Shari'a law at that time were the Quran, the Sunna and *ijtihad* only, as the other sources were developed at a later period.

14 Supra n. 2, Alqurashi.

15 The Quran 4: 35.

16 The Quran 4: 58.

you.'[17] The applicable law under the Quranic provisions is the Quran itself and the Sunna of Prophet Muhammad; and then the other sources of Shari'a as they have developed over time from the understanding of these two sources.[18]

> If you fear a breach between them (the man and his wife), appoint (two) arbitrators, one from his family and the other from her family; if they both wish for peace, Allah will cause their reconciliation. Indeed Allah is ever all-knower, well acquainted with all things.[19]

With reference to the latter Quranic verse, commentators emphasized the appointment of arbitrators in family disputes as one of the judge's duties and as part of the usual procedure that should be resorted to after exhausting the primary remedies.[20] In this verse, the Quran used the word 'eb a'tho', which is an order to send rather than appoint, adding more strength to the arbitral award issued by the arbitrators. Ibn Qodamah, in his comprehensive work *Almoghni*, which is the main textbook in comparative fiqh under the Hanbali school, cited two main arguments regarding the nature of the mission of arbitrators in the light of the previous Quranic verse:

Arbitrators are agents of the disputed parties According to this view, acceptance of the arbitration and appointment of the arbitrators are compulsory elements for the parties to the dispute, because the appointment is established by judicial order. However, acceptance of the award requires the parties' consent. The exception to the requirement for the parties' consent is where there are disqualified parties.[21] In this case, acceptance of the decision will be subject to the consideration of their guardian or of the judge.[22]

Arbitrators are judges According to this view, reference to arbitration is compulsory, as is acceptance of the award, which is considered final and binding in the same way as court judgments. Supporters of this view quote the following Quranic verse: 'Appoint (two) arbitrators, one from his family and the other from her family; if they both wish for peace.'[23] They add that the Quran calls them arbitrators, not conciliators, and that arbitrators are judges. Thus, arbitrators have freedom in their judgment with no need for the disputed parties' authority or

17 The Quran 4: 105.

18 These also form the basis of Saudi law.

19 The Quran 4: 35.

20 A. Al-Kenain, *Altahkeem fe AlShari'a Alislamiyah: Altahkeem Al'am, wa Altahkeem fe Alshiqaq Alzaouji* (1st edn., Dar Alasimah, 2000).

21 The general rules of disqualification of legal personality will be discussed later.

22 M. Ibn Qodamah, *Almoghni* (1st edn., Hajar Publications, 1992), Vol. 10, p. 263.

23 The Quran 4: 35.

consent. Ibn Qodamah added that the last sentence in the Quranic verse, 'if they both wish for peace', is directed to the arbitrators, not to the couple.[24]

> Surely, Allah commands you to deliver trusts to those entitled to them, and that, when you judge between people, judge with justice. Surely, excellent is the exhortation Allah gives you. Surely, Allah is All-Hearing, All-Seeing.[25]

> If they come to you, judge between them or turn away from them. If you turn away from them, they can do you no harm. But if you judge, judge between them with justice. Surely, Allah loves those who do justice.[26]

Although the above-quoted verses use the verb 'to judge', they distinguish between arbitration and litigation by giving arbitration a voluntary nature, in the sense that arbitrators are given a choice between accepting the position and rejecting it, which is exactly the same concept applied by modern arbitration. Unlike judges, who do not have the choice of declining jurisdiction over a case, if an arbitrator declines there is no way to force him to accept the arbitration, just as a court judge cannot decline jurisdiction over a case without a valid reason.[27] If the arbitrator accepts office, he has the duty to arbitrate with due observance of the rules of fairness and justice; he also has the right to resign at any time.[28] 'And when you pronounce judgment, pronounce it with justice even if a near relation is concerned, and fulfil the covenant of Allah.'[29] The Quran establishes the principle of the impartiality of arbitrators in this verse, and the issue as a whole received a great deal of attention from Muslim scholars, as the following passage demonstrates.

> O you who believe, do not kill game when you are in Ihram (state of consecration for Hajj or "Umrah"). If someone from among you kills it deliberately, then compensation (will be required) from cattle equal to what one has killed, according to the judgement of two just men from among you.[30]

This verse of the Quran gives individuals the right to appoint someone to judge in estimating the amount of compensation without the supervision of a judge or the authority. In the light of this verse, the mistaken party should appoint two qualified arbitrators and execute their decision without resorting to the authority, which is

24 See, in general, supra n. 22, Ibn Qodamah, Vol. 14.

25 The Quran 4: 58.

26 The Quran 5: 42.

27 I. Alastal, *Altahkeem fe AlShari'a Alislamiyah* (1st edn., Maktabat Alnahdah Al Arabiyah, 1986), p. 36. Such reasons vary from a fear of bias to being subject to actual duress.

28 S. Saleh, *Commercial Arbitration in the Arab Middle East: A Study in Shari'a and Statute Law* (1st edn., London, Graham & Trotman, 1984), p. 16.

29 The Quran 6: 152.

30 The Quran 5: 95.

evidence of the legality of ad hoc arbitration in the Quran.[31] The guidance provided by this Quranic verse is similar to the principles established by the UNICTRAL model law on International Commercial Arbitration, in the sense that the parties to the arbitration administer the proceedings themselves without the supervision of a judicial body.[32]

Arbitration in the Sunna

Definition of Sunna As mentioned above, the Quran contains general guidance and broader concepts regarding all legal aspects. These principles have been illustrated in the Sunna, which is the second source of Islamic law after the Quran. The Quran mentions: 'And whatever the Messenger gives you, take it, and whatever he forbids you, leave it.'[33] The Sunna can be defined as a collection of the sayings of Prophet Muhammad, examples of his behaviour, things he approved and things he condemned during his lifetime.[34] The Sunna can be divided into three types: Alsunna al qawliah, which is the sayings and statements of the Prophet; Alsunna al fi'liyah, which is the deeds of the Prophet; and Alsunna al taqririah, or the Prophet's silence or tacit approval regarding deeds that occur with his knowledge. There is a dispute between scholars as to whether the Sunna is a direct revelation of Allah or just a reasoning of the Prophet. Some scholars argue that the Sunna is not a direct revelation of Allah, as is the Quran, but that it is just a reasoning of Prophet Muhammad. However, this opinion contradicts the following verse of the Quran: 'He, Prophet Muhammad, does not speak out of his own desire. It is but revelation revealed to him.'[35] It is believed among the majority of Muslims that the Quran is literally the word of Allah, whereas the Sunna, though inspired by Allah, is the wording and actions of the Prophet.[36]

The Sunna also contains the Hadeeth, which is a more specific term. Hadeeth refers to the direct report of the sayings and teachings of Prophet Muhammad. In the Sunna, reference is made to arbitration. The administration of justice is mainly subjective, descriptive of judges' (arbitrators') ideal behaviour, generally in the form of broad thoughts and prescriptions. Saleh (1984) summarized the most cited references to arbitration in the Sunna as follows:

- The Prophet disliked endless litigation, especially litigation of an oral nature.
- The Prophet's continuous effort to conciliate between litigants and the swift procedure of conciliation is reported to have been established by

31 The Quran 5: 95.

32 See the UNICTRAL Model Law on International Commercial Arbitration, especially article 5.

33 The Quran 7: 59.

34 Supra n. 7, Ibn Hisham, 'The Life of Prophet Muhammad in Medina'.

35 The Quran 53: 3–4.

36 A. Hourani, *A History of the Arab People* (1st edn., Warner Books, 1991), pp. 59–71.

him between creditors and debtors. It is reported that he discounted the claim of a creditor in order to reach a rapid payment. '"Reduce your debt to one half", gesturing with his hand. Kab said, "I have done so, O Allah's Apostle!" On that the Prophet said to Ibn Abi Hadrad, "Get up and repay the debt, to him".'[37]

- Stringent sanctions would befall a litigant who did not abide by the ruling of the Prophet acting as a conciliator.
- The determination of disputes is according to the rules of the Quran, with no room for innovation.
- The repeated requirement that resources should be given to the Prophet as a judge (arbitrator) is authorized as a sign of faith.
- The remuneration of the judge (arbitrator) is authorized as long as it is not excessive.
- The important aspect of the Prophet's realistic and transcendental view on litigation (also valid for arbitration) is worth quoting:

> Allah's Prophet said, "I am only a human being, and you people (opponents) come to me with your cases; and it may be that one of you can present his case eloquently in a more convincing way than the other, and I give my verdict according to what I hear. So if ever I judge (by error) and give the right of a brother to his other (brother) then he (the latter) should not take it, for I am giving him only a piece of Fire."[38]

It is true that this statement stresses the weakness of judges (arbitrators), but it also throws light on the transcendental ethics of the Islamic sense of justice beyond the judicial mechanism.[39]

The Practice of Arbitration at the Time of Prophet Muhammad and his Companions

Unlike the legal scholars of Rome and medieval Europe, Prophet Muhammad was not interested in developing a dispute settlement mechanism that was isolated from political control. On the other hand, Prophet Muhammad needed to control the legal system and, through that, control the development of the law itself.[40] Arbitration was not isolated from the general improvement of the law. Practised

37 A. Albukhari, *Aljame' Alsaheeh (Saheeh Albukhari)* (1st edn., Dar Aljeel, 2005), Vol. 3, Chapter 40, No. 600.

38 Ibid., Vol. 9, Chapter 89, No. 281.

39 Supra n. 28, Saleh, p. 16.

40 G. Sayen, 'Arbitration, Conciliation and the Islamic Legal Tradition in Saudi Arabia', *University of Pennsylvania Journal of International Business Law*, 9/2 (1987), pp. 211–27.

by Prophet Muhammad and his companions, arbitration was a successful and flexible dispute settlement mechanism. Arbitration at that time can be divided into two main sections: general arbitration and arbitration in political disputes.[41] The general arbitration did not lose the voluntary character that it had during the pre-Islamic age; even Prophet Muhammad preferred to resolve disputes by proposing an amicable settlement (*sulh*) rather than by imposing a judgment on unwilling parties; however, a decision can be imposed if the parties do not accept the proposed settlement. This latter type of dispute settlement has been reported in the following Hadeeth:

> An Ansari man quarrelled with Azzubair in the presence of the Prophet about the Harrah Canals which were used for irrigating the date-palms. The Ansari man said to Azzubair, "Let the water pass", but Azzubair refused to do so. So, the case was brought before the Prophet who said to Azzubair, "O′ Zubair! Irrigate (your land) and then let the water pass to your neighbour." On that the Ansari got angry and said to the Prophet, "Is it because he [i.e., Zubair] is your cousin?" On that the colour of the face of Prophet changed (because of anger) and he said, "O′ Zubair! Irrigate (your land) and then withhold the water till it reaches the walls between the pits round the trees." Zubair said, "By Allah, I think that the following verse was revealed on this incident: But no, by your Lord they can have No faith until they make you judge in all disputes between them."[42]

Arbitration in war had a different character and applied in different circumstances from modern arbitration. It referred to the settlement of political and military disputes inside and outside the territory of the state, between the state and other states, or between the state and individuals who have military power. Shortly after the foundation of Islam, the treaty of Medina of AD 662, which was a security pact among the city's Muslims, non-Muslim Arabs and Jews, included an arbitration clause. The clause provided that in the case of a dispute between the inhabitants of the city with regard to a political matter, the dispute should be settled through arbitration by Prophet Muhammad personally or, subject to the approval of the parties, by an arbitrator appointed by Prophet Muhammad.[43] In accordance with the treaty of Medina, Prophet Muhammad resorted to arbitration in his dispute with the Jewish tribe Banu Qurayza.[44] With regard to that incident, the Jews agreed to name Muhammad as a sole arbitrator on the condition that he referred the decision of the case to another Muslim named Sa′ad ibn Moazz, who had once been an ally of the Jews. Even after Sa′ad rendered his decision, Muhammad formally ratified

41 Supra n. 28, Saleh, p. 17.

42 Supra n. 37, Albukhari, Chapter 40, No. 548.

43 Supra n. 7, Ibn Hisham, 'The Treaty of Medina'.

44 C. Brower and J. Sharpe, 'International Commercial Arbitration and the Islamic World: The Third Phase', *American Journal of International Law*, 97 (2003), pp. 643–56.

it, saying that it was in accordance with his own opinion.[45] The procedure of the latter case was described by Sayen (1987) as follows:

> This is evidence that if the parties submit to the judgment of a certain man and he refers judgment to a third person with their acceptance, then that is lawful. He should not refer judgment to third persons without their acceptance because Sa'ad, between the arms of the Prophet, took from them the oath that they would accept his judgement, and the prophet did not object to that. This is because people have different opinion regarding the law and this is a judgment that requires an opinion. So their acceptance for the judgement of one person is not acceptance of the judgment of another, and if he refers judgment to some one else without their consent and he judges in a certain way, then that judgment should not be enforced unless the first hakam approves it after he learns of it. Then it should be enforced because his approval gives it the same status as if he made it himself and because the judgment was in accordance with his opinion and they had accepted that.[46]

As mentioned above in the case of family dispute arbitration, the two appointed arbitrators have to agree on the judgment. This method was used in the well-known incident of *Tahkeem*, between Ali the fourth Caliphate and Mu'awiyah the governor of Syria in the year AD 659. This arbitration was an effort to stop the civil war that erupted as an impact of the assassination of the third Islamic Caliphate Othman, lasting for more than two years. The dispute was submitted to arbitration by written agreement; the two parties agreed to appoint two arbitrators in a written deed, which stated the names of the arbitrators, the time limit for making the award, the applicable law and the place of issuing the award.[47] The arbitrators had been given full power to determine the dispute; however, the provision of the applicable law provided that the decision should be based on the Quran and the Sunna. The two arbitrators agreed in private that both claimants be deposed and a new Caliphate be chosen by a general election. Ali's arbitrator announced the decision first; however, when Mu'awiyah's arbitrator followed, he said that he agreed that Ali should be deposed but affirmed Mu'awiyah's claim to the Caliphate.[48] The award was easily set aside on the grounds of violating the Quran and the Sunna.

The above incident shows the main features of a political arbitration during the first few decades of the life of Islam. When looking at the story, as narrated by different historians, in comparison with modern arbitration agreements, it can be said that both agreements share many characteristics:

---

45 See, generally, supra n. 40, Sayen.

46 Ibid.

47 Supra n. 2, Alqurashi.

48 Supra n. 40, Sayen, p. 229.

- defining the disputing parties precisely by name, place of residence and occupation;
- identifying the precise issue of the dispute;
- including the choice of the arbitrator(s);
- taking the form of a written contract;
- determining a deadline for issuing the final award;
- determining the applicable law in the arbitration proceedings;
- determining the seat of the arbitration;
- defining the supervisory authority;
- determining the authority responsible for the execution of the final award; and
- determining the terms of reference of the arbitral tribunal.

A few decades after this incident, Islamic jurisprudence started to develop through the understanding of Shari'a texts covering various areas of law. Arbitration received a good deal of attention as a supplementary mechanism to the official litigation, as will be seen later on. The questions of what Islamic jurisprudence is and how it evolved and developed, as well as the question of whether it can accommodate modern commercial practices, will be answered in the following chapter before proceeding to examine arbitration rules under the different schools of jurisprudence.

Chapter 3
Arbitration in the Fully Developed Islamic Law

By the end of the ninth century, fiqh and Sunna literature started to develop and take the form that we have nowadays. Scholars realized the importance of arbitration as an alternative for litigation and an essential step in the procedure of solving family disputes. This chapter analyses the arbitration rules under Shari'a as the base for the current arbitration rules in Saudi Arabia and many other Muslim countries. The chapter will start by showing the difference between arbitration and litigation. After that arbitration will be defined and then the chapter will compare the arbitration rules under the four schools of fiqh. The comparison will cover most of the important aspects of arbitration under Shari'a, from the arbitration agreement to the enforcement of the final arbitral award.

The Difference between Arbitration and Litigation

The Islamic law of arbitration regulates all arbitration proceedings. Some scholars do not distinguish between arbitration and litigation at all, describing arbitration as litigation, while others give arbitration many of the features of litigation, as will be seen below. Before examining arbitration regulation under classical Islamic law, the difference between arbitration and litigation should be clarified. According to different fiqh sources, there are six main differences between arbitration and litigation, which are as follows:

- Unlike litigation, the submission of a case to arbitration needs the disputants' acceptance.[1]
- The arbitrator's jurisdiction does not exceed to any issue other than the stipulated case in the arbitration agreement. Meanwhile, the judge has the authority to adjudicate in any case brought before him without the requirement of a prior agreement.[2]
- An arbitrator has no authority to make an injunction on any party other than the parties to the dispute.

1 Z. Ibn Nujaim, *Albahr Alraeq Sharh Kanz Aldaqaek* (2nd edn., Dar Alma'refah, 1993), Vol. 7, p. 27.

2 M. Alatasi, *Sharh Almjallah* (1st edn., Maktabah Haqqaniyah, 1949), article 1842.

- An arbitral award against a guardian of an incapacitated person is not valid if it provides for any damage against his interest unless approved by a judge.
- Unlike a judge, an arbitrator has the authority to deal with disputes even if one of the parties domiciles in another country.
- Unlike court judgments, arbitral awards can be enforced extraterritorially.[3]

The Differences between Judge and Arbitrator

There are some differences between a judge and an arbitrator, even in the opinions of the scholars who consider arbitration as a form of litigation, give arbitrators the same authority as court judges and give the arbitral award the same power as a court decision. First of all, an arbitrator does not have immunity; if it is proved that he is corrupt, he will be punished like any ordinary man. An arbitrator's witness summons is not compulsory and witnesses are not obliged to attend. This is explained by some classical jurists as follows: 'An arbitrator cannot force someone to attend the hearing either as a witness, expert or as a party to the dispute.'

An arbitrator does not have the authority to imprison anyone, because that would encroach on the competence of the court. An arbitrator cannot refer the dispute to another arbitrator without the approval of all the parties to the dispute. An arbitrator does not have the power to enforce an award and his duty ends by issuing the final arbitral award. Finally, an arbitrator cannot change his decision after issuing the award; if he does, the latter award is void.[4]

Definition of Arbitration

Although arbitration is recognized by all sources of Shari'a, it does not receive exclusive attention in the treatises and doctrinal literature of the four schools of fiqh, for the reason that many scholars deal with arbitration as a branch of litigation. Reference to arbitration is often made in chapters dealing with the administration of justice 'Al-Qada'. This might also be owing to the fact that the Islamic judiciary was sufficient and flexible enough to provide suitable solutions to all types of problems arising from social life during that time.[5] There are many different definitions for arbitration under the Islamic fiqh; each definition gives arbitration a different scope and even a different nature from the others. It is difficult to find a comprehensive definition for arbitration in the classical Shari'a texts, as each school defines it in accordance with the scope that it gives to arbitration. The Hanafi school defines arbitration as the process of choosing a person to settle a dispute. The Maliki school refers to arbitration in a fairly specified manner, defining it as

---

3 Ibid., p. 28.

4 M. Ibn Qodamah, *Almoghni* (1st edn., Hajar Publications, 1992), Vol. 14.

5 Y. Al-Samaan, *The Legal Protection of Foreign Investment in The Kingdom of Saudi Arabia* (1st edn., Dar Alandalus for Publication and Distribution, 2000), p. 248.

the process of choosing a person to settle a dispute between two or more parties. Arbitration requires both parties to agree on the arbitrator and the decision taken by the arbitrator.[6] The Shafi'e school defines it differently and does not put restrictions on the choice of arbitrator. Their definition reads as follows: 'Arbitration is the process of choosing a person among the community to judge between disputants and settle their differences.'[7] The Hanbali school defines arbitration as choosing an individual for the purpose of settling a dispute between two other parties and enforcing the judgment on them.[8]

When looking at the above-quoted definitions, we can see that the four schools define arbitration in very similar ways. It can also be seen that arbitration under Shari'a is not restricted to commercial disputes, as scholars leave room for arbitration to encompass almost all kinds of disputes. At a later stage, arbitration has been described as a spontaneous, and more or less ad hoc, move by two or more parties to a dispute to submit their case to a third party called hakam or muhakkem (arbitrator). The most comprehensive definition formulated by a modern author is: 'Arbitration is the submission by two or more parties to a third party of a dispute to be adjudicated according to Shari'a.'[9]

The Legal Status of Arbitration under Shari'a

As a general rule, the arbitrator is an ordinary man; however, the conflict here is about whether the arbitrator is required to possess all the qualifications of a judge, 'qadi', or not. The disagreement regarding the latter point led to arbitration having a different scope and characteristics. Moreover, scholars from different schools disputed over arbitration, whether it is litigation, agency, a combination of both, or a conciliation of the four main opinions, which are:

- Arbitration is litigation. This opinion was reported by the Malikies, some Shafi'es and the Hanbalies. They justified that the arbitrator adjudicates on the dispute and that is litigation. The Hanbalies added that the arbitral award is a binding judgment on all the parties.[10]
- Arbitration is an agency contract. This opinion has been reported by some Malikies. They added that the arbitrator is a private judge in a specified

6 B. Ibn Farhoun, *Tabsirat Alhokkam Fe Usul Alaqdiyah Wa Manahej Alahkam*, ed. Taha Abdulraouf Sa'ad (1st edn., Maktabat Alkolliyat Alazhariyah, 1986), Vol. 1, p. 43.

7 A. Almawardi, *Adab Alqadi* (4th edn., Dar Alani Liltiba'a Publishers, 1972), Vol. 2, p. 379.

8 Supra n. 4, Ibn Qodamah, Vol. 11, p. 843.

9 S. Saleh, *Commercial Arbitration in the Arab Middle East: Shari'a, Syria, Lebanon and Egypt* (2nd edn., Heart Publishing, 2006), p. 20.

10 Supra n. 4, Ibn Qodamah, Vol. 11, p. 484.

dispute and so needs the disputants' approval and acceptance in order to render a valid judgment.[11]

- Arbitration is conciliation. According to the Hanafies, arbitrators are appointed with the disputants' acceptance and each party can decline and deny the arbitration before the issuance of the award, exactly like conciliation.[12]
- Arbitration is a combination of litigation and agency. This is one of the Hanafies' opinions. They justified that arbitrators act on behalf of the parties and so are agents; on the other hand, the award is binding, so it is litigation.[13] This opinion is contrary to the doctrine of the impartiality of arbitrators, for the reason that arbitrators are appointed to give a fair judgment, not to act on behalf of the parties.

From these definitions, we can see that there are five main elements in any arbitration agreement under Shari'a, which are:

- the disputants, whether they are legal or natural persons with clear intentions and the full capacity to enter into the arbitration agreement;
- the arbitration agreement;
- a dispute;
- arbitrator(s); and
- applicable law.

Following the above opinions, some Hanafies emphasize the contractual nature of arbitration and compare it to contracts of agency (*wakalah*). In other words, they assume that an arbitrator acts as an agent on behalf of the disputants who appoint him. They also stress the close connection between arbitration and conciliation (*sulh*). Accordingly, an arbitral award, which is closer to conciliation than a court judgment, is of a lesser force than a court judgment, but the losing party is obligated to abide by the award because the arbitration agreement binds the parties like any other contract.

One of the interesting facts about arbitration under the Hanafi teachings is the mechanism of issuing the award. The award must be rendered unanimously, otherwise every arbitrator would be considered to have made his award separately. This would be inconsistent with the will of the disputing parties to have an award decided by the arbitrators together.[14] Under article 1847 of the Majalla, a disputant may revoke the appointment of an arbitrator at any time before the issuance of the final arbitral award, unless the appointment of the arbitrator is confirmed by a judge, because in this case the arbitrator would be regarded as the judge's representative

11 Ibid.

12 Supra n. 1, Ibn Nujaim, pp. 19–20.

13 Supra n. 2, Alatasi, article 1850.

14 Supra n. 7, Almawardi, pp. 247–59.

and therefore could not be revoked during the arbitration proceedings.[15] All these factors constitute major obstacles to arbitration as an effective method of dispute settlement and weaken arbitration as a whole.

Under the Maliki school, a disputing party can be brought to arbitration by the other disputing party in the same dispute that he is party to. The Malikies also hold an extreme position compared with other schools when dealing with some other crucial issues, such as the revocation of the appointment of the arbitrator, as the appointment of the arbitrator cannot be revoked after the commencement of arbitration proceedings.[16]

The Shafi'es consider arbitration an inferior system compared to the judiciary. This is because the appointment of the arbitrator can be revoked at any point up to the time of the issuance of the final award, which shows that an arbitrator is at a lower grade than a court judge.

The Hanbalies consider arbitration to be litigation; therefore, an arbitrator must possess the same qualifications as a court judge and arbitral awards should carry the same strength as a court judgment.[17]

The above examples of conflict among the schools can be regarded as advantages for arbitration under Shari'a, as parties can apply any opinion that belongs to any of the four schools on an equal basis without violating the law, for the reason that all the opinions are correct and the difference is merely in the interpretation of the same legal texts.

Arbitration regulations under the different schools of Islamic law, as are found in the classical treatises, are the basis of the current arbitration acts in many Muslim countries in general and in Saudi Arabia in particular. The following section examines the legal rulings on arbitration under Islamic Shari'a, from the arbitration agreement to the enforcement of the final arbitral award.

The Capacity of Parties to Enter into an Arbitration Agreement

Types of Legal Capacity

As with other types of contract, parties to an arbitration agreement should possess all the qualities of a capable personality. Such persons should also be competent enough to enter into the arbitration agreement, as well as being able to execute and accept the arbitral award. Under Shari'a, the legal capacity to enter into an arbitration agreement, *alahliyah* in Arabic, does not differ from the legal capacity to enter into any other agreement. In order to be able to enter into a contractual relationship, a party to a contract should each be capable of being defined as an

15 Supra n. 2, Alatasi, article 1847.

16 A. Saiyed, *Arbitration Rules: A Comparative Study between Shari'a, Kuwaiti and Egyptian Law* (1st edn., Aleman Publishers, 2000), pp. 46–47.

17 Ibid.

entity able to bear the legal aspects of Shari'a; able to acquire rights; able to bear obligations; and able to conduct legally effective actions and transactions.[18]

A personality can be either a natural or a legal personality. The term 'natural personality' corresponds to the living status of a human being as it starts at birth and ends at death. Nonetheless, a natural personality can be presumed a legal personality that might be present before birth or after real death.[19] A 'legal personality' is a personality presumed to exist separately from the individuals who established them but without human qualities.[20]

Alahliyah can appear in several forms depending on age and mental ability. Muslim scholars have identified two main sub-concepts of legal capacity, which are divided into five different levels, each level representing a different form of alahliyah.[21] The first sub-concept of alahliyah is ahliyat aluojoup, or the eligibility to qualify as a natural or legal person. Ahliyat aluojoup can be defined as the ability of a person to acquire rights and bear obligations. Ahliyat aluojoup has been divided into full (kamilah) and restricted (naqisah). Restricted capacity imposes limitations on a person's ability to acquire some rights and bear certain obligations. The latter level of capacity is restricted to the foetus and embryo during pregnancy, as an unborn human being has the full right to inherit.[22] Full capacity is attributed to every living human being from the moment of birth till death.

The second sub-concept of legal capacity in Islamic law is ahliyat al adaa′; the possession of ahliyat al adaa′ qualifies a person to conduct and execute his own affairs. It has also been defined as the 'ability of a person to initiate actions, the considerations of which depend on a sound mind'.[23] Ahliyat al adaa′ can be obsolete, restricted or full. Obsolete ahliyat al adaa′ was referred to by Muslim scholars as the state of non-existence of the capacity, or in'idam. Alahliyah is associated with people who have not yet reached the age of discernment, or who have reached it but for some reason cannot satisfy its requirements, such as children under the age of seven and insane people. Restricted ahliyat al adaa′ applies to persons who satisfy some of the discernment requirements but have not yet attained a sufficient level of mental and physical maturity; discerning children can be a good example.[24] Ahliyat al adaa′, mainly, concerns the presence of a

18 See, in general, M. Zahraa, 'The Legal Capacity of Women in Islamic Law', *Arab Law Quarterly*, 11 (1996), pp. 245–63.

19 See, in general, M. Zahraa, 'Negotiating Contracts in Islamic and Middle Eastern Law', *Arab Law Quarterly*, 13 (1998), pp. 265–77.

20 Supra n. 18, Zahraa, p. 253.

21 A. Alsamnani, *Rawdat Alqodat wa Tarwwq Alnajat*, ed. Salahaddin Alnahi (2nd edn., Moassasat Alrisalah, 1984), Vol. 1, p. 52.

22 Ibid., p. 56.

23 Supra n. 18, Zahraa, p. 251.

24 Shari'a scholars distinguish between the age of maturity and the age of discernment. Scholars dispute the age of maturity, as some fix it at 15 to 18, while the majority of scholars recognize maturity to be attained by physical puberty. All scholars agree on the age of seven as being the age of discernment.

sound mind, intellectual capacity and discernment. Any person who lacks one of these qualities is presumed to have a restricted ahliyat al adaa', provided that such a person reaches the age of discernment. Any human being will be presumed to have full ahliyat al adaa' upon reaching the age of maturity and satisfying its requirements.

It has been alleged that Islamic law does not recognize the concept of legal personality. Such a view can be generally rejected as incorrect. Although classical Muslim scholars did not apply this concept to partnerships, this fact can be explained by the social and economic conditions of their time, when partnerships generally comprised a limited number of individuals. In contrast, the concept of the legal personality is well-established under Shari'a with respect to such institutions as the public treasury, the waqf 'charitable trust', schools, hospitals and mosques, all of which are recognized as having the capacity to hold and exercise rights, and accept liability for obligations independent of their administrators. Parties to arbitration should have full capacity in order to be able to exercise their rights.[25] Alahliyah, as represented above, is only theory, as when it comes to actual application, the law summarizes Alahliyah in two main contexts only: majority and prudence. In the next few paragraphs, the requirements of majority and prudence under Shari'a as applied in Saudi Arabia will be examined.

The Legal Capacity Requirements for Natural Persons

In addition to satisfying the requirements of Shari'a contract law, a valid arbitration agreement requires the parties to the agreement to satisfy the requirements of legal capacity, i.e., to have reached a certain age and have a certain level of mental ability at the time of concluding the contract. Classical Islamic scholars tend to treat every case on its own merit, identifying the criteria according to age, sign of puberty and also on the attainment of a defect-free physical and mental maturity with which the person can reach a reliable standard in transactional matters.[26] A general legal competence to engage in legal transactions requires two basic qualifications: majority and prudence.

Majority

'Make trial of orphans until they reach the age of marriage; if then ye find sound judgment in them, release their property to them.'[27] The majority age is not exactly fixed under Shari'a law, neither by classical scholars nor today; however, the above-quoted verse indicates that it is around the age of puberty. Unlike most

25 A. Lerrick and Q. Mian, *Saudi Business and Labour Law* (2nd edn., Graham & Trotman, 1987), pp. 106–107.

26 Ibid.

27 The Quran 4: 6.

Western legal systems, Shari'a did not fix an exact age of majority. Some early Muslim scholars such as Abo Hanifa fixed the age of majority at 18 for males and 17 for females.[28] The most general support was given to the age of 15 for both males and females, by reason of the act of Prophet Muhammad. The Prophet did not allow anyone under the age of 15 to join the army during his lifetime. The Islamic fiqh rejected the fixing of any definite age for legal majority and adopted the principle that legal majority is attained with physical puberty. In Saudi Arabia nowadays, the majority age is a matter of dispute between different public authorities. The Ministry of Justice follows the teachings of Shari'a and accepts it as the age of physical puberty, which varies from one person to the other. This discussion does not relate to the recent controversy regarding marriageable age, because marriageable age varies according to the time, place and circumstances of each case. Such issues are left to local custom and tradition.

Before the age of 15, a person needs to obtain permission from his guardian in order to perform a valid action. In this case, the father of a minor is his guardian by default, following the Hadeeth of the Prophet when he said: 'You and your property belong to your father.' If the father is not present, the testamentary guardian appointed by him should have priority over anyone else. In the absence of the father and testamentary guardian, the paternal grandfather and the court-appointed guardian will follow respectively.[29] On the other hand, a person will have some restrictions on his actions until the age of 18, like the ability to work in the public sector. The restriction might also extend to the age of 21 for travelling outside the country.

Prudence

The Arabic legal term for prudence is *rushd* and a prudent person is called *rashid*. Ibn Qodamah described a prudent person as the person who shows protective safeguarding of his property and soundness in the ordering of his income.[30] The general trend restricts the scope of prudence to being required in financial matters only, whereas some scholars argue that prudence means sound judgment with regard to religion as well as property, so that a sinful or religious hypocrite may not be qualified as rashid, just as he may not qualify as a witness. The latter argument has been generally rejected in favour of the view that an impious Muslim might lack prudence in matters of religion, but if he has prudence in property dealings, then he has full competence to transact.[31]

---

28 Y. Haddad and B. Stowasser, *Islamic Law and the Challenges of Modernity* (1st edn., Altamira Press, 2004), pp. 222–24.

29 J. Nasir, *The Islamic Law of Personal Status* (2nd edn., Graham & Trotman Ltd, 1990), p. 215.

30 Supra n. 4, Ibn Qodamah, Vol. 6, p. 610.

31 N. Coulson, *Commercial Law in the Gulf States: The Islamic Legal Tradition* (1st edn., Graham & Trotman, 1984), pp. 32–36.

Incapacitated Persons

Muslim scholars have identified several mental and physical defects that constitute impediments to legal capacity; consequently, those who suffer such defects have a restricted legal capacity. These defects can be either natural or incidental defects.

Natural Defects

Minority and insanity Infants and insane people are not allowed to conclude any kind of contract and they must be represented by their guardians. The actions of infants and insane people are null and void and not capable of ratification. The incompetence of the insane does not require the prior issue of a judgment to the effect that the party is insane, except in the Maliki teachings.[32]

Mental derangement is a weakness of mental faculties causing a person to have a limited ability in understanding, mixed reasoning and a defective ability of execution. Mental derangement could be severe, similar to insanity; and in this case such mentally deranged persons would have the legal status of insane persons, causing their ahliyat al adaa′ to be obsolete. Alternatively, it could be slight mental derangement; in this case mentally deranged persons would have a restricted capacity similar to that of discerning children.[33]

Mortal illness According to article 1595 of the Majalla, mortal illness, 'maradh almout', is 'a sickness where, in the majority of cases, death is very likely to happen [… I]n the case of a male, [… he would] become unable to deal with his affairs outside his home, and in the case of a female, she [… would become] unable to deal with her domestic duties, death having occurred before the expiration of one year by reason of such illness whether the sick person has been confined to bed or not'.[34] Mortal illness might deprive the individual of the capacity to contract; mortal illness is an original concept of Shari′a. From the above-quoted definition, for a person to be declared incapacitated, four requirements should be fulfilled: it should be a hopeless illness such as cancer or AIDS; the patient should be aware of his illness; the death of the patient as a result of his illness should be expected within one year; and he must have committed a detrimental act towards his heirs or creditors. An arbitration agreement can be annulled by the patient's heirs or creditors if it contains a present or harmful action against their interests.[35] Annulment of an arbitration agreement requires a court order.

---

32 Supra n. 9, Saleh, p. 27.

33 Supra n. 18, Zahraa, p. 253.

34 A. Arrawi, 'Principles of the Islamic Law on Contracts', *George Washington Law Review*, 36 (1953), pp. 32–36.

35 Ibid.

Incidental Defects

Intoxication As a general rule, a person under the influence of alcohol or drugs loses his legal capacity for as long as remains intoxicated. An incapacitated person under this category, as it has been defined by Abo Hanifa, is a person who is unable to distinguish the earth from the sky.[36] The Hanafi school holds an extreme position with regard to intoxicated people. According to the Hanafies, the legal competence of a man is not affected when intoxication results from a voluntary act. It is affected only when alcohol is taken by accident or for medical reasons. To a lesser degree, the Malikies give an intoxicated person the option to ratify his action after regaining his consciousness. The Shafi'es and the Hanbalies deny the legal competence of an intoxicated person and disregard his acts.[37]

Insolvency An insolvent '*moflis*' is a person whose debt exceeds his assets and who is therefore unable to discharge his liability for such debts. It has been argued that a person may be regarded insolvent if he attempts to place his assets beyond the reach of his creditors. In some cases, when a debtor delays payment, a judge may, upon the petition of the creditors or heirs, issue an injunction forbidding the insolvent person from disposing of his assets.[38] This anticipatory restriction of legal capacity is called *hajr*; scholars have based it on the practice of Prophet Muhammad and his companions. All forms of commercial conduct of the insolvent are invalid unless approved by a judge or by the creditors.[39]

Shari'a Contract Law in Relation to Arbitration Agreements and Arbitration Clauses

Parties to the dispute should agree to arbitrate as a prerequisite for the commencement of arbitration proceedings. Such an agreement takes the form of either an independent agreement or a contractual clause incorporated within the main contract. Unlike arbitration under the Code of the Commercial Court of 1931, the Arbitration Act of 1983 regards arbitration agreements and clauses as binding and enforceable. As a general rule, we can say that all contracts and transactions are lawful and binding unless someone finds clear evidence to the contrary. Prohibition of the contract should be established by a clear Shari'a text or through accurate reasoning.[40] Shari'a maintains the parties' freedom to contract.

36 Supra n. 9, Saleh, p. 28.

37 Supra n. 29, Nasir, p. 47.

38 N. Aghndies, *Islamic Theories of Finance: With an Introduction to Islamic Law and Bibliography* (1st edn., Gorgias Press, 2005), pp. 215–16.

39 See Diwan Almazalim, Decision No. 60/D/4 of 1989.

40 S. Mahmoud, *Arbitration Codes: Comparative Study between the Arbitration Codes of Saudi Arabia, Kuwait and Egypt* (2nd edn., Dar Alkotob Alqanoniyah, 2007), p. 56.

In relation to the Hanbali school, Ibn Taymiyyah concluded that a contract cannot be revoked without the mutual consent and satisfaction of all the parties, except when it provides for an obvious violation of Shari'a law, i.e., it prohibits a lawful issue or legalizes a prohibited one.[41] The important aspects of Shari'a contract law in relation to arbitration agreements and arbitration clauses will be examined with reference to the fiqh treatises and common practice in Saudi Arabia. This is because there is no code or act to regulate commercial contracts, the practice being totally based on the traditions of Shari'a.

Contract under Shari'a

The Meaning of 'Contract'

Shari'a recognizes a contract as a legally valid activity and encourages the parties to any agreement to perform their obligations in accordance with the terms of the contract. The Quran states: 'You who believe, fulfil any contracts you may make.'[42] The Arabic term *aqd* is translated into English as 'contract'; however, it carries a deeper meaning than a normal contractual relationship. The literal meaning of the word aqd is 'tie' or 'bond'. There is no precise equivalent of the technical term 'contract' in Western jurisprudence, as a contract under common law involves, in addition to the intention to create a legal relation, the basic requirements of offer, acceptance and consideration. Under Shari'a contract law, however, a contract does not necessarily require the agreement of all the parties, because the term aqd may describe a unilateral action that is binding and effective even without the consent of the other parties in some events. For instance, a gift contract and the dissolution of a marriage by the husband are valid actions with no need for the other parties' acceptance.[43] The juristic use of the word aqd might lead to a presumption that scholars have been using the word in its etymological sense, i.e., following the root of the word rather than its technical use.[44]

Unlike other legal systems, a contract under Shari'a covers all kinds of obligations in all aspects of life such as religious obligations to Allah, the political obligations expressed in treaties, the obligation of *Bay'ah* to the political leader and commercial obligations.[45] The following Quranic verse supports the view that a contract involves all aspects of life including faith and personal religious

---

41 Ibid.

42 The Quran 5: 1.

43 Supra n. 31, Coulson, p. 18.

44 M. Hamid, 'Islamic Law of Contract or Contracts', *Journal of Islamic and Comparative Law*, 3 (1969), pp. 1–11.

45 N. Mohammed, 'Principles of Islamic Contract Law', *Journal of Law and Religion*, 6 (1988), pp. 115–16. Bay'ah is an Arabic term describing the oath of allegiance to the political leader. Bay'ah has been in practice since the time of Prophet Muhammad.

affairs: 'Fulfil the covenant of God when you have entered into it, and break not your oaths after you have confirmed them.'[46] There is no precise definition for contract in Shari'a treatises but most of the classical scholars define it as 'offer and acceptance'. Some scholars require the intention to enter into the contract except in issues related to personal status, i.e., marriage and divorce where the contract will form even if there is no intention.[47] Some Western scholars assume that a contract in Islamic law is merely a legal undertaking – there is a dispute among the different schools of fiqh over the essentials, which are different from the Western definition of a 'binding promise'.[48]

Formation of a Contract

To form a contract under Shari'a, a number of conditions have to be fulfilled. First of all, for a contract to be valid, it should not contradict Shari'a principles. This means that the contract should not involve any prohibited subject matter and should be procedurally valid in the sense that there should be no uncertainty, or '*gharar*'. Moreover, a commercial contract is of no value without satisfying the essential conditions of offer and acceptance.[49] Shari'a contract law is far easier than modern Western laws; however, this simplicity may turn into complexity in modern commercial contracts, especially when the contract is to be concluded by means other than the traditional one of having the parties to the contract physically gather and conclude the contract with the witness of other qualified persons. In addition to the parties' legal capacity requirements to join the contract, Shari'a requires that the parties should sustain mutual agreement during the transaction session, known as Khiar Almajlis.

Mutual Consent

The most important condition for the validity of any contract is the mutual consent of the parties to the contract. The legal basis of this rule is the following Quranic verse: 'O you who believe! Transfer not unjustly the property of one another among yourselves except by your mutual consent.'[50] In accordance with the teachings of this verse, a contract concluded under duress is null and void. Consent should be voluntary and parties should freely choose to make the promise. In addition to mutual consent Shari'a requires mutual satisfaction, as contracts concluded against

46 The Quran 16: 91.

47 A. ben Gasim, *Hashiyat Alraoud Almourbi' Sharh Zad Almostaqna* (1st edn., Almatba'a Alahliyah Liloffset, 1976), Vol. 4, p. 327. See also, supra n. 4, Ibn Qodamah, Vol. 4, p. 271.

48 Supra n. 31, Coulson, p. 18.

49 A. Alkhenain, 'Contracts Involving Uncertainty', *Ministry of Justice Journal, Saudi Arabia*, 13 (2002), pp. 170–73.

50 The Quran 4: 29.

the will of one of the parties can be revoked if one of the parties challenges it. Classical Shari'a scholars distinguished between consent and satisfaction, because consent can be obtained without satisfaction, as in the case of hard bargaining, which is considered to be a sort of duress. The only exception to this requirement is contracts made by an authority against insolvents to pay off creditors – these require neither consent nor satisfaction.[51]

Mutual agreement is the foundation of most kinds of contract under Shari'a. Mutual consent happens when one party gives an explicit offer, in Arabic called ijab. The party who receives the offer should give an unequivocal acceptance, or qoboul. If these two steps are taken correctly, the contract will be legally binding as long as the parties do not change their minds before leaving the place at the conclusion of the contract. In normal circumstances, if a contract has been concluded in conformity with all the relevant provisions of Shari'a, not only is the contract valid and binding on the parties, but its conclusion is also permissible, albeit with certain performances having become obligatory.[52]

Khiar Almajlis

Khiar Almajlis is another important doctrine under Shari'a contract law. Khiar Almajlis is the option of cancelling a contract after its conclusion without bearing any liability. This cancellation method is available in the period between the moment of concluding the contract and the time of leaving the place at the conclusion of the contract. The option of Khiar Almajlis is available to all the parties to a contract – when one of them decides to use it, the contract will be annulled without any liability. The concept of Khiar Almajlis is similar, to some extent, to the cooling-off period in Western laws. The basis for this doctrine came from the following Hadeeth of Prophet Muhammad, in which he said: 'The buyer and the seller have the option to cancel or to confirm the contract before they separate from each other.'[53]

With regard to a conditional sale, the Prophet said: 'No deal is settled and finalized unless the buyer and the seller separate, except if the deal is conditional.'[54] In this case, the validity of a contract depends on the conditions stipulated in it. Furthermore, Khiar Almajlis is not the only cancellation method under Shari'a

51 Supra n. 47, ben Gasim, Vol. 5, p. 332. See also I. Algari. 'The Formation of the Contract in Islamic Shari'a', *Ministry of Justice Journal, Saudi Arabia*, 11 (2001), pp. 1–13.

52 J. Schacht, 'Problems of Modern Islamic Legislation', *Studia Islamica*, 12 (1960), pp. 99–129.

53 A. Albukhari, *Aljame' Alsaheeh (Saheeh Albukhari)* (1st edn., Dar Aljeel, 2005), Vol. 3, Chapter 34, Hadeeth No. 320.

54 Ibid., Vol. 3, Book 34, Hadeeth No. 326.

contract law; other forms of Khiar apply to some cases such as conditional sales, fraud, defects, mistakes and misrepresentations.[55]

In circumstances where one of the parties to the agreement wishes to cancel or amend the contract on one of the cancelling grounds, the damaged party will have the option of cancelling the contract without bearing any liability toward the other parties.[56] After the end of the cooling-off period, i.e., leaving the venue after concluding the contract, the contract is final and ready for execution.

Nominate and Innominate Contracts

Unlike other laws, Shari'a pays very little attention to the distinction between nominate and innominate contracts. Shari'a established the rule that in matters of civil and commercial dealings, any agreement not specifically prohibited by Shari'a is valid and binding on the parties and can be enforced by the court. In the Aramco Award of 1958, the arbitration tribunal stated: 'Aramco's concession must be considered as an innominated contract sui generis.' Moreover, the law gives full recognition to the rule *Pacta Sunt Servanda* with a few moral and religious exceptions in cases where the execution of the contract leads to a violation of Shari'a.[57]

Nominated commercial contracts under Shari'a law are:

- *Bai'* – a sale, which is the transfer of the subject matter of the contract for consideration;
- *Hibah* – a gift, which is the transfer of the subject matter without consideration;
- *Ijara* – a lease, which is the transfer of the right of using the subject matter for consideration;
- *Ariyyah* – a loan, which is the transfer of the right of using the subject matter without consideration; and
- *Salam* – such contracts can be equivalent to futures contracts.

Contracts other than these five are innominated and are permissible only as long as they do not violate the principles of Shari'a and public order.

55 In addition to Khiar Almajlis, there are a few types of options mentioned in Shari'a treatises, namely: Khiar Alshart – conditional sale; Khiar Ala'ib – where the buyer has the option of cancelling the contract for a defect in the subject matter; Khiar Alro'yah – where the validity of the contract is subject to the inspection of the goods; Khiar Ghalat or 'mistake' – where the parties reserve the right of cancelling the contract if it is concluded by mistake, i.e., if one of the parties buys the wrong goods; Khiar Altadlees – where the parties have the right to cancel the contract in case of fraud.

56 See, generally, supra n. 31, Coulson, pp. 56–74.

57 See, generally, S. Habachy, 'Property, Right, and Contract in Muslim Law', *Columbia Law Review*, 62 (1962), pp. 450–73.

Special Conditions – 'Shorout'

Fiqh treatises define special conditions as conditions that are irrelevant to the fundamental nature of the contract. Some scholars do not accept such conditions, an attitude that shows how far Shari'a law tries to keep commercial contracts as simple as possible. However, simplicity can work as an impediment in some modern transactions.[58] In this sense, a loan agreement should not involve a condition that is not reasonably relevant to the concept of loan, such as sale or lease, as, if the parties wish to stipulate something other than the main subject matter of the contract, they should do so in a separate agreement. For instance, hire-purchase contracts were the subject of much debate in the last decade because the condition of obligatory sale of the subject matter after the termination of the lease period was not relevant to the lease contract under Shari'a. Scholars who opposed such contracts argued that having two different kinds of obligations, i.e., sale and lease, under the same contract may create a degree of uncertainty. Hire-purchase contracts were eventually legalized under the condition that the provisions related to the sale of the subject matter after the termination of the lease period changed to be a non-binding promise; otherwise, such contracts are null and void.[59]

With regard to banking transactions, the known practice of *Altawarrouq* is debated continually among scholars nowadays – some prohibit it, while others allow it with restrictions. An Altawarrouq transaction is a contract wherein a customer requests a bank to acquire a specific commodity, usually one with a stable price such as metals, on his behalf. The customer will repay the bank the cost of the commodity plus an agreed margin in instalments. The customer then requests the bank to sell the commodity right away in the commodity spot market.[60] An Altawarrouq contract involves three main irrelevant obligations, as the bank will be seller, broker and agent at the same time. First, the bank will act as broker and seller in the credit sale of a commodity from the bank to the client. Second, the bank will act as agent for the client in the second sale of the commodity. When looking at the nature of Altawarrouq, the reasoning of the scholars who prohibit it is obvious, because the purpose behind this transaction is not interest in the commodity at issue but the acquisition of immediate financing without having to take out a loan and pay interest. Although such transactions do not involve interest, they do involve a great deal of prohibited gharar, or uncertainty, as a result of having two or more different irrelevant obligations in one contract.[61]

---

58 Supra n. 4, Ibn Qodamah, Vol. 4, p. 224.

59 See the Council of Senior Ulama of Saudi Arabia, Decision No. 52 dated 29/10/1420 H. (2000) Riyadh, Saudi Arabia.

60 J. Sole, *Introducing Islamic Banking into Conventional Banking System* (IMF Working Paper No. WP/07/175, International Monetary Fund, 2007).

61 '*Majma' Alfiqh Alislami*', the Islamic Fiqh Council of the Muslim World League, Decision No. 19 dated 22/10/1428 H. 3/11/2007. Makkah, Saudi Arabia.

Prior to the enactment of the Arbitration Act of 1983, Shari'a courts failed to recognize arbitration clauses as valid dispute settlement clauses. This was because judges regarded them as conditions that were irrelevant to the nature of the contract.[62] However, there is no doubt that arbitration agreements and arbitration clauses are valid agreements as long as the dispute is solvable through conciliation.

Termination of the Contract

Shari'a contract law shares many of the common grounds for dissolving a contract with Western laws. As with English law, a contract will be discharged when both parties have satisfactorily performed their contractual obligations. Furthermore, in accordance with the principle of freedom of contract, parties to the contract can terminate it by mutual agreement in the same way that they established it.[63] Under Saudi law, mutual agreement to terminate a contract is treated, to some extent, in a way similar to a conciliation award, because the law does not provide any teachings with regard to remedies and liabilities in such instances. However, Shari'a did introduce the principle of Aloqoud Aljai'za. There is no exact equivalent of this term in Western laws, as the direct translation of this group of contracts is 'permissible contracts', which is meaningless for the reason that entering into most kinds of contracts is permissible. However, the term may be used to describe non-binding contracts. The most popular forms of non-binding commercial contract are wakalah, or 'agency', and the mudarabah company.[64] The most important feature of these kinds of contract is unilateral termination, except in mudarabah where the only condition is to give notice to the other party unless the terms of the contract provide for certain obligations. Shari'a scholars restrict the principle of freedom of contract by the doctrine established by the 'La Dharar wa La Dhirar' Hadeeth of Prophet Muhammad, which translates as 'there shall be neither unfair loss nor the causing of such loss'. This doctrine is important not just in the field of contracts, but also as one of the main bases of fiqh teachings in all aspects of life. Accordingly, the principle of 'La Dharar wa La Dhirar' allows any party to annul a contract if they have experienced serious prejudice as a result of the execution of the contract.[65]

In relation to arbitration, some fiqh schools consider appointing arbitrators for non-binding contracts, as the parties can revoke them at any time during arbitration

---

62 N. Albejad, *Arbitration in Saudi Arabia* (1st edn., Institute of Public Administration, 1999), p. 30.

63 See, generally, G. Samuel, *Contract Law: Cases and Materials* (1st edn., Sweet and Maxwell, 2007), pp. 475–505.

64 A mudarabah company is a form of commercial partnership where one partner gives money to another for investing it in a commercial activity.

65 See, generally, S. Alsadlan, *Alqawaid Alfiqhiyah Alkubra wa Matafarra' Minha* (1st edn., Dar Balancia, 1997), especially Chapter 5.

proceedings. However, the arbitration agreement is a binding agreement, as will be seen when discussing the arbitration law of Saudi Arabia.

The Arbitration Agreement and the Arbitration Clause in Islamic Law

The Arbitration Agreement

There is no mention of a model arbitration clause or agreement in the classical Shari'a treatises; however, the general rules of Shari'a contract law are applied to arbitration agreements. An arbitration agreement can be formed by an offer and an acceptance or by any word or action that indicates the intention of the parties to refer the dispute to arbitration.[66] The Majalla set a few conditions for the validity of the arbitration agreement, which are:

- the dispute must already have arisen and be clearly defined;
- the parties must have agreed to arbitration by a reciprocal offer and acceptance and they must say the following to the arbitrator – 'arbitrate between us because we have appointed you as an arbitrator';
- the arbitrator must be appointed by name; and
- the arbitrator must have the capacity to be a witness.[67]

With the exception of the Maliki school, which considers the appointment of an arbitrator as irrevocable, the appointment of an arbitrator is revocable up to the point of the issuance of the award, except where the appointment has been confirmed by a court or if the arbitration agreement contains a provision for the non-revocation of the arbitrator. The Maliki school stresses the irrevocability of the appointment of arbitrators and the arbitration agreement in the light of the following Quranic verse: 'O you, who believe, fulfil the contracts.'[68] This verse calls for the fulfilment of all contractual obligations, and the arbitration agreement is a binding contract. In addition, assuming that the arbitration agreement is not a binding obligation, it will undermine the strength of arbitration as an effective dispute settlement mechanism.

The arbitration agreement should be documented in writing to prevent any future disputes regarding the arbitration.[69] Islamic law encourages the recording of all debts and contracts, as the Quran states: 'When you deal with each other, in

66 M. Ibn Taymiyyah, *Majmou' Alfatawa* (2nd edn., The Ministry of Islamic Affairs of Saudi Arabia, 1995), Vol. 29, p. 20.

67 A. Alahdab, *Altahkeem Ahkamouh wa Masaderouh* (1st edn., Naoufal Publications, 1990), p. 26.

68 The Quran 5: 1.

69 See, generally, A. Al-Kenain, 'Tadween Almorafa'a Alqadaiyah', *Al-Adl Journal*, 2 (1999), pp. 76–115.

transactions involving future obligations in a fixed period of time reduce them to writing. Let a scribe write down faithfully as between the parties.'[70]

The Arbitration Clause

One of the conditions of the validity of an arbitration agreement is to have an existing dispute; therefore, the legality of the arbitration clause is controversial. Under Shari'a, there are two grounds on which to challenge the legality of the arbitration clause. First, the submission of a non-existing dispute to arbitration might involve uncertainty (*gharar*), which is prohibited in Shari'a contract law. Under Shari'a, a contract whose subject matter did not exist at the time of the conclusion of the contract is not acknowledged and is similar to the prohibited contracts of selling unborn animals.[71] Also, the enforcement of the arbitration clause is suspended on the occurrence of disputes between the contracting parties – this is contrary to the fact that contractual obligations under the arbitration clause are among the obligations that cannot be conditional, according to the four schools.[72]

The previous view counters the basic principles of Shari'a contract law; according to the principle of freedom of contract, parties to the contract are free to include any term or condition as long as these terms and conditions are not contrary to the mandatory principles of Islamic law, such as those providing for the payment of interest, resulting in a risk or any practice involving any kind of speculation where the parties become unable to predict the result of the contract.[73]

When looking at the sources of Islamic jurisprudence, especially the doctrines of istihsan and urf, it is difficult not to allow the use of arbitration clauses for the following reasons:

- They are necessary in commercial contracts in general and in international commercial contracts in particular, as they enable justice to be achieved more quickly.
- They are commonly used in commercial transactions.
- They do not really involve uncertainty or risk because arbitration clauses provide that the contracting parties should choose an authority other than the court to resolve their disputes.

Although the teachings of the Hanbali school are very strict in matters that relate to rituals and beliefs, they are very flexible in commercial and financial transactions.

70 The Quran 1: 282.

71 See, in general, M. Wohidul Islam, 'Dissolution of Contract in Islamic Law', *Arab Law Quarterly*, 13 (1998).

72 Y. Al-Samaan, *The Legal Protection of Foreign Investment in the Kingdom of Saudi Arabia* (1st edn., Dar Alandalus for Publication and Distribution, 2000), pp. 253–54.

73 Supra n. 67, Alahdab, pp. 28–30.

According to the Hanbali teachings, contractual clauses are valid as long as they are not contrary to the purpose of the contract. Ibn Taymiyyah added that a contractual clause is valid even if it is not necessary, appropriate or even relevant to the contract. Al-Sanhury made the following comment:

> With the renewal brought about by Ibn Taymiyyah, the Hanbali doctrine made a great step forward [i]n the way of evolution. It has shed the prohibition of double contracts and restricted the number of defect clauses as it is held that a clause is only defected if it is contrary to the object of the contract or the provisions of Shari'a, i.e. the law public order or good morals. In this, the Hanbali doctrine has come quite close to the [W]estern doctrines: any clause which accompanies the contract is valid unless it is impossible or contrary to public order or good morals. Said clause is then set aside but the contract remains valid unless this clause condition is the determinating motive of the contract: in this case, the contract is also set aside.[74]

To sum up, arbitration clauses are recognized as valid by all the schools as long as they are not contrary to public order and do not permit an action prohibited under Shari'a. Risk and uncertainty make a transaction void and it is obvious that an arbitration clause does not involve any risk.[75]

The Scope of Arbitration

Unlike Western laws, Shari'a does not restrict arbitration to commercial matters only. It gives arbitration the full competence to work as a real alternative to the judiciary. The scope of arbitration in Islamic law is a matter of disagreement between the four schools; the differences in the scope of arbitration given by each school are a result of the different definitions applied to it; nonetheless, arbitration in its narrowest sense under Shari'a is wider and more comprehensive than arbitration in Western legal systems. The scope of arbitration under each school of fiqh will be examined in the following few paragraphs.

The Hanafi School

The Hanafies have two opinions regarding the scope of arbitration. The first permits arbitration in all subject matters except Hodoud and Qissas; some scholars permit arbitration in the case of murder by error.[76] They consider Hodoud as crimes

74 A. Al-Sanhury, *The Sources of Truth in the Muslim* Fiqh (1st edn., Maktabat Alhalabi Alhoqouqiyah, 1998), Vol. 2, p. 102. Cited by Alsamaan, supra n. 72, p. 254.

75 Ibid.

76 The term Hodoud describes crimes which are punishable by a pre-established punishment found in the Quran, and the execution of the punishment is definite; examples

against God and they have fixed punishments that have been set by Him and are found in the Quran and in the Sunna. The second does not allow arbitration to cover Hodoud but does allow it in Qissas. The supporters of this division argue that because Hodoud are crimes against God there is no way to arbitrate in them. Qissas, however, are crimes committed against other human beings; those victims or their heirs therefore have the right to decide on the punishment, and on whether to execute it or not. They add that if the family of a murdered person were to take revenge on the murderer prior to the case appearing before the court, their action would be considered acceptable and they would have no criminal liability.

The Maliki School

The Malikies restrict the application of arbitration to commercial matters only; they say that cases involving any issue other than money must be decided by a judge. In their view, the arbitrator has limited jurisdiction on the given case and the disputed parties only; subjects other than money are of the competence of the judicial authority. The Malikies do not put limitations on the terms of reference of the arbitral panel. For instance, if an arbitrator renders a correct judgment on a case that is outside his jurisdiction, the judgment would be valid subject to the ratification of a court judge; nonetheless, he would be warned not to do it again.[77]

The Shafi'e School

The Shafi'es have three main opinions regarding the scope of arbitration; some of their scholars deny the validity of arbitration if there is a court in the town, because arbitration might weaken the power of the court. Another group of scholars give arbitration the same scope and power as litigation; they argue that the appointed arbitrator has the same power as the appointed judge, as both have been appointed; and the validity of arbitration is not restricted to commercial disputes. The third group of scholars allows arbitration to proceed in all subject matters except in criminal disputes.

The Hanbali School

The Hanbalies largely give arbitrators the same jurisdiction as court judges. Some scholars do not allow arbitration in criminal matters because the nature of criminal cases is different from that of commercial disputes. Ibn Taymiyyah did not restrict the scope of arbitration and he gave it the same scope as litigation; however,

---

are rape, theft and terrorism. Qissas is a term to describe revenge crimes; in Qissas crimes, the victim or his family has a right to seek retribution and retaliation, and also a right not to execute the judgment, as in the case of murder and injury.

77 Supra n. 6, Ibn Farhoun, p. 145.

according to him, an arbitral award has no value without judicial review, which is the same concept followed by the Saudi legal system nowadays.[78]

Applicable Law

The concept of the conflict of laws under Shari'a has different dimensions in contrast to modern Western laws. All four schools of fiqh insist on the mandatory application of procedural and substantive Shari'a rules; the application of any law other than Shari'a or any custom or practices that are not in compliance with Shari'a on a dispute between Muslim parties within the Muslim state is totally prohibited. The ban has been brought about by the following Quranic verses: 'Those who do not judge according to what Allah has sent down, they are the unjust.'[79] 'Those who do not judge according to what Allah has sent down, they are the sinners.'[80]

Islamic law pays no attention to states, borders and other concepts such as nationality and domicile; it only recognizes two main categories of legal subjects, Muslims and non-Muslims. With regard to Muslims, Shari'a is a personal law and is applicable regardless of whether the Muslim travels or resides in or outside Islamic territory. In other words, Shari'a applies extraterritorially to Muslims. Regarding non-Muslims, Shari'a is a territorial law, as it applies to anyone travelling or residing in Islamic territory, with the exception of family law and religious affairs.[81] In the latter cases, Islamic conflict law adheres to the personality of laws by allowing non-Muslims a relative legislative and judicial autonomy. If a Muslim party is involved in any dispute, Shari'a will be the applicable law; however, there are some cases where the dispute involves non-Muslims only, which will be given more attention when discussing the qualifications of arbitrators.

The conflict of laws under Shari'a arises to some extent between the rules of the different Shari'a schools, but it should be noted that the problem of the conflict of laws is not so material in arbitration, because each party will nominate its arbitrator, which can be considered as an implied choice of school. Article 1803 of the Majalla provides that the defendant in judicial proceedings is allowed to choose a judge from his own school if he has been brought before a judge from another school of law. The choice can be made if the application of the other school's teachings will result in a substantial change in the award or the judgment.[82] To overcome this problem, there are four judges belonging to the four schools of fiqh in major Muslim cities. Similarly, judges in Saudi Arabia have the

78 A. Al-Kenain, *Altahkeem fe AlShari'a Alislamiyah: Altahkeem Al'am, wa Altahkeem fe Alshiqaq Alzaouji* (1st edn., Dar Alasimah, 2000), p. 49.

79 The Quran 5: 45.

80 The Quran 5: 47.

81 M. Berger, 'Conflicts of Law and Public Policy in Egyptian Family Law: Islamic Law through the Backdoor', *American Journal of Comparative Law*, 50 (2002), pp. 555–56.

82 Supra n. 2, Alatasi, article 1803.

right to apply the teachings of the four schools on an equal basis. As a final remark, the application of the different schools results in a very minor difference and, in many cases, the four schools incorporate the opinions of each other within their teachings as different ways of interpreting the same legal text.

Arbitrators

Qualifications of Arbitrators

An important condition for the validity of arbitral awards is that they be awarded by a qualified arbitrator. Also, having an arbitrator that lacks one of the qualifications can be solid ground for challenging an arbitral award not just under Shari'a, but as a recognized concept in all civilized arbitration rules. There has been a dispute among the four schools of fiqh with regard to the required qualifications of arbitrators. There are two main views on whether the arbitrator should possess the qualifications of a judge or not. The difference in the requirements is based on the nature of the arbitration and whether it is similar to conciliation, agency or litigation. The first view does not require the arbitrator to possess all the qualifications of a judge – It is necessary for him to be a Muslim man only. This opinion has been supported by some Malikies and by Ibn Taymiyyah from the Hanbali school, justifying arbitration as a kind of agency. For this reason, Ibn Taymiyyah held that an arbitral award is of no affect without judicial review.[83] The second opinion represents the view of the majority of Muslim scholars, which requires the arbitrator to possess all the qualifications of a judge.[84] There are eight qualifications of a judge under the four schools' law, which will be elaborated in turn.

The arbitrator should be Muslim There is no doubt among all the scholars that a non-Muslim is not allowed to adjudicate in any dispute involving a Muslim element if the dispute concerns an action performed within Muslim territory. According to the Malikies, the Shafi'es and the Hanbalies, arbitration proceedings in Muslim territory must be adjudicated by a Muslim arbitrator and non-Muslims should not serve as judges or as arbitrators, even to arbitrate between non-Muslims.[85] However, banning non-Muslim arbitrators from arbitrating in a totally non-Muslim dispute might contradict the following Quranic verse: 'So let the People of the Gospel judge according to what God has sent down therein.'[86] The Hanafies have no restrictions on this issue and permit non-Muslims to arbitrate

83 Supra n. 66, Ibn Taymiyyah, Vol. 35, p. 355.
84 Supra n. 78, Al Kenain, p. 58.
85 Ibid.
86 The Quran 5: 47.

between non-Muslims in all subject matters in accordance with the above-quoted Quranic verse.[87]

According to the Hanbali school, apart from settling personal status disputes, non-Muslims are not allowed to serve as arbitrators inside Islamic territory. If the arbitration agreement provides for the settlement of the dispute by conciliation, then the arbitrators/conciliators can be non-Muslims because the agreement is considered to be an agency agreement that can be executed by them. Moreover, oral testimony and expert opinion from non-Muslims are assumed to be valid in commercial matters.[88]

The arbitrator should be mature Muslim scholars agree that maturity is one of the most important qualifications of judges and arbitrators. Shari'a law assumes underage people to be under the authority and guardianship of others, so they cannot have authority over people themselves.[89] The Hanafies, the Malikies and the Hanbalies prohibit child arbitration because children lack the necessary technical qualifications and experience. Some Malikies approve the arbitration of a child if he renders a correct judgment.[90]

The arbitrator should be prudent As an essential condition for the acceptance of a testimony and oath, prudence is also required in arbitrators by all four schools.[91] It is not sufficient for a judge/arbitrator to use his five senses like any ordinary man. He must have the ability to understand, analyse and solve complicated problems, although some Maliki scholars do not like too much cleverness.[92] Prudence and Adalah share many common aspects, but Adalah is more comprehensive, including prudence in addition to matters of religion and behaviour.

The arbitrator should be knowledgeable about Shari'a law An arbitrator must have sufficient understanding of Shari'a law, especially the Quran, the Sunna, the ijma' and the qiyas. A judgment without reference to one of these sources will be considered null and void and will not be approved by the judge for enforcement. The Shafi'es, the Hanbalies and some of the Malikies and Hanafies require a judge/arbitrator to be a 'mujtahid', i.e., to have the ability to exercise ijtihad.[93] The majority of Hanafies and some of the Malikies and Hanbalies, however, do not require him to be so. Ibn Taymiyyah from the Hanbali school argued that arbitrators should be specialists and so should have knowledge in their areas of specialization only. He added that a general knowledge of Islamic law should be obtained by the arbitrator

87 Supra n. 78, Al Kenain, p. 59.
88 Supra n. 4, Ibn Qodamah, Vol. 14, p. 170.
89 Supra n. 21, Alsamnani, Vol. 1, p. 52.
90 Supra n. 78, Al Kenain, p. 61.
91 Supra n. 4, Ibn Qodamah, Vol. 10, p. 45.
92 Ibid.
93 Supra n. 7, Almawardi, Vol. 2, p. 380.

in order to enable him to render a valid judgment that does not contradict the main principles of Islamic Shari'a. The Malikies allow non-specialists to arbitrate provided that they seek specialists' consultation and the award is based totally on the experts' testimony, otherwise the award will be void.[94]

The arbitrator should possess the characteristics of adalah The word *adalah* is a comprehensive term to describe a person's character. Honesty, a stable mind, decent behaviour, good moral values and avoidance of forbidden things and major sins all make up the character of an adl person.[95] In contrast, the term *fasiq* is used to describe the opposite qualities and is usually reserved for those whose moral character is corrupt. According to the Malikies, the Shafi'es and the Hanbalies, if the authority appoints a judge who is not adl, he will have no valid authority and judgments.[96] The Hanafies and some Malikies do not require a judge to be adl – a non-adl person can still have a valid authority and judgment if he has been appointed by the authority. In addition, some Malikies, Shafi'es and Hanbalies use the concept of 'necessity judge' to describe either an appointed judge who does not possess all the required qualifications or a powerful person without the legal authority needed to help run people's daily lives.[97]

Though adalah is a requirement for a court judge whether an arbitrator has to be adl or not is still a matter of dispute. Some Hanafies, the majority of the Malikies and the Hanbalies do not recognize the appointment and the judgment of a fasiq arbitrator because they consider arbitration to be equivalent to litigation. The other view recognizes the appointment and the judgment of a non-adl or fasiq arbitrator provided he is professionally qualified.[98] It can be said that if a person's testimony is accepted, his arbitration should be recognized.

The arbitrator should be male Shari'a requires an arbitrator to be a man; the appointment of a woman as a judge/arbitrator is considered null and void even if she gives a correct judgment.[99] Scholars support this opinion with the following Hadeeth: 'When the Prophet heard the news that the people of Persia had made the daughter of Khosrau their Queen, he said, "Never will succeed such a nation as makes a woman their ruler".'[100] They also apply the general principles of the following Quranic verse: 'Two men shall serve as witnesses; if not two men, then a man and two women whose testimony is acceptable to all. Thus, if one

94 Supra n. 4, Ibn Qodamah, Vol. 14, pp. 5–37.

95 Supra n. 9, Saleh, p. 36.

96 Supra n. 78, Al Kenain, p. 73.

97 S. Alramly, *Nihayat Almohtaj Ila Sharh Alminhaj* (3rd edn., Dar Ihya' Altorath, 1993), Vol. 8, p. 240.

98 H. ben Maza, *Sharh Adab Alqadi*, ed. Abilwafa Alafgani and Abibakur Alhashimi (1st edn., Dar Alkotoub Al Ilmiyah, 1994), Vol. 4, p. 66.

99 Supra n. 4, Ibn Qodamah, Vol. 11, p. 380.

100 Supra n. 53, Albukhari, Vol. 9, Chapter 88, Hadeeth No. 219.

woman becomes biased, the other will remind her.'[101] According to this verse, a male's testimony is equal to that of two women; therefore women are not as competent as men in certain roles, such as judge and arbitrator. Not all schools of fiqh think the same, however. The Hanafies do not require judges/arbitrators to be men – they permit women to arbitrate in all cases except crimes. The Hanafies' practice contradicts their opinion, though, as the Hanafies ruled Islamic countries for centuries during the Ottoman Empire and never appointed a woman as a judge. The vast majority of Muslim scholars do not recognize the appointment of women arbitrators because women are not qualified to be judges.[102]

The issue of employing women in the judiciary as judges carries a great deal of controversy in Saudi Arabia. In the past, restrictions on female employment in the judiciary were criticized by many international human rights organizations. These days the issue is being raised within the kingdom, too, asking for women to be given the right to become arbitrators and even judges. Such an issue seems to be more about social nature than about legal or religious matters, as it relates to the common culture and traditions that are important sources of public policy in modern Saudi law. Moreover, customs and practices are sources of Islamic law just as any fatwa, ijtihad or ijma' should fit within the overall social order. What can be said about female arbitration can also be said about other issues, such as women driving in Saudi Arabia, although there is no religious objection regarding the latter.

The arbitrator should not be blind, deaf or mute A judge should not be blind, deaf or mute as such disabilities can impede him from rendering accurate judgments. Partial hardness of hearing and sight can be tolerated as long as it does not affect the arbitration.[103] With regard to hearing and sight, scholars are divided amongst three opinions, The Hanafies, the Shafi'es and some Hanbalies require the arbitrator not to be deaf or blind as one of these disabilities nullifies his appointment and can be grounds for challenging the judgment.[104] The second opinion is propounded by the Maliki school, which says that sight and hearing are very important conditions that should be met in an arbitrator. If deafness or blindness occurs during the course of his appointment, the arbitrator should be replaced as soon as possible, yet if he renders a judgment it will be considered valid. They also apply the same conditions for talking disability. The third view is that of some Hanbalies, who do not see blindness and deafness as obstacles to the appointment of an arbitrator. A mute person cannot be appointed at all except in the view of some Shafi'es, which requires the arbitrator to be able to communicate by understandable sign language.[105]

101 The Quran 1: 282.
102 Supra n. 78, Al Kenain, pp. 77–79.
103 Supra n. 4, Ibn Qodamah, Vol. 11, p. 381.
104 Supra n. 98, Ibn Maza, Vol. 4, p. 61.
105 Supra n. 16, Saiyed, p. 47.

The arbitrator should be impartial Muslim scholars pay a great deal of attention to the principle of the impartiality of judges and arbitrators. The reasons behind such regulations are to promote justice and to give confidence in the legal system. A few issues might harm the impartiality of the arbitrator and might prevent his appointment or serve as grounds for challenging the arbitral award. The first impediment is hostility. The Shafi'es see no problem if the award is in favour of the arbitrator's opponent, but if it is not in his favour they have two opinions: some of them do not allow the appointment on the ground of hostility, because enemies are not allowed to be witnesses against each other; while others believe the ratification to be subject to the disputant's permission. The second impediment is dispute, which refers any normal dispute even if it does not reach the level of hostility.[106] There is a great deal of conflict regarding this issue but, briefly, if the arbitrator is in dispute with both parties, some scholars reject his appointment and do not recognize his awards, while others allow him to arbitrate without conditions. If the arbitrator is in dispute with one of the disputants, there is unanimity on banning his arbitration.

If the arbitrator is one of the parties to the same dispute, there are four views regarding the validity of his appointment. The first view allows one of the parties to the dispute to act as an arbitrator as long as he is adjudicating in equity. The second does not allow a party to the dispute to serve as an arbitrator; the Hanafies justify this opinion by saying that a party to the dispute is not allowed to be a witness against the other party, thus he is not allowed to arbitrate. The third opinion does not encourage one of the parties to be an arbitrator in the dispute, but if this happens the award is valid. The fourth does not allow one of the parties to serve as an arbitrator in the same dispute unless he is willing to issue an award in favour of his opponent, as it will be considered as a form of admission (*iqrar*).[107] The main view encourages the parties to avoid any suspicion with regard to the impartiality of the arbitrators; if they both agree on an arbitrator, his award will be valid.

The third impediment to the impartiality of the arbitrator is kinship. The kinds of relationship that annul the appointment are fatherhood, motherhood, including grandfathers, grandmothers, great-grandfathers and great-grandmothers, in Arabic called '*alosoul*'. This category also includes children, grandchildren, and their children as well as the wife and husband in Hanafi teachings. Scholars have two opinions regarding kinship: some Shafi'es and Hanafies allow kin to judge against family members only; others allow family members to be chosen as arbitrators.[108]

106 Ibid.

107 Ibid.

108 Supra n. 1, Ibn Nujaim, Vol. 7, pp. 26–27.

The Appointment of Arbitrators

The appointment of an arbitrator is a contractual act entered into by two or more parties involved in a judicial or extrajudicial dispute.[109] All parties should consent to the appointment of the arbitrator; there are some differences of opinion among the four schools as to whether the consent of the parties is required at the time of the appointment only or whether it should continue until the arbitrator makes his award. The appointment should be made in the arbitration agreement subject to the acceptance of the arbitrator as mentioned above.[110] The Hanafies require an arbitrator to be known to the parties to avoid uncertainty; however, if a person arbitrates between two parties, without an appointment, and they accept his award, his appointment will apply retroactively.[111] Some modern texts deny the institutional appointment under Shari'a and argue that arbitration is an independent mechanism for settling disputes and it should not fall under the influence of any official institution.[112] This argument contradicts the Quran, in which the appointment of arbitrators in family disputes should be done through the court judge as seen above.

The Number of Arbitrators

Multiple arbitrators' proceedings were unknown pre-Islam. Traditionally, arbitrators had to settle disputes alone, acting as single judges.[113] All four schools permit the parties to have more than one arbitrator; the Shafi'es permit two arbitrators; the Hanafies, the Hanbalies and the Malikies allow parties to have more than two arbitrators.[114] Some Hanbalies do not recommend the appointment of an even number of arbitrators for the sake of reaching unanimity when issuing the award. This approach was adopted by the Arbitration Act of 1983 in Saudi Arabia, which will be seen below.

Remuneration of Arbitrators and Administration Fees

The issue of judges' remuneration has been recognized by all four schools, which have recommended that a suitable remuneration be drawn from the public treasury to ensure judges' impartiality. The case is different with arbitration, though, as it is a private dispute settlement method. Under all the schools, the parties to the arbitration agreement should bear the fees of the arbitrators. The Hanbali scholar Ibn Qayem Aljaoziyah set two conditions for the arbitrator's

---

109 Supra n. 9, Saleh, p. 39.
110 Supra n. 16, Saiyed, pp. 38–40.
111 Supra n. 78, Al Kenain, p. 100.
112 Supra n. 9, Saleh, p. 39.
113 This effect can be seen in article 4 of the Arbitration Regulation of Saudi Arabia.
114 Supra n. 78, Al Kenain, pp. 105–106.

remuneration: first, that an arbitrator should not receive any money from the public treasury for arbitration; and second, that the money should be deposited with an impartial party before the commencement of the arbitral proceeding in order to guarantee the payment of the fees.[115] Classical Shari'a treatises do not mention anything regarding administration fees and experts' remuneration. It seems that if the arbitration agreement does not state that the parties are going to bear the administration fees, such fees should be paid by the parties.

Termination of the Office of Arbitrator

Under Shari'a, the arbitrator's appointment may end before or after the settlement of the dispute. One reason that the appointment of an arbitrator may end is the issuance of the arbitral award – this puts an end to the dispute, called 'raf' alneza'' in Arabic, as the parties to the dispute are no longer in need of the services of the arbitrators.[116] The second reason for the termination of the arbitrator's appointment is reaching a settlement outside the arbitral tribunal, which can be described as compulsory termination. Examples are reaching an amiable settlement outside the tribunal, exemption or rescheduling of debt.[117]

The appointment of an arbitrator can be terminated before reaching a settlement. The termination in this case can take the following forms:

- Disqualification of an arbitrator: losing one or more of the required qualifications of an arbitrator disqualifies him from continuing in office and annuls the arbitration and the award. The concept of the continuity of the qualifications requires an arbitrator to be qualified throughout the arbitral procedure, from the date of the arbitration agreement until the issue of the award.[118]
- The absence of the arbitrator: if the arbitrator's absence affects the parties to the dispute, they have the choice of annulling his appointment.[119]
- The expiration of the arbitrator's appointment: the parties to the dispute have the choice of appointing an arbitrator for a limited period of time. The arbitrator has no jurisdiction over the dispute after the designated date unless the parties to the arbitration extend it, which will be considered as a new appointment.[120]

---

115 Ibn Qayem Aljaoziyah, *Bada'I Alfawaid*, ed. Hisham Ata, Adil Adawi and Ashraf Ahmad (1st edn., Nizar Mustafa Albaz Publishers, 1996), Vol. 3, p. 146.

116 Supra n. 2, Alatasi, article 1842.

117 Supra n. 4, Ibn Qodamah, Vol. 5, p. 2.

118 Supra n. 16, Saiyed, pp. 41–42.

119 Supra n. 1, Ibn Nujaim, Vol. 7, p. 28.

120 Ibid.

- Termination by the arbitrator's death or insanity: it is obvious that an arbitrator's appointment terminates at the moment of his death or insanity.[121]
- Revocation of the arbitrator's authority: the arbitrator is not authorized to exercise his function without the continuing consent of either of the parties to the arbitration. The consent must continue until the issue of the arbitral award; however, the Malikies do not agree with this concept and consider the appointment to be irrevocable.[122] The issue of the revocability of an arbitrator's appointment of the can be summarized by saying that the parties to the dispute can terminate the appointment of the arbitrator at any time – if the arbitrator issues an award after the revocation the award will be considered void. On the other hand, if the appointment has been made through a judge (or in an institutional arbitration nowadays), the revocation must be done through a judge again.[123] If one party revokes the appointment of the arbitrator and the other denies, there are three views. Each party to the dispute has the right to revoke the appointment of the arbitrator unilaterally at any time without any limitations because the arbitrator is an agent. The revocation is permissible before the commencement of the arbitration only. Parties to the dispute cannot revoke the appointment of the arbitrator after they accept it. A party to the arbitration cannot revoke the appointment unilaterally because that might be used fraudulently by the party that see the proceeding going not in their favour.[124]
- Resignation of the arbitrator: Malikies do not accept the arbitrator's resignation after the commencement of the arbitration without the parties' approval. Other schools have various opinions; some scholars allow the arbitrator to resign at any time. If the arbitrator refuses to perform his duty, either party can revoke the appointment without any remuneration.[125]

Rules of Evidence

Evidence can be defined as anything that tends to prove or disprove a fact at issue in a legal action.[126] The law on evidence in Islamic Shari'a has not changed much over the last 10 centuries, so it is, to some extent, out of date nowadays. There is a link between the concept of evidence and the definition of plaintiff in Islamic law. A plaintiff is not just the litigant who commences the judicial or arbitral proceedings. The plaintiff is the litigant who, by issuing the claim before the judge

121 Supra n. 9, Saleh, p. 45.
122 Ibid.
123 Supra n. 2, Alatasi, article 1847.
124 Supra n. 78, Al Kenain, pp. 159–60.
125 Ibid.
126 T. Buckles, *Laws of Evidence* (1st edn., Thomson Delmar Learning, 2003), p. 15.

or the arbitrator, disrupts an apparently normal state of affairs by alleging that this state of affairs does not conform to his rights. The defendant is the party who admits or denies the plaintiff's claim. Shari'a places the burden of proof on the plaintiff, justified on two grounds: the existing situation is presumed to be the original and the normal state of affairs, and it is up to the plaintiff to establish the contrary; and a person summoned before the judge/arbitrator is presumed to be free of liability.[127]

There are six types of evidence under Shari'a. These rules are firmly set out, leaving no room for the judge/arbitrator to choose the most convincing one; all of them have the same power. Apart from family disputes, the typical procedure before any Shari'a court consists of three stages. First the plaintiff lodges the claim which should be precise in all its details. The claim can be in writing or can be verbalized at the time of the trial. At the second stage, the judge invites the defendant to answer the plaintiff's claim. At this stage, the defendant will either admit the claim, '*iqrar*', or deny it, '*nokoul*'. If the defendant denies the claim, the judge will ask the plaintiff to adduce the evidence, '*baiyenah*'. The final stage starts if the plaintiff fails to provide the court with testimonial evidence; he may administer the oath, '*yameen or qasam*'. If the defendant swears that the claim is groundless, the claim will be dismissed; however, if the defendant refuses to take the oath, the case will be decided in favour of the plaintiff.[128] This is the normal procedure applied, since the time of Prophet Muhammad until today, in all Shari'a courts anywhere in the world.

Admission – 'Iqrar'

The iqrar, or admission, is ranked at the top of the types of evidence by Shari'a scholars, as there is a rule that 'admission is the master of all types of evidence'. Iqrar has been defined as an admission on the part of a person that he owes an obligation to another person. It is disputed whether the scope of the term includes a confession, either judicial or extrajudicial, or not. A recognizable admission is one that has been made by an adl defendant provided that he is not under duress; a valid admission should be precise with regard to specific facts and circumstances in order to enable the arbitrator to issue a correct award.[129]

Oral Testimony – 'Shahadah/Baiyenah'

In Shari'a, oral testimony, or *shahadah,* is the primary means of evidence, prevailing over all other forms of evidence. The classical juridical reading of the Quranic verses privileges the oral testimony, shahadah, of two male witnesses over

127 Supra n. 9, Saleh, p. 60.

128 See, generally, supra 4, Ibn Qodamah, Vol. 14.

129 R. Peters, *Crimes and Punishment in Islamic Law* (1st edn., Cambridge University Press, 2005), p. 82.

the written deed as the primary form of legal proof in general.[130] 'The witnesses should not refuse when they are called on [to give their testimony].'[131]

The Quran gives oral testimony a sacred character and obliges witnesses to perform it as a religious duty. Moreover, Shari'a sets a strict punishment for giving a false statement with intention, ranging between seven and 75 lashes in a public place. In addition to the physical punishment, the false witness would be slandered and would lose his credibility before courts forever; in other words, his testimony would not be accepted before any court or arbitration tribunal for the rest of his life.[132] The punishment for bearing false witness was determined in principle in the following Quranic verse: 'And those who launch a charge against chaste women, and produce not four witnesses "to support their allegations" lash them with eighty stripes; and reject their evidence ever after.'[133] The interpretation of this principle in cases other than the accusation of adultery depends on the discretion of the court. The qualifications of a witness vary from one school to another; however, a witness should be a trustworthy Muslim person who has reached the age of puberty and he should not be subject to any incapacity. The testimony of non-Muslims is accepted in all subject matters except Hodoud. The four schools of fiqh require a thorough investigation of a witness's trustworthiness; if there is any doubt about it the witness will not be heard. Oral testimony is administered on the spot by the arbitrator and, according to the Hanafies, at the request of the witness. Disqualified witnesses are not allowed to participate as arbitrators in a dispute. According to the Quran, a male's testimony is equal to that of two women; the Quran states that a woman may forget an incident so the second one is needed to remind her.[134]

Oath – 'Qasam/Yameen'

According to the reported practice of Prophet Muhammad, the oath is the final step in any court proceeding. Arbitrators resort to the oath by special request from the plaintiff in cases where he is unable to adduce evidence of his rights or where his evidence is incomplete, such as when he has one male and one female witness or two females only. The qualifications of a party to be able to give a credible oath are the same as those of the witness. If the defendant takes the oath, the arbitrator may decide on the case in his favour; however, some Hanafies consider the oath to be a second-class form of evidence and allow the plaintiff to challenge the oath.[135] Scholars of other schools, however, require an additional oath to be taken by the plaintiff, subject to a request from the defendant, in case the arbitrator decides

130 O. Arabi, 'Orienting the Gaze: Marcel Morand and the Codification of Le Droit Musulman Algerien', *Journal of Islamic Studies*, 11/1 (2000), pp. 43–72.

131 The Quran 1: 282.

132 Supra n. 4, Ibn Qodamah, Vol. 14, p. 262.

133 The Quran 24: 4.

134 The Quran 1: 282.

135 Supra n. 9, Saleh, p. 64 and supra n. 4, Ibn Qodamah, p. 145.

the case in favour of the plaintiff.[136] The Quran gives the oath a sacred nature and warns parties about lying under oath as in the following Quranic verse:

> [S]urely, those who take a small price by (breaking) the covenant of Allah and their oaths, for them there is no share in the Hereafter, and Allah will neither speak to them, nor will He look towards them on the Day of Judgment, nor will He purify them. For them there is a painful punishment.[137]

A Muslim party taking the oath has to swear on the Quran; in the case of a non-Muslim party, he should swear on something sacred to him, such as the Bible for Christians and the Torah for Jews.[138]

Written Evidence

The Quran encourages parties to any contract to write it down. Classical scholars disputed whether it is a binding condition for the validity of a contract or just a recommendation. The division in opinion is owing to the understanding of the following verse, which is the longest verse in the Quran:

> O you who believe, when you contract a debt for a fixed time, write it down. And let a scribe write it down between you with fairness; nor should the scribe refuse to write as Allah has taught him, so let him write. And let him who owes the debt dictate and he should observe his duty to Allah, his Lord, and not diminish anything from it. But if he who owes the debt is unsound in understanding or weak, or [if] he is not able to dictate himself, let his guardian dictate with fairness. And call to witness from among your men two witnesses; but if there are not two men, then one man and two women from among those whom you choose to be witnesses, so that if one of the two errs, the one may remind the other. And the witnesses must not refuse when they are summoned. And be not averse to writing it whether it is small or large along with the time of its falling due. This is more equitable in the sight of Allah and makes testimony surer and the best way to keep away from doubts. But when it is ready merchandise which you give and take among yourselves from hand to hand, there is no blame on you in not writing it down. And have witnesses when you sell one to another. And let no harm be done to the scribe or to the witnesses. And if you do [it], then surely it is a transgression on your part. And keep your duty to Allah. And Allah teaches you. And Allah is Knower of all things.[139]

---

136 Ibid.
137 The Quran 2: 77.
138 Supra n. 4, Ibn Qodamah, p. 145.
139 The Quran 1: 282.

Presumptions – 'Qara'en'

It has been reported that Prophet Muhammad and his companions decided some cases on the basis of presumptions, or the legal method of istis'hab. The use of presumptions in giving judgments has been given a wider scope by Hanbali scholars; according to them, the refusal of the defendant to take an oath is a presumption in favour of the plaintiff. It also constitutes a presumption of ownership if a property is in possession of one of the parties for a long time with no proof to the contrary.[140]

Personal Knowledge of the Judge or Arbitrator

Giving a judgment on the basis of the judge/arbitrator's personal knowledge is prohibited in all the schools except Hanafi. Basing a judgment on the judge/arbitrator's own knowledge raises suspicion of bias and can be grounds for challenging an award. The Hanbalies leave no room for the arbitrator's own knowledge relating to the dispute, as he is totally forbidden to rely on it in rendering the award without evidence.[141]

Rules of Fair Trial

Islamic law establishes its own rules of fair trial to guarantee justice and equality. Some of these rules have been derived from the pre-Islam practices of Arabs and have been upheld by Shari'a. According to the Shari'a view, the choice of a qualified and impartial judge is the first step in achieving justice. Thus, Shari'a concentrates first on the impartiality of judges and arbitrators, governing their social lives. A judge – any official, really – is forbidden to accept gifts while he is in office from anyone with whom he did not exchange gifts before his appointment, because such an act might raise the suspicion of bias.[142] Hanafi scholars discourage judges from receiving gifts while other scholars consider any gift to a judge as a bribe.[143] Prophet Muhammad gave the prohibition of accepting gifts a religious character in the following Hadeeth:

> What is wrong with the employee whom we appoint that he returns to say, "this is for you and that is for me?" Why didn't he stay at his father's and mother's house to see whether he will be given gifts or not? By Him in Whose Hand my

140 See, in general, supra n. 4, Ibn Qodamah, Vol. 14, p. 156.
141 Ibid.
142 Supra n. 4, Ibn Qodamah, Vol. 14, p. 58.
143 Ibid., p. 59.

> life is, whoever takes anything illegally will bring it on the Day of Resurrection by carrying it over his neck.[144]

Moreover, Hanbali scholars do not allow judges to conduct business. Bribery is totally prohibited by the Quran and the Sunna; the punishment expands to cover the corrupter and the corrupted and all persons in connection with it.

The principle of the equal treatment of parties to a dispute has various forms under Shari'a. All litigants, without exception, must be granted reasonable access to the place of hearing. The procedure must be carried out with equal speed; no priority should be given except in cases where a delay might harm the litigants, such as in the case of travellers and ill people. In the course of the hearing, the judge/arbitrator should address each litigant in an equally composed tone; equality should also be reflected in the way that litigants are seated. The judge/arbitrator should not greet one litigant with undue warmth, nor engage in a personal conversation, as it might seem unjust to the other litigant.[145] If one of the parties to the dispute does not speak Arabic and the judge/arbitrator does not know his language, two translators – only one is required by the Hanafies and some Hanbalies – must attend the hearing to translate between the litigants and the judge/arbitrator. The translators should possess the characters of adalah as they will be considered as witnesses to the statements of the parties.[146]

Under Shari'a, an arbitrator is not allowed to decide a dispute without hearing all the parties and giving them the chance to present all their evidence. There are strict conditions for issuing a judgment in absentia, as such a judgment requires judicial review before its execution because the defendant might have a defence against the claim. However, according to the Malikies and some Hanbalies, a judge/arbitrator is not allowed to issue a judgment *in absentia* at all.[147]

Shari'a understands that parties have different abilities in representing their cases. Therefore, Shari'a assumes that substantive truth should prevail over procedural technicalities as embodied in the following Hadeeth:

> You people present your cases to me and some of you may be more eloquent and persuasive in presenting their argument. So, if I give some one's right to another [wrongly] because of the latter's "tricky" presentation of the case, I am really giving him a piece of fire; so he should not take it.[148]

144 Supra n. 53, Albukhari, Chapter 8, Hadeeth No. 162.

145 The Ministry of Justice of Saudi Arabia, *Litigation in Saudi Arabia, History, Institutions and Principles* (1st edn., The Ministry of Justice of Saudi Arabia, 1999).

146 Supra n. 4, Ibn Qodamah, Vol. 14, p. 84.

147 Ibid., Vol. 14, p. 96.

148 Supra n. 53, Albukhari, Chapter 3, Hadeeth No. 845.

This Hadeeth affects the *res judicata* aspects of a judgment/award but only to a limited extent and no more than the Western concept of retrial would affect the award.[149]

Enforcement of Arbitral Awards under Shari'a

The Nature of the Arbitral Award

The objective of an arbitral award is to settle the dispute and put an end to the conflict between the parties, known as 'raf' alneza'' in Arabic. Arbitration loses its objective of settling disputes if arbitral awards lack enforceability.[150] Despite some scholars requiring the disputants' approval, an award is enforceable and binding on the parties from the moment it becomes final and has the same effects and power as a court judgment. The arbitrator has no right to decline his award; even if he declines and issues another award in favour of the other party, the latter award will be void. No third party would be affected by the arbitral award because the arbitrator has no jurisdiction over anyone but the parties to the dispute who agreed to obey the arbitrator's decision and execute it on themselves. Hanbali scholars require ratification from a judge before enforcing any arbitral award.[151]

The Content of the Arbitral Award

The content of an arbitral award does not differ from any ordinary court judgment. The award should include a sufficient description of the merits of the dispute at issue, the findings of fact substantiated by Shari'a rules of evidence, the reasoning under usul alfiqh with references to Shari'a sources and finally the decision. An award that lacks the findings of fact under Shari'a rules of evidence or a valid reasoning according to Shari'a substantive rules will not be accepted. The arbitrators have the right to correct material errors in the award from the time of issuing the award until referring to the court for an enforcement order.[152]

Challenge of the Arbitral Award

Parties to the dispute may accept the arbitral award and execute it, or they may ask for further judicial review. Each school has its own view regarding the ability of parties to challenge the arbitral award. Maliki scholars consider arbitral awards to be unchallengeable – a judge cannot revoke an award as long as it does not

149 Supra n. 9, Saleh, pp. 70–71.

150 Supra n. 78, Al Kenain, pp. 141–45.

151 Ibid.

152 See, generally, A. Al Kenain, *Tasbeeb Alahkam Alqadaiyyah fe AlShari'a Alislamiyah* (1st edn., Al Kenain, 1999).

contradict the main sources of Shari'a, the only exception being if it entails serious prejudice. According to Hanbali scholars, an arbitral award carries the same influence as a court decision and can be revoked under the same conditions that revoke a court judgment. The Hanafies recognize the possibility of revoking an arbitral award in cases where the award is not in compliance with the appellant's mathhab, or school. However, the revocation is not mandatory; it is up to the judge, who should pay attention to the relevant circumstances when reviewing the award. The Shafi'es have two opinions with regard to the strength of the arbitral award. One gives the arbitral award the same strength as a court judgment, in which case the judge has to treat the arbitral award in the same way as any other judgment. The other view requires the parties to accept the award or reject it. In such a case, there is no challenge of the arbitral award because the award is not binding; therefore, there is no need to challenge it.[153]

Judicial Remedies

After the issuance of the arbitral award, parties who are not satisfied with the outcome have two options available to them.

Revocation

Parties to the dispute may ask for the revocation of the arbitral award. This issue takes us back to the nature of arbitration under the teachings of each school; if arbitration is similar to conciliation or to agency contract the award can be revoked on the same grounds of revoking any normal contract. If the arbitration is judicial in nature it cannot be revoked without there being an obvious error in the award or at any stage of the arbitral procedure. If the judge revokes the arbitral award, he is not obliged to decide on the case again unless he has been asked to do so by one of the parties to the dispute. On the other hand, if the judge upholds the arbitral award, his judgment will be treated as an enforcement order.[154]

Appeal

The parties to the arbitration may appeal to the arbitration panel or to the court. In this situation, the judge will revoke the arbitral award and issue a new award if he accepts the appeal.[155]

---

153 Supra n. 1, Ibn Nujaim, Vol. 7, p. 26; see also supra n. 4, Ibn Qodamah, Vol. 11, p. 484.

154 Supra n. 16, Saiyed, p. 74.

155 Ibid.

Miscellaneous Issues

The Seat of the Arbitration

The seat theory did not receive any attention from classical Muslim scholars because it has no affect on arbitration. None of the classical treatises mention anything with regard to the seat of arbitration; however, the seat of the arbitration is to be decided according to the parties as a clause in the arbitration agreement.

The Rights of Third Parties

Generally speaking, the effect of the arbitral award must not extend to anyone other than the parties to the dispute. If a third party has got an interest in the enforcement of the arbitral award, they can send their request to the court.[156]

The Unanimity of the Award

If the arbitration proceeds with a sole arbitrator, the problem of the conflict of opinions with regard to the final decision between the arbitrators will not exist – the task of making the award is an individual process. However, scholars agree that if multiple arbitrators fail to agree, the award will be void. An award needs to comply with the opinion of the majority of the arbitrators in order to be fair and just.

Hanbali treatises suggest that there are four methods of issuing the arbitral award if the arbitrators do not reach an agreement. First, when drafting the arbitration agreement, the number of arbitrators should be odd. Second, the assistance of an external arbitrator should be sought and the case should be decided according to his opinion, although the external arbitrator is not allowed to come up with a new opinion; his job is only to choose one of the available decisions. Third, if the arbitrators fail to issue the award, the dispute can be decided by another tribunal or by a sole arbitrator. This option may lengthen the dispute, which contradicts one of the main objectives of choosing arbitration as a swift dispute settlement mechanism. Fourth, if unanimity cannot be reached and the parties to the dispute have exhausted the above-mentioned methods, they can refer the dispute to litigation as a last resort.[157]

It has been shown that Islamic Shari'a regulates arbitration proceedings in a comprehensive way, covering all the important aspects from the formation of the arbitration agreement to the enforcement of the final arbitral award. The chapter has also shown arbitration to be a real alternative to litigation in all subject matters. Shari'a arbitration rules are not substantially different from other current rules, but they do form the basis for most arbitration regulations in most Muslim countries nowadays. Before looking at the arbitration regulations in Saudi Arabia, which are

156 Ibid.

157 Supra n. 4, Ibn Qodamah, Vol. 10, p. 546.

codifications of the Hanbali teachings as introduced by Ibn Taymiyyah and Ibn Qodamah, the next chapter will examine the regulatory attitude toward arbitration in Saudi Arabia.

Chapter 4

The Regulatory Attitude toward Arbitration in Saudi Arabia

Commercial arbitration has existed in the Saudi legal system since the enactment of the Code of Commercial Courts in 1931. Nonetheless, international arbitration was not always welcomed by the Saudi government. At first, the Saudi Government did not oppose resorting to international arbitration, although it did restrict it. This restriction started to relax from the mid-1970s, but very slowly. The main purpose of this chapter, which is divided into two parts, is to examine the regulatory attitude toward international arbitration in Saudi Arabia. The first part will discuss the regulatory attitude toward arbitration from the creation of the Saudi state in the 1930s to the first oil boom in the 1970s. It will examine arbitration cases to which the Saudi Government was party, such as the *Wahat Alburaimi* and the well-known case of *Arabian American Oil Company v. Saudi Arabia* (Aramco Case) and their impacts on the Saudi legal system. The second part will cover the period from the mid-1970s until now, a period which experienced a shift in attitudes toward attracting foreign investment.

The regulatory attitude toward arbitration in Saudi Arabia has gone through three phases. At first, international arbitration was welcomed – the first Saudi Government attempt to use arbitration was in the settlement of the *Wahat Alburaim* (Buraimi Oasis Case) in 1955. The arbitration took place in Jeddah, Saudi Arabia, with the British Government acting on behalf of the ruler of Abu Dhabi and the Sultan of Oman. The arbitration agreement established a tribunal consisting of five members for the settlement of the dispute as to the location of the common border between Saudi Arabia and Abu Dhabi, and as to the sovereignty of the Buraimi Oasis. According to the arbitration agreement, the tribunal had to give due regard to all relevant considerations of law, fact and equity, and in particular to the historical rights of the rulers in the area; the traditional loyalties, tribal organization and way of life of the inhabitants of the area; and the exercise of jurisdiction and other activities in the area.[1] The *Buraimi* arbitration did not have a significant impact on arbitration or the Saudi Arabian legal system, unlike the well-known arbitration between the Government of Saudi Arabia and Aramco in 1958, which changed the Government's attitude toward international arbitration for several decades,

1 The arbitration agreement between the Government of the United Kingdom (acting on behalf of the ruler of Abu Dhabi and His Highness the Sultan Said bin Taimur) and the Government of Saudi Arabia, Jeddah, 30 July 1954 (HMSO Cmd 9272, 1954) cited in J.B. Kelly, 'The Buraimi Oasis Dispute', *International Affairs*, 32/3 (July 1956), pp. 318–24.

in what can be called the second phase.[2] During this phase, Saudi Arabia looked at international arbitration as a threat to its national sovereignty. The Aramco award of 1958 had a significant impact on accepting arbitration agreements and clauses providing for international arbitration by governmental bodies; and will be discussed later in this chapter. The third phase started with the first oil boom in the 1970s and has continued up to now.[3] Economic expansion and infrastructure-building caused Saudi Arabia to relax its attitude toward international arbitration, by joining the ICSID convention, reforming the arbitration regulations and offering more protection to foreign investments. The first part of this chapter deals with arbitration from the creation of the Saudi legal system and the enactment of the Code of Commercial Courts in 1931 until the first oil boom in the mid-1970s. The second part deals with the current approach that started as a result of the oil boom.

Arbitration in the Saudi Legal System Prior to the Oil Boom

Arbitration under the Code of Commercial Courts 1931

The related provisions of the Code of Commercial Courts are concerned only with commercial arbitration between private parties. The Code includes nine brief articles for regulating arbitration proceedings. Article 493 allows disputants to stipulate to arbitrate in a written notarized deed. The parties to the arbitration are free to decide on the number of arbitrators, the timescale and the way of rendering the arbitral award, whether it is by unanimity or by majority. Arbitration under this Code is institutional,[4] and the proceedings are held under the supervision of the Commercial Court.[5]

Article 494 deals with the procedural law of arbitration. Arbitrators are required by this article to apply the provisions of the Code of Commercial Courts in the light of Shari'a procedural rules, with the support of the arbitration agreement.[6] As with the relevant provisions in the Arbitration Act of 1983, an arbitral award is not enforceable unless reviewed by the Commercial Court, which will either approve it for enforcement or repudiate it.[7] With regard to the revocability of the appointment of arbitrators, the Code prohibits the revocation of the appointment of the arbitrators by the parties after the Court's approval; nonetheless, the disputants

---

2 This case is also known as Aramco Case or the Onassis Case.

3 F. Sami, *International Commercial Arbitration in Arab Countries* (1st edn., Dar Althaqafa Li Nashr wa Altaouze', 2006), p. 423.

4 However, article 613 sets the administrative fees for enforcing arbitral awards that have not been supervised by the Court.

5 The Code of Commercial Courts of Saudi Arabia, article 493.

6 Ibid., article 494.

7 Ibid., articles 495 and 497.

have the right to challenge the award before the Court.[8] The Code also includes provisions to determine the administrative fees.[9]

However, these provisions were not available in real life because Shari'a courts at that time did not recognize the arbitration agreement or the arbitration clause in cases where the parties insisted on their right to arbitrate in accordance with the arbitration agreement. Even if the court approved an arbitration agreement or clause, enforcement of the arbitral award was voluntary. Accordingly, reference to arbitration was very limited; the conflict between the Commercial Court and Shari'a courts led arbitration to become ineffective, time-consuming and, in many cases, harmful to the parties involved. The Arbitration Act of 1983 superseded the arbitration provisions of the Code of Commercial Courts. However, ad hoc arbitration in cases of a non-commercial nature is still governed by the provisions of the Code.[10]

Arbitration Clauses in the Oil Concessions in Saudi Arabia

On 29 May 1933, the founder of the kingdom of Saudi Arabia, King Abdul-Aziz, concluded a contract on oil exploitation with the Standard Oil Company of California (Socal), the parent company of Chevron. Under that contract, the company was granted an exclusive concession for 60 years in the eastern province of Saudi Arabia.[11] In accordance with the concession agreement, Socal established a corporation, the California-Arabian Standard Oil Company (Casoc) and assigned to it all its rights and obligations under the agreement. In 1936, owing to the failure in locating oil and the high cost of operations, the Texas Oil Company acquired a 50 per cent stake in the concession, which had been ratified by the Government of Saudi Arabia. The company name was changed in 1944 from California-Arabian Standard Oil Company to Arabian American Oil Company (Aramco).[12] At the time of drafting the concession agreement, Saudi Arabia did not foresee the possibility of a dispute with Aramco, and so it left out a solid arbitration clause. However, article 31 of the concession agreement did state that any dispute would be settled through an arbitration panel consisting of three arbitrators and that Islamic law as taught by the Hanbali school would apply. The issue of the applicability of Islamic law was even clearly expressed in the arbitration agreement between the

---

8 Ibid., article 496.

9 Ibid., articles 610, 611, 612 and 613.

10 N. Albejad, *Arbitration in Saudi Arabia* (1st edn., Institute of Public Administration, 1999), p. 30.

11 In 1939, by a supplementary agreement, the concession area was extended to cover about 116,000 square miles and the period was extended to 65 years.

12 See, in general, Saudi Aramco. Available online at <http://www.saudiaramco.com> [accessed 8 April 2009].

Government of Saudi Arabia and Aramco in 1955; nonetheless, the arbitration tribunal failed to apply it in the dispute, as will be seen below.[13]

Owing to the outcomes of the Aramco arbitration and following the Council of Ministers Resolution No. 58 of 1963, Saudi Arabia avoided the possibility of not applying its law in disputes raised in the future. This was demonstrated by the great attention paid to the concession agreement between the Government of Saudi Arabia and Auxirap (French Red Sea). The Auxirap agreement of 1965 was outstandingly more favourable to Saudi Arabia than the Aramco one had been. Article 63 of the 1965 concession agreement provided that any dispute raised as a result of the interpretation or the execution of the agreement should be referred first to a committee of two experts, one chosen by the Government of Saudi Arabia and the other by the concessionaire. If the committee failed to reach an acceptable settlement, the dispute would be referred to the Committee of the Settlement of Mining Disputes in accordance with the Mining Act of 1963.[14] The agreement was altered later that same year after the participation of the Petromin Oil Company in the same concession,[15] owing to the distinction between the Auxirap and Saudi Government dispute and the Auxirap and Petromin one. There would have been no change in the dispute settlement procedure if the dispute had occurred between Auxirap and the Saudi Government; however, a dispute between Petromin and Auxirap would have needed to be settled by means of international arbitration just like any normal commercial dispute.[16] As an added security, Saudi Arabia obliged Auxirap, as the operating company for the concession, to incorporate a joint venture company in Saudi Arabia and to set the maximum foreign ownership limit at 60 per cent.[17] It can be seen from the arbitration clauses in other oil concessions (especially after the Aramco award) that Saudi Arabia tried not to refer to arbitration outside its jurisdiction. This is clear from the agreements with the Japan Petroleum Trading Co. of 1957, in which article 55 stated that disputes were to be finally resolved by a five-arbitrator panel sitting in Saudi Arabia. Article 23 of the agreement between Saudi Arabia and the Trans-Arabian Pipe Co. also provided for a three-arbitrator panel sitting in Jeddah. Thus the Saudi Government tried to secure its position in any possible conflicts to ensure the application of Saudi law in any future disputes, especially after the disappointing outcomes of the Aramco award.[18]

---

13 A. Ashoush, *The Law of the Oil Concessions in the Arab Countries* (1st edn., Alsharikah Almuttahidah Lelnashr Wa altawze', 1975), p. 415.

14 The committee is to be established by article 50 of the Mining Law of 1963.

15 The Saudi Arabian Lubricating Oil Company was formed in 1968 by a royal decree as one of the joint ventures of the General Organization of Petroleum and Minerals (Petromin). The company was renamed the Saudi Arabian Lubricating Oil Company in 1997 after Petromin's shares in the company were transferred to Saudi Aramco.

16 See supra n. 13, Ashoush, p. 415.

17 Ibid., p. 613.

18 A. Lerrick and Q. Mian, *Saudi Business and Labour Law* (2nd edn., Graham & Trotman, 1987), footnote 15, p. 153.

Aramco v. Saudi Arabia

Background

In January 1954 an agreement was concluded between the Government of Saudi Arabia and Aristotle Onassis, the Greek-born shipping tycoon. Hereinafter it will be referred to as the Onassis Agreement. The original deal was amended in April of the same year. It has been argued that the provisions of that agreement were only beneficial to Onassis and those middlemen who facilitated the deal. It was also argued that Onassis's main concern was to guarantee the employment of 10 oil tankers that he was chartered on in a long-term contract in a time when the global tankers market was experiencing overcapacity in addition to global depression in the demand for oil.[19] Others, however, argue that the agreement was an attempt to break Aramco's monopoly over Saudi oil.[20] Nevertheless, and away from politics, Saudi Arabia sought its own interests, as is clearly demonstrated in the provisions of the agreement.

The agreement granted Onassis the right to establish a private company in Saudi Arabia under the commercial name the Saudi Arabian Maritime Tankers Company (Satco). The newly formed company was bound to maintain a minimum of 500,000 tons of tankers under the Saudi Arabian flag and to register this tonnage in Saudi Arabia.[21] The agreement obliged Satco to establish a marine school in Jeddah and to employ its graduates onboard Satco tankers. Satco further undertook to give Saudi Arabian employees and workmen preference in working on its tankers.[22] Moreover, Satco was obliged to carry on its tankers, free of charge, 50,000 tons of oil and oil products from Saudi Arabian ports in the Gulf to any Saudi port in the Red Sea.[23] The Government of Saudi Arabia was entitled to receive a royalty of one shilling and sixpence for every ton shipped abroad in Satco tankers, as well as the payment of all port and harbour duties in Saudi Arabian ports.[24] The agreement foresaw a possible increase in Satco's fleet, which had to always represent a minimum of 500,000 deadweight tons of tankships during the life of the agreement.[25]

Satco's tankers had to bear Saudi Arabian names and Satco had the right to enjoy the Government's protection, which is the right of any Saudi Arabian

---

19 D. Holden and R. Johns, *The House of Saud* (1st edn., Sedgwick and Jackson, 1981), pp. 181–82.

20 Ibid.

21 Article 14 of the Onassis Agreement as quoted in the Aramco award 27 ILR (1963), pp. 116–27.

22 Ibid., articles 6 and 9.

23 Ibid., article 10; however, it did not state the frequency of this shipment, whether it will be for one time only or in a frequent manner.

24 Ibid., articles 11 and 12.

25 Ibid., article 14.

company.[26] The agreement obligated Saudi Arabia to enact a Maritime Law.[27] The controversial provisions of the agreement raising the dispute were articles 4 and 15. According to these provisions, the Saudi Arabian Maritime Tankers Company had the right of priority for the transport of oil for a period of 30 years from the date of signing the agreement, renewable for a further period by mutual agreement.[28]

The dispute at issue started when the Government of Saudi Arabia ordered Aramco to apply Royal Decree No. 5737 of 09/04/1954, which ratified the Onassis Agreement concluded on 20 January 1954. The royal decree gave the Onassis Agreement a legal status similar to that of the Aramco concession agreement of 1933. On 23 January 1954, the Saudi Minister of Finance advised Aramco of the signing of the agreement and informed it of the content of article 4. The letter read as follows:

> [I]it is taken for granted that the Saudi tankers have priority over other tankers for loading Saudi petroleum (in second place) after the tankers owned by your company or by companies which founded you and which have been actually transporting Saudi petroleum before December 31, 1953.[29]

Aramco's Response

Aramco rejected the Onassis Agreement and responded to the Minister of Finance's letter, saying that the implementation of the Onassis Agreement would be:

- contrary to and in violation of both the letter and the spirit of the existing agreement between the Government of Saudi Arabia and Aramco;
- contrary to the long-established business arrangements and procedures developed with reliance on these agreements;
- contrary to established worldwide custom and practice in the international oil industry;
- of a disastrous effect upon the presently established sales outlets for Saudi oil and the possible future development thereof; and
- wholly impractical.[30]

Aramco based its rejection on the above-mentioned grounds without any real justification. This carried on throughout the proceedings, as Aramco failed to prove that the Onassis Agreement would cause any injury to its interests.

26 Ibid., articles 2 and 3.
27 Ibid., article 5.
28 Aramco award, 27 ILR 117 (1963), p. 128.
29 Ibid., p. 130.
30 Ibid.

The Saudi Government's Position

After months of negotiations to reach an amicable settlement, the parties agreed to submit the dispute to an ad hoc arbitration tribunal in Switzerland. The arbitration proceedings started in 1954 but the award was not issued until 1958. Although it was only an arbitration relating to the interpretation of a concession agreement, many circumstances lengthened the proceedings to four years. Throughout, the Government of Saudi Arabia tried to reach an amicable settlement outside the tribunal. The arbitrator appointed by Saudi Arabia, Dr Badawi, died during the proceedings and was replaced by Mr Mahmoud Hassan; and both, in addition to the arbitrator appointed by Aramco, were Egyptian nationals. Dr Badawi and Mr Habachy, the arbitrator chosen by Aramco, appointed the Swiss Georges Sauser-Hall as a referee. The Saudi Government recognized that the concession agreement of 1933 gave Aramco very extensive rights, exclusive in character, in respect of the operations pertaining to its enterprise, but it contended that these rights did not include transportation of petroleum and petroleum products by sea. The Government contended that Aramco was granted an exclusive right to transport its oil and oil products only to the seashore including the exclusive area in Saudi Arabia and to the limit of the territorial waters of the state, but this grant did not include the right to cross Saudi Arabia's maritime frontier and reach the high seas.[31]

The Government based its argument on the text of the concession agreement, which did not expressly provide for granting Aramco the exclusive right of transportation by sea to foreign countries.[32] The Government also relied upon the principle of restrictive interpretation of the obligations assumed by a sovereign state in agreements with private individuals or companies, inasmuch as a government must always bear in mind and safeguard the interests of the community.[33] The Government took the position that it could withdraw from the arbitration any act performed under it to exercise its sovereign power. The Saudi Government concluded that, with regard to the transportation of oil and oil products to foreign countries, Aramco was in the same legal position as other inhabitants of Saudi Arabia; it therefore had to comply with any restriction adopted by the Government in connection with external transport of oil and oil products. The company had no ownership in these products or in any other property interest that would immunize it, or its buyers, from governmental action regulating such transport.[34]

31 Supra n. 28, Aramco award, p. 140.

32 Supra n. 28, Aramco award, p. 132. Aramco alleged that it has the exclusive right of transportation of Saudi oil; however, it has never exercised it, either by engaging in such transport or by exerting control over such transport.

33 Ibid.

34 Ibid. In support of the Government's point of view, some Muslim scholars exclude minerals from the scope of private ownership. See supra n. 18, Lerrick and Mian, pp. 170–71.

Saudi Arabia insisted that, in addition to the principles of Islamic and international law, the general principles of law recognized by civilized nations do not support the contention that the concession agreement of 1933 exempts Aramco from the regulatory power of the Saudi Government. The Government added that since the Onassis Agreement had been ratified by Royal Decree No. 5737, it had become the law of the land that everyone had to respect.[35] The Saudi Government contended, therefore, that Aramco could be lawfully bound to ship oil and oil products to foreign markets on Satco tankers, in conformity with the Onassis Agreement ratified by the royal decree. To exercise its sovereignty, the Government insisted that Aramco be forced to submit to any regulatory restriction providing for a preferential right in the transportation of its products from Saudi Arabia in favour of tankers flying the Saudi Arabian flag. Despite the fact that Saudi Arabia ratified the Onassis Agreement in the interests of its community, it guaranteed the minimum standard of protection to the rights of Aramco.[36] Royal Decree No. 5737 gave Satco's tankers a right of priority after Aramco's tankers and tankers owned by the owning companies of Aramco, which is a right that Aramco has never exercised since its creation. This means that the application of the royal decree caused no injury to Aramco. Moreover, under Islamic law, the 'generic terms of a contract must be interpreted extensively'. If Aramco was granted the right of transport, it should have exercised it; Aramco did not do so for more than 17 years. For the sake of the manifestation of the general principles of law recognized by civilized nations, the Government cited the French administrative law, as developed by the French Conseil d'État, to support its contention that a state has the right to exercise its regulatory powers in order to control, and if necessary adapt, the methods used by a company operating a public service. In the Government's opinion, the 1933 concession is included in the concept of public service.[37]

Applicable Law

According to article 4 of the arbitration agreement between Aramco and the Government of Saudi Arabia, dated 15 February 1955, the arbitral tribunal would have to decide on the dispute in accordance with Saudi Arabian law insofar as matters fell within the jurisdiction of Saudi Arabia. The tribunal would be free to decide the applicable law where matters were outside the jurisdiction of Saudi Arabia.[38]

---

35 Supra n. 28, Aramco award, p. 141.

36 Ibid., p. 140; the letter of the Saudi Minister of Finance quoted above.

37 Ibid.

38 Article 4 (b) of the arbitration agreement defined Saudi law as Muslim law under the teaching of the school of Imam Ahmad ben Hanbal, as applied in Saudi Arabia.

With regard to the procedural law, despite the fact that the parties agreed for the arbitration to take place outside Saudi Arabia, the law of the seat could not be applied to the arbitration. The tribunal stated:

> [C]onsidering the jurisdictional immunity of foreign states, recognized by international law in a spirit of respect for the essential dignity of sovereign power, the tribunal is unable to hold that arbitral proceedings to which a sovereign state is a Party could be subject to the law of another state.[39]

As mentioned above, the parties to the arbitration agreement agreed to apply the principles of Islamic law, as taught by the Hanbali school. The tribunal, though, supported Aramco's argument and stood against the application of Saudi law; however, it did explain its opinion in a 'more polite way' than Aramco.[40] The tribunal stated that:

> [T]he regime of mining concessions, and, consequently, also of oil concessions, has remained embryonic in Moslem law and is not the same in the different schools. The principles of one school cannot be introduced into another, unless this is done by the act of authority. Hanbali law contains no precise rule about mining concessions and [is] *a fortiori* about oil concessions.[41]

This quotation simply reveals a lack of knowledge of Islamic law, which has rules to govern all kinds of contract. If, for instance, the Hanbali school is unable to govern a concession agreement, resorting to other schools through the method of qiyas can solve the dispute. As was mentioned in a previous chapter, using qiyas does not require any act of authority. It needs only adequate knowledge of the situation and accurate reasoning, without any resort to official authority, because it is the law of God, not of the state. The rules apply to the exploitation of hidden wealth such as gold and silver, can apply to oil and gas by means of analogical reasoning. The law applicable to this case under all conflict of laws theories can only be Saudi law. The tribunal denied the application of Saudi law in the dispute and claimed that Saudi law has no rules for governing oil concessions.

The concession agreement of 1933 was an agreement between a state and a private American party and so could not be subject to public international law. The tribunal quoted: 'Any contract which is not a contract between states in their capacity as subjects of international law, is based on the municipal law of some country.'[42] But if international law cannot be applied because of the nature of the dispute, and other municipal laws cannot be applied because a state cannot fall under a jurisdiction of another state, what is the applicable law? Even the general

39 Supra n. 28, Aramco award, p. 154.
40 Ibid., pp. 162–63.
41 Ibid.
42 See, in general, supra n. 28, Aramco award.

principles of law recognized by civilized nations cannot be applied in this case because, in the end, the tribunal would be imposing the municipal law of one state on to a sovereign state. Moreover, when the tribunal denied the application of Saudi law and applied British and Swiss practices, it implied that Saudi Arabia is not a civilized nation, which was discrimination not just against Saudi Arabia, but against Islamic law as a whole.[43]

The tribunal contradicted itself when denying the application of Saudi law. No other law could be really relevant other than Saudi law for the following reasons:

- the contract was concluded in Jeddah, in Saudi Arabia;
- it came into force after its ratification and publication in the Saudi official gazette;
- the characteristic performance of the contract took place in Saudi Arabia; and
- the concession of 1933 is a contract concerning immovable property situated in Saudi Arabia.

The tribunal's competence was to specify the rights and obligations of both parties under the concession agreement and to determine whether the Onassis contract did infringe Aramco's rights.[44] The tribunal determined that it could only decide on certain disputes, such as the five questions submitted by the parties, and could find whether the two contracts were compatible or in conflict. The tribunal was not authorized as an amiable compositeur; however, it was competent to find a method for reconciling or harmonizing the two agreements. Consequently, the tribunal rejected the suggestion that it had wider powers than those bestowed upon it by the parties' agreement. Despite the disagreement of one of the arbitrators, the tribunal concluded the case in Aramco's favour and stated in the award that the Onassis Agreement was neither a law of the state of Saudi Arabia nor a governmental regulation.[45] The general principles of law relied on by the tribunal were neither clear nor coherent and were not, logically, suitable for the situation. Although the arbitral award was not binding on Saudi Arabia, the Saudi Government abided by it, voluntarily announcing the death of the Onassis Agreement and of Satco.

Comments on the Case

The relationship between the Government of Saudi Arabia and Aramco was based on mutual understanding of each other's needs. The Saudi Government understood the American thirst for oil and facilitated Aramco's operations in the Saudi deserts. Aramco understood the Saudi Government's need for cash and arranged for loans, constructions and the employment and training of Saudi nationals. If Aramco had

43 Ibid.
44 Ibid., p. 202.
45 Ibid., p. 220.

given preferential treatment to Satco, it would have at least reduced the amount of loans it gave to the Government, bearing in mind the financial difficulties that Saudi Arabia faced during the early 1950s.[46] However, Onassis had a long history of legal troubles with the US Government, which may be the reason behind Aramco's rejection, giving the impression that if someone else other than Onassis had made the agreement with the Saudi Arabian Government, Aramco would not have opposed applying Royal Decree No. 5737. The FBI investigated Onassis several times since 1943 for charges ranging from fraud to the possession of fascist ideas. Moreover, in 1953 Onassis was charged, along with some other individuals and companies, with conspiracy to defraud the United States Government in multi-million-dollar deals to buy surplus US ships after the war. The US Government found him to be in violation of the law forbidding the sale of US ships to aliens.[47] In the following year, Onassis was charged for another related fraud against the US Government. He was charged with violating the shipping law citizenship provision, which requires that all ships displaying the American flag be owned by United States citizens. Onassis pleaded guilty and agreed to pay seven million dollars to the Government of the United States.[48]

The arbitrators chose the Swiss Sauser-Hall as a referee. Georges Sauser-Hall was a professor of international law at Geneva and Neuchatel Universities; he was also a Member of the Permanent Court of Arbitration and the Institute of International Law. He engaged in many cases of international arbitration, such as the dispute between Albania and Italy in 1951, but there was still considerable doubt as to his knowledge of Islamic law and the Arabic language – the official language of the contracts and one of the languages of the hearings. One of the main points of controversy in this case was the interpretation of article 1 of the concession agreement of 1933; for example, whether the Arabic word '*moutlaq*' is a synonym of 'exclusive' in English, and whether '*moua'malat*' has the same meaning as 'treat'. An arbitrator would need a good grasp of both languages in order to reach the correct interpretation of the texts, and the tribunal failed to achieve this.

Saudi Arabia claimed that the wording of the 1933 concession agreement did not give Aramco an exclusive right for transport. This opinion was supported by one of the arbitrators, Mr Hassan, who quoted:

> Signing the Award, I state that I am in disagreement particularly with the interpretation contained therein of Article 1 of the Aramco Concession Agreement of 1933. That article is the key to the solution of the present dispute

46 See, generally, supra n. 19, Holden and Johns. The situation was even worse before the 50/50 profit-sharing agreement.

47 'Time Clock', *Time Magazine* (15 February 1954).

48 Federal Bureau of Investigation United States, *Published Materials under the Freedom of Information Act 2000*. Available online at <http://foia.fbi.gov/foiaindex/aonassis.htm> [accessed 9 April 2009].

> and to the answers to be given to the questions submitted to the tribunal. In my opinion, article 1, when read in its proper context, covers an Oil Concession with its various technical ramifications. The word "transport" which occurs in the nomenclature of Aramco's exclusive rights can only cover transport which pertains to operations to be performed in the exclusive are of the Concession.[49]

Mr Hassan added:

> Maritime transport is a vast worldwide operation which is independent from the industrial enterprise of the concessionary company and cannot therefore be mentioned casually. The rights granted to Aramco in article 1 are recited in technological order. They correspond to the logical sequences of the successive operations of the enterprise which move with clockwork regularity from one stage to another. Had the parties intended the "transport" to mean transportation by sea, that word should have been the last in the enumeration of the exclusive rights granted to Aramco. This is because transport by sea is the final act in the process covered by the enterprise. Moreover, had the Parties envisaged transport by sea in the 1933 Concession Agreement, they would have mentioned this *expressis verbis*, as such a right cannot be granted to Aramco by implication.[50]

The tribunal cited the award of *Petroleum Development Ltd v. Sheikh of Abu Dhabi* as a precedent to support the rejection of the application of the principle of restrictive interpretation of the contractual obligation of a government toward a private individual.[51] The latter case cannot be treated as such, however, because it has a different nature. Unlike Saudi Arabia, Abu Dhabi was not a sovereign state at that time – it was under British protection to the extent that the British Government acted on its behalf in the *Buraimi* arbitration with Saudi Arabia.[52]

Lack of experience played an important role in Saudi Arabia losing this case, from the submission of the case to arbitration outside Saudi Arabia to the voluntary enforcement of the award. The case was between a sovereign state and a private party; thus, if the dispute had occurred nowadays, it would have been governed by ICSID arbitration rules and Saudi Arabia would have got a better deal. Saudi Arabia should not have involved Onassis in the dispute because Satco was, in theory, a Saudi company. It should have granted complete protection as a Saudi company. Saudi Arabia was in the stage of creating or modernizing its legal system, though, so such mistakes were common. Despite the fact that the award was not in favour of Saudi Arabia, Saudi Arabia did benefited from the lesson when building its legal regime. The award encouraged Saudi Arabia to be more cautious when dealing with foreign parties in any contract, especially when the oil

49 Supra n. 28, Aramco award, pp. 228–29.

50 Ibid.

51 Ibid., p. 194.

52 See, in general, supra n. 1, Kelly.

industry is involved, and not to put its national sovereignty at dispute again. This trend is evident from the Saudi reservation relating to the ICSID Convention.

The Legal Impacts of the Aramco Award 1958 on Arbitration in Saudi Arabia

The Council of Ministers Resolution No. 58 of 1963

The Aramco award affected many different areas of law and legal practice, especially international arbitration and economic policy. The direct regulatory response to the award was the Council of Ministers Resolution No. 58 of 1963, which was supplemented by the Ministry of Commerce Circular of 1979 and which imposed some restrictions on the acceptance of arbitration clauses and agreements.

The Council of Ministers Resolution No. 58 of 1963 concerns arbitration when the Government of Saudi Arabia or any governmental entity is party to a dispute. Prior to 1963, the Government frequently provided for arbitration as a means of settling disputes between itself and private parties; however, owing to the disappointing outcomes of the Aramco award of 1958, Resolution No. 58 prohibited resorting to arbitration to settle disputes between the Saudi Government (including its ministries, departments or agencies) and individuals, companies or private organizations.[53] The regulation did not distinguish between foreign and local entities. The Resolution provides the following:

- No government agency shall conclude a contract with any individual, company or private organization that includes a clause subjecting the government agency to any foreign court of law or any judicial body.
- Except in concessions granted by the Government,[54] no government agency shall accept arbitration as a means of settling disputes that may arise between it and any individual, company or private organization.
- The most important principle of private international law is the principle of application of the law of the place of performance; government agencies may therefore not choose any foreign law to govern their relationship with any individual, company or private organization.
- The above provisions shall apply to contracts concluded after the issuance of this resolution.[55]

---

53 The Resolution is incorporated in article 3 of the Arbitration Act of 1983.

54 The exceptions here are technical disputes and disputes arising out of concession agreements that have been exempted for their important interest to the country.

55 See the Ministerial Resolution No. 58 dated 17/01/1383 (1963).

Ministry of Commerce Circular No. 31/1/331/91 of 1979

The Ministry of Commerce Circular No. 31/1/331/91 of 1979 confirmed the Council of Ministers Resolution No. 58 of 1963 in prohibiting or restricting recourse to international arbitration. The Circular stated that a clause providing for arbitration (outside the kingdom) included in the articles of association of Saudi companies would be considered absolutely void. Articles of association containing such clauses would neither be approved nor registered.[56] As a result, reference can be made to domestic arbitration in the articles of association of a joint company formed by foreign and local businessmen for the purpose of carrying out investment operations in Saudi Arabia. This restriction includes all forms of joint companies, whether they are formed by foreign investors and a private party or by a foreign investor and the Government of Saudi Arabia.[57]

Other Impacts: The Establishment of OPEC

Following awards involving the sovereignty, such as the Aramco award, the Saudi Minister of Oil and Mineral Affairs of that time, Abdullah Al Tirigi (sometimes spelled 'Al-Tariki') was deeply inspired by the revolutionary ideas of Juan Pablo Pérez Alfonso, the then Venezuelan Oil Minister and Frank Hendryx, who was a former Aramco employee employed by the Minister.[58] The Venezuelan Minister came up with the idea of forming OPEC to enhance national sovereignty over natural resources and profit-sharing with the foreign concessionaires. Hendryx put forward the proposition that all petroleum agreements should be periodically re-negotiated when they no longer suit one of the parties, or when conditions change to such a degree that the agreement becomes out of date.[59] According to Hendryx:

> An oil producing nation by the law of civilized nations may clearly, in a proper case, modify or eliminate provisions of an existing petroleum concession which have become substantially contrary to the best interests of its citizens. Financial

56 Ministry of Commerce, Companies Department Circular No. 31/1/331/91 dated 22/02/1399 H. (1979).

57 Y. Al-Samman, 'The Settlement of Foreign Investment Disputes by Means of Domestic Arbitration in Saudi Arabia', *Arab Law Quarterly*, 9 (1994), pp. 217–20.

58 Hendryx was legal adviser to the Saudi Arabian Directorate General of Petroleum and Mineral Affairs. The Directorate General was replaced by the Ministry of Petroleum and Mineral Wealth in 1960.

59 See, generally, S. Duguid, 'A Biographical Approach to the Study of Social Change in the Middle East: Abdullah Tariki as a New Man', *International Journal of Middle East Studies*, 1/3 (1970), p. 195.

interest must certainly be included in the classification of matters of vital interest to a nation's citizens.[60]

The Change in the Governmental Attitude toward Arbitration: 1970s until Now

Reasons for the Change

In the aftermath of the first oil boom, Saudi Arabia accumulated enormous financial surpluses that made it the strongest of the OPEC group.[61] The financial ability characterized Saudi Arabia as a major capital-exporting country exporting to the world, especially to the United States and Europe.[62] The main objective behind the statutory reform was to attract foreign investment. Saudi Arabia at that time did not lack financial capital, but it was in need of technology and expertise. In the late 1970s, Saudi Arabia started to transform its economy from overwhelming dependence on oil to a diversified industrial economy, with the ultimate aim of setting up a hydrocarbon-based petrochemical industry.[63] The flow of foreign investment would not have met the kingdom's economic needs without regulatory flexibility and sufficient protection of foreign investment. One of the fundamental requirements of any foreign investor is the existence of a fair and impartial dispute settlement mechanism, wherein the investor is not the weak party in the dispute.

The shift started when Saudi Arabia agreed to settle certain differences and claims relating to the Agreement on Guaranteed Private Investment and guarantees of Saudi public sector contracts and investments with the United States in 1975.[64] Saudi Arabia started a comprehensive reform, as a legal incentive to foreign investment, by joining the ICSID Convention in 1979–1980, issuing the Arbitration Act of 1983 and implementing a regulation in 1985, ratifying the New York Convention on the enforcement and recognition of foreign arbitral awards of 1958. It also contributed to the establishment of the GCC Commercial Arbitration

60 L. Kissam and E. Leach, 'Sovereign Expropriation of Property and Abrogation of Concession Contracts', *Fordham Law Review*, 28 (1959–1960), pp. 177–200.

61 That also led to so-called petrodollar recycling, as a result of having quite a small population and/or underdeveloped infrastructure and the availability of extra financial resources even with intensive development plans.

62 F. El Sheikh, *The Legal Regime of Foreign Private Investment in the Sudan and Saudi Arabia: A Case Study of Developing Countries* (2nd edn., Cambridge University Press, 2003), p. 11.

63 Ibid.

64 The Overseas Private Investment Corporation (OPIC) no longer provides coverage in Saudi Arabia. In 1995, OPIC removed Saudi Arabia from its list of countries approved for OPIC coverage because of Saudi Arabia's failure to take steps to comply with 'internationally recognized labour standards'. See the US Department of State website at <http://www.state.gov/e/eeb/ifd/2005/43038.htm> [accessed 1 May 2009].

Centre, giving effect to some regional arbitration-related conventions and adopting a number of bilateral investment agreements.[65]

Saudi Arabia Joins the ICSID Convention

The International Centre for the Settlement of Investment Disputes is an autonomous international organization with close links to the World Bank. All of the members of the ICSID Convention are also members of the World Bank. According to the ICSID Convention, which came into force on 14 October 1966, the Centre provides facilities for the conciliation and arbitration of disputes between member countries and investors who qualify as nationals of other member countries. Recourse to ICSID services is entirely voluntary. However, a party to a dispute cannot withdraw its consent unilaterally, and member states are required to enforce ICSID arbitral awards.[66] The acceptance of ICSID jurisdiction was seen as an important instrument in giving investors the confidence to continue with existing investments as well as a tool for attracting further investments.[67] Saudi Arabia signed the Convention in September 1979 and it entered into force in June 1980.[68]

Pursuant to article 25(4) of the Convention, any contracting state may notify ICSID of the class or classes of dispute that it may or may not be willing to submit to ICSID arbitration. Accordingly, Saudi Arabia, in its ratification instrument, reserved the right not to submit to ICSID questions pertaining to oil and to acts of sovereignty, whether by way of conciliation or arbitration.[69] Investment arbitration in Saudi Arabia is to be governed by ICSID rules in contrast to commercial arbitration, which is governed by the Arbitration Act of 1983 or other rules provided that they are recognized by Saudi authorities. *Ed. Züblin AG v. Kingdom of Saudi Arabia* is the first case in which the Saudi Government was party to ICSID arbitration. The construction of university facilities was the subject matter of the dispute. On 28 January 2003, the Secretary General registered a request for the constitution of the arbitration panel. However, a settlement was reached by the parties and the proceeding discontinued at the request of the claimant in accordance with article 44 of the Arbitration Rules.[70] This case is an example of the dispute settlement approach of the Government of Saudi Arabia, which

65 Saudi Arabia has ratified 17 investment promotion and protection agreements other than the agreements formed under the GCC and the Arab League.

66 See, in general, the International Centre for the Settlement of Investment Disputes (ICSID) website at <http://www.worldbank.org/icsid> [accessed 26 April 2009].

67 J. Lew, L. Mistelis and S. Kroll, *Comparative International Commercial Arbitration* (1st edn., Kluwer Law International, 2003), p. 22.

68 See the Council of Ministers Resolution No. 372 of 15/03/1394 H. (1974). See also Royal Decree No. M/8 of 22/02/1394 H. (1974).

69 G. Delaume, 'ICSID Arbitration and the Courts', *American Journal of International Law*, 77/4 (1983), pp. 784–96.

70 See the list of the concluded cases of the ICSID, Case No. (ARB/03/1). Available online at <http://www.worldbank.org/icsid/cases/conclude.htm> [accessed 25 April 2009].

performs its obligation under any contract adequately and in good faith. In the case of a dispute, the Government prefers to settle it amicably and in private, which was one of the reasons behind the length of the proceedings in the Aramco case.[71]

The Arbitration Act of 1983

Regardless of the impractical provisions in the Code of Commercial Courts of 1931, article 183 of the Labour Law of 1969[72] and article 3 of the Chamber of Commerce and Industry Regulation of 1980,[73] Saudi Arabia lacked comprehensive arbitration regulation. The Arbitration Act of 1983 repealed the related provisions in the Code of Commercial Courts of 1931. The Implementing Regulation of 1985 was brought about to answer all the related questions that had not been covered by the Act and to describe various aspects of arbitration proceedings. In many ways it is a codification of the Hanbali law of arbitration. The Act provides a framework for commercial arbitration in a flexible way that makes arbitration a real alternative dispute resolution mechanism, as will be seen in the next chapter.

Conventions on the Recognition and Enforcement of Foreign Arbitral Awards

The New York Convention 1958

The United Nations Convention on the Recognition and Enforcement of Foreign Arbitral Awards of 1958, known as the New York Convention, requires signatories to enforce arbitral awards issued by other member nations. Saudi Arabia ratified the Convention on 18 July 1994 to become the 94th party to the Convention.[74] The main purpose of the Convention is to facilitate the enforcement and recognition of arbitral awards made in the territory of a state other than the state wherein the recognition and enforcement of such awards are sought.[75] The main feature of this Convention is article 5.2, which gives the member states two grounds to refuse the enforcement of any foreign arbitral award. Article 5.2 (a) states that a member

71 See supra n. 28, Aramco award. It is also the reason for the very small number of disputes against the Saudi Government, bearing in mind the intensive constructions and governmental contracts during the 1970s and 1980s.

72 See Royal Decree No. (M/21) of 06/09/1389 H. (1969). Article 183 provides for arbitration as an alternative to the Committee for the Settlement of Labour Disputes.

73 Royal Decree No. (M/6) dated 60/04/1400 H. (1980). According to article 5 of Chambers of Commerce and Industry Regulation, the Chambers of Commerce and Industry are competent to resolve business disputes by arbitration if the parties agree to it.

74 See the United Nations Commission on International Trade Law (UNCITRAL) at <http://www.uncitral.org> [accessed 30 April 2008].

75 Article 1 of the United Nations Convention on the Enforcement and Recognition of Foreign Arbitral Awards (New York Convention) (10 June 1958).

state can refuse the enforcement of a foreign arbitral award if the subject matter of the dispute is not capable of settlement by arbitration under its municipal law. Article 5.2 (b) gives the member state the right not to enforce foreign arbitral awards that are contrary to public policy.[76] The defence of public policy can be used intensively and there are many aspects of public policy in Saudi Arabia that can set aside any foreign arbitral award. Accordingly, it has been argued that Saudi Arabia joined the New York Convention without being obliged to enforce foreign arbitral awards and that the scope of article 5 (b) of the Convention should be restricted.[77] Saudi judges do not set aside foreign arbitral awards on the grounds of being 'foreign' or having been issued by a non-Muslim arbitrator, as many foreign practitioners claim. In cases where an award is rejected, it is usually because it is not suitable to be enforced domestically. Arbitrators should therefore bear in mind the public policy of the place of enforcement of any award.

The Convention of the Arab League of Nations on the Enforcement of Judgments of 1952

Although this Convention was replaced by the Riyadh Convention for Judicial Cooperation of 1983, it might be useful to give a brief outline about the Convention. The Convention of the Arab League of Nations on the Enforcement of Judgments of 14 September 1952 was ratified by Saudi Arabia on 18 July 1954. Saudi Arabia was the first country to ratify the Convention. The Council of Ministers Resolution No. 50 dated June 25/12/1379 H. (1960) gives *Diwan Almazalim* the competence to examine the petitions for the enforcement of Arab League judgments. Prior to the enactment of the previous resolution, Arab League arbitral awards were not to be tried *de novo* except in the circumstances stated below. The Council of Ministers Resolution was complemented by Royal Decree No. (M/51), which expanded the jurisdiction of *Diwan Almazalim* to cover the enforcement of all foreign arbitral awards and judgments. The royal decree abolished the discrimination between arbitral awards issued in a member state to the Arab League and non-Arab arbitral awards.[78] The Convention provides for the direct enforcement of any court decision issued in any court in any member state of the Convention. The Convention left the competent authority with a limited scope for judicial review for the reason that most Arab countries have their laws based on the same principles.[79] With

76 Ibid., article 5.2.

77 K. Roy, 'The New York Convention and Saudi Arabia: Can a Country Use the Public Policy Defence to refuse Enforcement of Non-Domestic Arbitral Awards?' *Fordham International Law Journal*, 18 (1994–1995), pp. 920–26.

78 See, generally, A. Alfahal, *Qada' Almazalim Fe Almamlakah Al Arabiya Al Saudiya* (1st edn., Dar Alnawabig, 1994).

79 See article 1 of the Basic Law of Saudi Arabia, which states that Shari'a rules are the only source of legislation in Saudi Arabia, See also article 2 of the Egyptian Constitution, as amended in 1980, which states that Islamic jurisprudence is the principal source of legislation; article 2 of the Constitution of Kuwait of 1962, which states that

regard to arbitration, the competent authority in Saudi Arabia is *Diwan Almazalim*. According to article 3 of the Convention, the competent authority does not have to review the arbitral award; however, it does have the right to refuse the enforcement in the following cases:

- if the subject matter of the dispute is not arbitrable under the law of the state where the enforcement is sought;
- if the arbitral tribunal exceeds its jurisdiction;
- if the award is issued under a non-valid arbitration clause or agreement;
- if the award is issued *in absentia*;
- if the award is not final in the country where it is rendered; and
- if the award is contrary to public policy or to the law of the country wherein the enforcement is sought.[80]

The Gulf Cooperation Council (GCC) Commercial Arbitration Centre

The GCC Commercial Arbitration Centre was established as an independent, non-profitable organization by the leaders of the GCC states in December 1993 during the 14th GCC Summit in Riyadh, Saudi Arabia, with its headquarters situated in Bahrain.[81] The arbitration rules of the Centre were issued in November 1994 and the Centre was fully functional by March 1995. The Centre is the most active arbitration centre in the GCC area owing to its understanding of the legal systems of its member states. Moreover, arbitration through the Centre is considered the most advantageous foreign solution for parties with regard to enforcement in Saudi Arabia.[82] In relation to the enforcement of the Centre's awards, article 36 of the rules of procedure of the Centre provides:

> [A]n award passed by the Tribunal pursuant to these Rules shall be binding and final. It shall be enforceable in the GCC member States once an order is issued for the enforcement thereof by the relevant judicial authority.[83]

The rules set the grounds of setting aside an arbitral award in article 36, which are:

Shari'a shall be a main source of legislation; and article 3 of the Constitution of Yemen of 1994, which provides that Islamic Shari'a is the source of all legislation.

80 The Convention of the Arab League of Nations on the Enforcement of Judgements of 14 September 1952.

81 GCC stands for Gulf Cooperation Council, which is a 1981 agreement among the six Arab countries of the Gulf region – Bahrain, Kuwait, Oman, Qatar, Saudi Arabia and the United Arab Emirates – aimed at coordinating and integrating their economic policies.

82 See, in general, the GCC Commercial Arbitration Centre website at <http://www.gcac.biz/en> [accessed 30 April 2009].

83 Arbitral rules of procedure adopted by the GCC Commercial Cooperation Committee in November 1994 in Riyadh, Saudi Arabia.

- when it is passed in the absence of an arbitration agreement or in pursuance of a null agreement, or if it is prescribed by the passage of time or if the arbitrator goes beyond the scope of the agreement;
- when the award is passed by arbitrators who have not been appointed in accordance with the law, or when it is passed by those who are unauthorized to hand down a ruling in the absence of others, or when it is passed pursuant to an arbitration agreement in which the issue of the dispute is not specified, or when it is passed by a person who is not legally qualified to issue such an award.

Bilateral Investment Treaties

Apart from the regional agreements concluded under the Arab League and the GCC, Saudi Arabia concluded an investment promotion and protection agreement with the following 17 countries: Italy, Germany, Belgium, Taiwan, China, France, Malaysia, Luxembourg, Spain, Turkey, India, Republic of Korea, Philippines, Switzerland, Egypt, Singapore, and Austria. These agreements aim to promote and protect the investments of nationals and the enterprises of one contracting party in the territory of another by providing an appropriate legislative environment in which to stimulate and increase investment, trade and industrial activity. With the recession in Western economies and its own ambitious development plans, Saudi Arabia is assuming the role of capital-exporting country. Many Western countries such as the US and the UK are keen to share part of its wealth by any means. In relation to dispute settlement, all the treaties provide for arbitration as a method of settling any dispute arising out of the interpretation of the agreements.[84] The agreements also provide for arbitration under ICSID for the settlement of disputes between the host state and the private parties of another state, as well as ad hoc arbitration under the UNCITRAL arbitration rules for settling disputes between private parties.[85]

84 See for example, article 9 of the agreement between Saudi Arabia and the Belo-Luxembourg economic union (bleu) concerning the reciprocal promotion and protection of investments signed in Jeddah on 22 April 2001; article 10 of the agreement between Saudi Arabia and the Republic of Austria concerning the Encouragement and Reciprocal Protection of Investment signed in Riyadh on 30 June 2000; article 10 of the agreement between the Saudi Government and the Government of Malaysia concerning the promotion and reciprocal protection of investment signed in Kuala Lumpur on 10 October 2000.

85 Ibid. Moreover, article 11.2.b of the Agreement between Saudi Arabia and Austria provides for an ad hoc arbitration tribunal to be established under the rules of UNCITRAL for the purpose of settling disputes between host states and private parties.

The Saudi Arbitration Team

On 24 August 2002 a royal decree was issued under number 7/5/23165 calling for the establishment of the Saudi Arbitration Team. According to some of its members, the main duties of the team are: advertising for arbitration in Saudi Arabia as an auxiliary mechanism to litigation; and attending and holding conferences on issues related to arbitration in Saudi Arabia. In addition, the team's policy aims at encouraging the business community to pay more attention to arbitration in Saudi Arabia in order to take away part of the caseload from local courts and committees. The team has so far achieved moderate success at bringing arbitration into the limelight.[86] The legal community is expecting more from the team than just advertising, because it is the only organized entity which is able to develop and work on the idea of establishing independent arbitration courts and centres.

Conclusion

The attitude of the Saudi Government toward international arbitration has been strongly influenced by the outcome of the Aramco award of 1958. At first, the Government welcomed international arbitration, as seen in the *Buraimi* case of 1955. After the Aramco award, international arbitration was viewed by the Saudis as a breach of their national sovereignty, manifested in terms of disrespecting their laws and regulations and applying foreign laws to their national wealth. It was also suspected that international arbitration was being used by Western parties wishing to escape the application of Saudi law. Some evidence of this lies in the arguably unfair tactical use of arbitration by some Western companies.[87] The disappointing outcomes of the Aramco arbitration were expected, owing to the lack of legal experience and naïve or 'too honest' conduct towards Aramco. Some of the members of the arbitration tribunal in the Aramco case lacked basic knowledge of Islamic Shari'a and its principles. The arbitration tribunal was unfair in judging Shari'a and refused to apply its principles when the application was due. The Aramco award changed the Government's attitude toward arbitration as the Aramco award was followed by the Council of Ministers Resolution No. 85 of 1963, which prohibited the Government and its agencies from accepting arbitration clauses and agreements. Later, the Ministry of Commerce Circulation complemented the Council of Ministers Resolution and prohibited foreign arbitration clauses in the articles of association of joint ventures registered within the kingdom. This approach did not last for long because the oil boom started to relax it. Saudi Arabia agreed to settle certain differences and claims relating to the Agreement on Guaranteed Private Investment and guarantees of Saudi

86 I would like to thank judges I. Alhowaimil, A. Alrudhaiman and E. Alsheikh, who are members of the team, for their useful help on this point.

87 Supra n. 57, Alsamman, p. 219.

public sector contracts and investments with the United States in 1975. Having previously contracted with an individual country, the comprehensive reform, as a legal incentive to foreign investment, began when Saudi Arabia joined the ICSID Convention in 1979–1980. The impacts of the Aramco award were obvious in the reservation made by the Government regarding oil and acts of sovereignty. This step was followed by expanding the jurisdiction of *Diwan Almazalim* to include the enforcement of foreign judgments and arbitral awards in 1982. The Arbitration Act of 1983 and its Implementing Regulation in 1985 were the first comprehensive arbitration regulations in the kingdom still in force today. The real interaction with the world in the field of international commercial arbitration came after the ratification of the New York Convention on the enforcement and recognition of foreign arbitral awards of 1958, regardless of its limited application in Saudi Arabia and the intensive use of the public policy defence. The New York Convention is still the main international instrument for the enforcement of foreign arbitral awards. Saudi Arabia also contributed to the establishment of the GCC Commercial Arbitration Centre, which works as a fully functioning arbitration centre for the GCC countries, with easier and more direct enforcement of its awards in Saudi Arabia. The last few years have witnessed the adoption of several bilateral investment agreements for the protection of foreign investment. These include arbitration as the main method of dispute settlement. The quality of the regulatory relaxation differs between the 1970s and the current phase, which is owing to economic circumstances. In the 1970s, Saudi Arabia needed to attract foreign expertise and technology to contribute to the building of its infrastructure. After the collapse of the global oil market in the 1990s, the objective of attracting foreign capital was added to the Saudi agenda. Despite the fact that Saudi Arabia relaxed its regulation toward foreign elements and showed more tolerance toward foreign arbitral awards, the impact of the Aramco award was still evident in the limitations on arbitration in governmental contracts, such as those demonstrated in article 3 of the Arbitration Act of 1983 and in the reservation made when ratifying the ICSID Convention. Nevertheless, the arbitration clauses in the Gas Concessions of 2004 do show more openness toward the outside world in this area.

Chapter 5

Saudi Law as *Lex Arbitri*: Evaluation of Saudi Arbitration Law and Judicial Practice

The Arbitration Act of Saudi Arabia was adopted by Royal Decree No. M/46, issued on 12/07/1403 H. (1983), repealing in the process the relevant provisions of the Commercial Court Code of 1931.[1] The Implementing Rules of the Act were subsequently adopted by royal decree in 1985.[2] The purpose of the Implementing Rules was to supplement lacunae in the Act and provide guidance on particular aspects of Saudi arbitral proceedings. More specifically, the Act is silent regarding numerous procedural issues, such as the rules pertaining to the delivery of arbitral awards, notifications as to the process and communication between the parties and the arbitral tribunal and between the arbitral tribunal and third parties, the seat of the arbitral tribunal, and others. It will be demonstrated that the Act constitutes a codification of the Hanbali law of arbitration,[3] as elaborated by Ibn Taymiyyah (1263–1328) in his collection of *Fatwas*,[4] and Ibn Qodamah (1146–1223) in his comprehensive work *Almoghni*, which has been considered the most authoritative source of Hanbali teachings until the present day.[5]

As mentioned above, the Act provides a framework for flexible commercial arbitration with a view to establishing it as a real and effective alternative dispute resolution mechanism. Prior to the adoption of the 1983 Act, arbitration existed only as a theoretical possibility on account of several factors. Firstly, the courts at the time did not recognize arbitration agreements or clauses, even where the parties claimed a contractual entitlement to arbitrate as a result. Even where the court approved the arbitration agreement or clause, the subsequent enforcement of the arbitral award was wholly voluntary.[6] Accordingly, reference to arbitration was

1 Part of this chapter was published in the following article: Abdulrahman Baamir and Ilias Bantekas, 'Saudi Law as *Lex Arbitri*: Evaluation of Saudi Arbitration Law and Judicial Practice', *Arbitration International*, 25/2 (2009), pp. 239–70. The Code of Commercial Courts was reprinted in *Umm Alqura Gazette*, issue No. 2969 of 22/08/1403 H. (1983).

2 Royal Decree No. M/7/2021, of 08/09/1405 H. (1985), reprinted in *Umm Alqura Gazette*, issue No. 3069 of 10/10/1405 H. (1985).

3 S. Saleh, *Commercial Arbitration in the Arab Middle East: Shari'a, Syria, Lebanon and Egypt* (2nd edn., Heart Publishing, 2006), especially Chapter 20, pp. 290–325.

4 M. Ibn Taymiyyah, *Majmou' Alfatawa* (2nd edn., The Ministry of Islamic Affairs of Saudi Arabia, 1995), Vol. 29.

5 M. Ibn Qodamah, *Almoghni* (1st edn., Hajar Publications, 1992), Vol. 10.

6 N. Albejad, *Arbitration in Saudi Arabia* (1st edn., Institute of Public Administration, 1999), p. 30

very limited. Secondly, the jurisdictional conflict between the Saudi Commercial Court[7] and Shari'a courts culminated in rendering arbitration ineffective and time-consuming. Although the Arbitration Act of 1983 supersedes the arbitration provisions of the Commercial Court Code of 1931, ad hoc arbitrations lacking a commercial character are still governed by the provisions of the Commercial Court Code.[8] While one generally speaks of either ad hoc or institutional arbitration, in Saudi Arabia there is yet another classification on the basis of the nature of the dispute as either compulsory or voluntary arbitration. As a general rule, resort to arbitration is voluntary,[9] except where the regulator recommends the compulsory route in a particular case. The rationale behind this classification is to restrict the jurisdiction of Shari'a courts with respect to certain controversial matters under Shari'a and also to avoid the conflict between Shari'a and Saudi law on the one hand and Saudi law and some customs and traditions on the other.[10]

The Arbitration Act of 1983 is relatively brief and ambiguous in parts and, as already stated, lacks detail with respect to key issues of arbitration proceedings. Most of the ambiguous issues were ironed out in the Implementing Rules of 1985. The Implementing Rules are elaborate and highly influential for both arbitral tribunals and the judicial bodies overseeing the arbitral process in Saudi Arabia. However, even the Implementing Rules did not give a clear answer to some essential aspects, such as the question of arbitrability, which will be examined in detail in the next chapter. Arbitration regulation is in the redrafting stage and a new act is expected to be issued soon. However, the ratification of a new act will not make any considerable change to current law and practice because it will be a different interpretation to Shari'a law on arbitration, as discussed in previous chapters.

The following sections provide an analysis of the Rules with reference to Hanbali arbitration law and the relevant laws in Saudi Arabia, especially the Law of Procedure before Shari'a Courts.[11]

---

7 Upon its establishment, there was only one commercial court seated in Jeddah, which was later substituted by the Commission for the Settlement of Commercial Disputes under the supervision of the Ministry of Commerce and Industry.

8 Supra n. 6, Albejad, p. 30.

9 Article 1, 1983 Arbitration Act of Saudi Arabia

10 Supra n. 6, Albejad, p. 51. For instance, disputes related to tobacco products and musical instruments are compulsorily referred to arbitration.

11 As we have already noted, under Hanbali teachings arbitration is equivalent to litigation and the arbitrator is thus analogous to a private judge having specific jurisdiction only over the issue at hand. Article 36 of the Implementing Rules provides that the arbitral tribunal should comply with the litigation principles of Shari'a. The Implementing Rules were issued in 1985 prior to the enactment of the 2000 Law of Procedure before Shari'a Courts. Prior to the enactment of the 2000 Law, arbitrators relied on Shari'a principles in order to find governing rules for arbitral proceedings.

Arbitration, Arbitrators and Parties

Article 1 of the Implementing Rules concerns the scope of arbitration. According to the article, arbitration is not permitted in matters in which conciliation is not permitted such as hodoud,[12] accusation of adultery between spouses and all matters relating to public order.[13] The Hanbalies mainly give the arbitrator the same jurisdiction as a court judge. Ibn Taymiyyah does not restrict the scope of arbitration and gives it the same scope as litigation; however, according to him an arbitral award has no value without judicial review.[14] The Act follows the restriction made by some Hanbali scholars and does not allow arbitration in some criminal matters because it has a different nature from commercial disputes and is related to state power.[15]

Article 2 deals with the capacity of parties to arbitrate. Like any normal contract, an arbitration agreement is not valid unless it is made by a person with the full legal capacity to conclude a valid contract. In order to conclude a valid agreement under Shari'a, the parties to the dispute must satisfy the requirements of legal capacity, i.e., they must have reached a certain age and have a certain level of mental ability at the time of concluding the contract.[16] Neither the guardian of a minor nor the trustee of charitable trust, called '*waqf*' in Arabic, can conclude an arbitration agreement unless authorized to do so by the court.[17] Even after being authorized to resort to arbitration, an arbitral award against the guardian of an incapacitated person is invalid if it provides for any damage against their interest unless approved by a judge.[18] In accordance with article 5 of the Arbitration Act, the arbitration agreement should be sent to the competent authority for approval, i.e., to the authority having jurisdiction on the dispute originally.[19] When reviewing arbitration agreements, the competent authority decides whether they entail any contradiction with the substantive and the procedural law of arbitration as well as public policy.

After approving the arbitration agreement, the authority, which is mainly *Diwan Alamzalim* (the Board of Grievances) or the Chamber of Commerce and Industry, should inform the arbitral tribunal of the approval and advise it to proceed in looking at the dispute at issue. Alternatively the refusing party may be forced by the *Diwan* to prepare it in accordance with the Arbitration Act.[20] If one of the

12 Hodoud are crimes for which the Quran provides punishments such as theft, adultery and accusation of adultery.

13 Article 1 of the Implementing Rules of the Arbitration Act.

14 A. ben Mofleh, *Al-forou'* (4th edn., A'alam Alkotoub, 1985), Vol. 6, p. 440.

15 Supra n. 5, Ibn Qodamah, Vol. 11, p. 484.

16 M. Zahraa, 'The Legal Capacity of Women in Islamic Law', *Arab Law Quarterly*, 11 (1996), pp. 245–63.

17 Article 2 of the Implementing Rules of the Arbitration Act.

18 See, in general, the Implementing Rules of the Arbitration Act.

19 See article 5 of the Arbitration Act and *Diwan Almazalim* decision No. 59/T/4 of 1412 H. (1992).

20 *Diwan Almazalim* decision No. 184/T/4 of 1412 H. (1992).

parties refuses to arbitrate after concluding a binding arbitration clause, the other party will prepare the arbitration agreement unilaterally but under the supervision of the authority. If the agreement meets the legal requirements and the denying party rejects it, the authority will approve it, inform the arbitral tribunal and ask it to proceed normally following the related provisions of the Arbitration Act and the Implementing Regulations.[21]

Under Saudi law, the existence of the arbitration clause does not affect the right of parties to resort to litigation. It can be understood from case law that referring the dispute to litigation with the existence of an arbitration clause is an implied waiver of the parties' right to arbitrate. In decision number 29/T/4 of 1413 H. (1993), the *Diwan* emphasized the parties' right to insist on arbitration as a means of settling a dispute relating to a valid agreement;[22] however, the action of referring the dispute to litigation is a waiver of the parties' right to arbitrate and the arbitration clause will be of no avail.[23] This view was further supported by decision number 72/T/4 of 1411 H. (1991), in which the *Diwan* denied jurisdiction over the dispute because of the existence of the arbitration clause. When the case was referred to the Review Committee of the *Diwan*, however, it was found that one of the defendants was insisting on his right to arbitrate despite referring the case to litigation, an action which annuls his right to arbitrate. The Committee upheld the nullification of the arbitration clause because the defendant raised his claim after referring the dispute to litigation.[24] The moment when the right to arbitrate is waived by referring the dispute to litigation is not clearly determined but it might be subject to the time of filing the dispute to litigation before the Shari'a court or *Diwan Almazalim*.

It is not a matter of public policy in Saudi Arabia that the arbitration clause waives the parties' right to refer to litigation. In Saudi law, if one of the parties wants to insist on his right to arbitrate, his claim should be made before referring the dispute to litigation, as seen in decision numbers 95/T/4 of 1413 H. (1993) and 142/T/4 of 1409 H. (1989).[25] In the latter decision the Review Committee of the *Diwan* added that the parties to the arbitration have the right to refer the case to litigation even if they have a valid arbitration clause. Litigation is the original method for settling disputes – arbitration is an option only when it has nothing to do with public policy.[26] On the other hand, referring a dispute to litigation does not affect the right of the parties to resort to arbitration. In case number 27/T/4 of 1411 H. (1991), the defendant argued that the plaintiff sued him before a court in the

21 See *Diwan Alamzalim* decision No. 150/T/4 of 1413 H. (1993).

22 *Diwan Almazalim* decisions No. 113/T/4 of 1416 H. (1996) and No. 38/T/4 of 1409 H. (1989).

23 *Diwan Almazalim* decision No. 29/T/4 of 1413 H. (1993).

24 *Diwan Almazalim* decision No. 72/T/4 of 1411 H. (1991).

25 *Diwan Almazalim* decisions No. 95/T/4 of 1413 H. (1993) and No. 142/T/4 of 1409 H. (1989).

26 Ibid.

United States, which is a waiver of his right to arbitrate. The Committee decided that referring the dispute to litigation has no effect on parties' right to arbitrate.[27] As has been seen above, case law carries some contradiction when determining whether referring a dispute to arbitration could annul the arbitration clause or whether the arbitration clause remains valid. Such a conflict may be owing to the fact that precedent cases have little effect on legal practice – the emphasis is placed instead on reasoning and the understanding of judges and arbitrators.

Article 3 determines the nationality of arbitrators as well as other matter of public policy regarding the character of arbitrators. The arbitrator should be a Muslim male of Saudi nationality or a Muslim male of any other nationality of a liberal profession; otherwise he may be a public official upon the approval of the department to which he belongs. If there is more than one arbitrator, the chairman should be knowledgeable about Shari'a rules and the commercial regulations, custom and tradition in effect in the kingdom.[28] Article 4 of the Act adds that in the case of multiple arbitrators the number should be odd.[29] The appointment of a sole arbitrator as well as the validity of arbitral awards rendered by a sole arbitrator is upheld by the common practice and decisions of the *Diwan*.[30] The requirement to have an odd number of arbitrators facilitates the issuing of the arbitral award in the case of conflict in the judgments of arbitrators.[31] Islamic law clearly elaborates the issue of non-Muslims acting as arbitrators and there is no doubt among all the scholars that non-Muslims are not allowed to adjudicate in any dispute involving a Muslim element within Muslim territory. This opinion is based on the assumption that arbitration is another form of litigation.[32]

If the arbitration agreement provides for the settlement of the dispute by conciliation, then the arbitrators/conciliators can be non-Muslims because the agreement is considered to be an agency agreement which can be executed by them.[33] In relation to Saudi law, arbitrators working in the settlement of any dispute within the kingdom must be Muslims in accordance with article 3 of the Implementing Rules of Arbitration.[34] Residing in Saudi Arabia is not a condition for the validity of the appointment of arbitrators. The Arbitration Act is silent on the issue of the place of residence of arbitrators and it requires them to be Muslim males only. In case number 22/T/4 of 1413 H. (1993) *Diwan Almazalim* rejected the decision of the Committee for the Settlement of Commercial Disputes, which annulled the appointment of an arbitrator on the ground that he was not residing in

27 *Diwan Almazalim* decision No. 27/T/4 of 1411 H. (1991).

28 Article 3 of the Implementing Rules.

29 Article 4 of the Arbitration Act.

30 *Diwan Almazalim* decision No. 7/T/4 of 1419 H. (1999).

31 A. Al-Kenain, *Altahkeem fe AlShari'a Alislamiyah: Altahkeem Al'am, wa Altahkeem fe Alshiqaq Alzaouji* (1st edn., Dar Alasimah, 2000), p. 111.

32 A. Alfarra', Al-Ahkam Al-Sultaniyah, ed. Muhammad Hamid Al-fagy (1st edn., Dar Alkotoub Alilmiyah, 1983), p. 61.

33 Supra n. 5, Ibn Qodamah, Vol. 14, p. 170.

34 See article 3 of the Implementing Rules.

Saudi Arabia, even though he was a Muslim. The Review Committee added that the rejection imposed an unnecessary restriction.[35]

Article 4 provides for some restrictions on the appointment of arbitrators. According to the article, if a person having an interest in a dispute has been convicted of a *hadd* (single of hodoud) or a crime of dishonour, or has been dismissed from public office by punitive decision or adjudicated bankrupt, he may not be an arbitrator unless relieved from such a condition.[36] The concern here is with the issues of impartiality and credibility. Moreover, most of the latter issues can be used as grounds for the challenging of witnesses. The appointment of an arbitrator possessing one of these characteristics violates the principle that the arbitrator must be an adl.[37] The appointment of a fasiq[38] is void because arbitration under Hanbali teachings is litigation – therefore the arbitrator should possess all the characters of a court judge.[39]

Article 5 obliges the authorities to issue an official updated list of licensed arbitrators. The list should be prepared by agreement among the Minister of Justice, the Minister of Commerce and Industry and the Chairman of the Board of Grievances. The courts, judicial commissions and Chambers of Commerce and Industry shall be notified of the list and disputants have liberty to choose arbitrators from such lists. The Ministry of Justice criterion for prospective arbitrators is that they have to pass an exam before they qualify as arbitrators. The exam covers various topics such as the mandatory rules of Shari'a and arbitration procedure under the Arbitration Act and its Implementing Rules, in addition to the valid laws and customs relating to the area in which the arbitrator wants to practise.[40] The test is multiple-choice, with 20 questions. Candidates can download it from the website of the Ministry of Justice and then fax or post in their answers. This process might not be the most appropriate way of qualifying arbitrators, because the test does not cover many important arbitration issues such as public policy, the issuance of the award or even the rules of procedure. For instance, some questions deal with issues like the number of articles in the Arbitration Act and the Implementing Rules, the date of ratifying the New York Convention of 1958, what does UNCITRAL stands for, etc. The Ministry is about to revise the criteria for qualifying arbitrators and a new regulation will be enacted by 2011.

The credibility of such a procedure is also disputed because anyone can answer it on behalf of a candidate. According to the Ministry of Justice website,

35 *Diwan Almazalim* decision No. 22/T/4 of 1412 H. (1992).

36 Article 4 of the Implementing Rules.

37 Supra n. 3, Saleh, p.36. In general, the term adl refers to someone who does not violate Shari'a law and who has decent mental abilities.

38 Fasiq is a term describing someone guilty of openly and flagrantly violating Islamic law and/or someone whose moral character is corrupt.

39 Supra n. 31, Al-Kenain, pp. 77–79.

40 See article 5 of the Implementing Rules. The list of arbitrators is available from the website of the Ministry of Justice at <www.moj.gov.sa> [accessed 22 September 2009].

if a candidate fails in answering one of the questions, he will have to attend an interview that might be nothing more than a repetition of the test he already sent to the Ministry.[41] Although non-Saudis are allowed to arbitrate if they are chosen by the parties to a particular dispute, the Ministry of Justice requires all applicants to be of Saudi nationality.[42]

Arbitration Clause

Article 6 overcomes one of the main impediments to arbitration in Saudi Arabia, i.e., the recognition of arbitration clause. The article also sets the minimum amount of information that should be included in the arbitration agreement According to the article, arbitrators shall be appointed by agreement of the parties in the arbitration agreement, which should adequately define the subject of the dispute and the names of the arbitrators. An agreement to arbitrate may also be made by a contractual clause – an 'arbitration clause' – relating to disputes arising out of the execution of the contract.[43]

The failure of courts to recognize arbitration clauses characterized arbitration under the Code of Commercial Courts of 1931 as an impractical and time-consuming dispute settlement mechanism.[44] Courts did not recognize the arbitration clause because they doubted its validity under Shari'a (most arbitrations at that time were rejected on the ground of uncertainty). One of the conditions of the validity of an arbitration agreement is to have an existing dispute; therefore, the legality of the arbitration clause is controversial. Under Shari'a, a contract whose object did not exist at the time of the conclusion of the contract is not acknowledged, which is similar to the prohibited contracts related to selling fish in the sea or birds in the sky. Hanbali teachings, as the most flexible school in commercial transactions, consider the arbitration clause to be a contractual clause that is valid as long as it does not contradict the purpose of the contract and is not prohibited under Shari'a.[45] Any rejection may be a result of judges' misunderstanding of the contractual nature of arbitration clauses.

Traditionally, an arbitration agreement should include the names of the arbitrators, the subject of the dispute, the applicable law and the time of rendering the arbitral award, as well as the seat of the arbitration.[46] It can be seen in the

41 The Ministry of Justice of Saudi Arabia website at <www.moj.gov.sa> [accessed 17 May 2009].

42 Ibid.

43 Article 6 of the Implementing Rules.

44 See, in general, supra n. 6, Albejad, p. 30.

45 See, in general, supra n. 5, Ibn Qodamah, Vol. 14.

46 G. Sayen, 'Arbitration, Conciliation and the Islamic Legal Tradition in Saudi Arabia', *University of Pennsylvania Journal of International Business Law*, 9/2 (1987), pp. 211–27.

famous incident of *Tahkeem* between Ali the fourth Caliphate and Mu'awiyah the governor of Syria in AD 659.[47] The arbitration agreements between the Government of Saudi Arabia and Aramco and between the Government of Saudi Arabia and the ruler of Abu Dhabi and the Sultan of Oman in the 1950s followed the same model.[48] Under Saudi arbitration law there is no need to determine the applicable law in the arbitration agreement or clause because it will be, by default, Shari'a or Saudi law. Moreover, Hanbali teachings give total freedom to the parties to the agreement to include any condition in their agreement, even if the condition is irrelevant to the dispute at issue, as long as it is not contrary to Shari'a principles.[49]

Article 7 of the Implementing Rules deals with the role of the supervisory authority to the arbitral proceedings. The supervisory authority over the arbitration proceedings is the authority originally having jurisdiction over the dispute. The authority originally having jurisdiction over the dispute should issue a decision approving the arbitration agreement within 15 days and should notify the arbitral tribunal of its decision.[50] This article codifies the opinion of Ibn Taymiyyah, which was that the arbitral award is without value without judicial review.[51] *Diwan Almazalim* and the Ministry of Commerce are the competent authorities to deal with commercial dispuites in the kingdom. Regardless of the very recent change in the charter of *Diwan Almazalim*, which moved the competence of settling commercial disputes to the Ministry of Justice, the supervision of arbitration has been one of the *Diwan*'s competences up till now.[52] As a general rule, all the parties to the arbitration and the arbitral tribunal are bound by the Arbitration Act and the Implementing Rules, meaning that any clause, agreement or action found to be in violation of the law is null and void. The *Diwan* in its decision number 53/T/4 of 1414 H. (1994) nullified an arbitral award made without the supervision and approval of the competent authority. In this case, the parties to the arbitration agreed to arbitrate under the supervision of entities other than the competent authority originally having jurisdiction over the dispute. The Review Committee of the *Diwan* set aside the award, stating that, as terms and conditions in the arbitration agreement contradict the Arbitration Act and related law, the award was null and void. As a result, it is prohibited to have a person, legal or natural, as a supervisor for arbitration in the kingdom other than the competent

47 Z. Alqurashi, 'Arbitration under the Islamic Shari'a', *Oil, Gas and Energy Intelligence*, 1/2 (March 2003), pp. 30–44.

48 See Aramco award 27 ILR 117 (1963), p. 128. See also the arbitration agreement between the Government of the United Kingdom acting on behalf of the ruler of Abu Dhabi and His Highness the Sultan Said bin Taimur the Sultan of Oman and the Government of Saudi Arabia signed in Jeddah on 30 July 1954 (HMSO Cmd 9272, 1954) cited in supra n. 347, Kelly, pp. 318–24.

49 Supra n. 46, Sayen, p. 220.

50 Article 7 of the Implementing Rules.

51 Supra n. 31, Al Kenain, p. 49.

52 *Umm Alqura Gazette*, issue No. 4170 dated 30/09/1428 H. 12/10/2007.

authority originally having jurisdiction over the dispute.[53] In another case, the *Diwan* nullified the arbitral award rendered without an approved arbitration agreement. In this case, the *Diwan* directed the arbitration tribunal to proceed in deciding the case even though there was no arbitration agreement approved by the *Diwan*. The arbitral tribunal proceeded, relying on the communication of the *Diwan*, including all the information that should be in the arbitration agreement; however, this action was in violation of the law and a mistake on the part of the *Diwan*, which should have informed the tribunal of the importance of having a valid arbitration agreement. As a result the award was considered null and void and the actions of the *Diwan* and the tribunal found in violation of the Arbitration Act and its Implementing Rules.[54]

It is disputed whether the competent authority has supremacy over the arbitration tribunal irrespective of the place of arbitration. When looking at the arbitration regulations, especially article 18 of the Arbitration Act,[55] it appears that the supervisory authority may act as an appellate body; however, case law regards the supervisory authority as the lower court and the arbitral tribunal as the supreme. Consequently, the *Diwan* will either uphold or reject an arbitral award without the competence to decide on the case anew. In decision number 53/T/4 of 1415 H. (1995) the Committee stated that, because the phrase 'competent authority' in the Arbitration Act and its Implementing Rules does not specify the required degree of the court, the supervisory authority should apply its own rules of procedure. The *Diwan* is seen as a second-degree court after the arbitration tribunal; therefore, the *Diwan* should apply its own rules of procedure and the *Diwan*'s duty is only to uphold or reject the decision of the arbitration tribunal.[56]

Article 8 demonstrates one of the impacts of the Aramco award of 1958. Both this article and article 3 of the Arbitration Act are incorporated in the Council of Ministers Resolution Number 58 of 1963 and the Deputy Minister of Commerce Circulation No. 3/9/sh/331/9/2903 of 13/03/1399 H. (1979).[57] In disputes to which a government authority is party and desires to resort to arbitration, such authority shall prepare a memorandum concerning arbitration in such a dispute, stating in it the subject of the dispute, the justification for arbitration and the names of the parties for submission to the President of the Council of Ministers to consider

---

53 *Diwan Almazalim* decision No. 61/T/4 of 1415 H. (1995).

54 *Diwan Almazalim* decision No. 99/T/4 of 1414 H. (1994).

55 Article 18 of the Arbitration Act reads as follows: 'All awards passed by the arbitrators, even though issued under an investigation procedure, shall be filed within five days with the authority originally competent to hear the dispute and the parties notified with copies thereof. Parties may submit their objections against what is issued by arbitrators to the authority with which the award is filed, within fifteen days from the date they are notified of the arbitrators' awards; otherwise such awards shall be final.'

56 *Diwan Almazalim* decision No. 53/T/4 of 1415 H. (1995).

57 See the Council of Ministers Resolution No. 58 dated 03/02/1383 H. (25/06/1963) and the Deputy Minister of Commerce Circulation No. 3/9/sh/331/9/2903 of 13/03/1399 H. (1979).

approval of the arbitration. The article allows some governmental entities to include arbitration clauses in their contract and, in all cases, the Council of Ministers should be notified of the award rendered in relation to all the disputes involving a governmental element.[58] In practice, if a governmental entity wants to resort to arbitration for the settlement of any dispute with another party, it should obtain approval from the President of the Council of Ministers; however, a governmental body may include an arbitration clause in its contracts.[59]

Proceeding

Article 9 specifies some of the responsibilities of the competent authority toward the arbitration proceedings. The arbitration proceedings shall be supervised by the authority originally having jurisdiction over the dispute. The authority shall appoint a clerk to act as secretary for the arbitral tribunal. The article sets the duties of the secretary, which include: establishing the necessary records to register the request for arbitration and submitting them to the competent authority for approval of the arbitration document; notifying and communicating in accordance with the Arbitration Act; and carrying out any other responsibilities determined by the competent minister.[60] Article 8 of the Arbitration Act states that the clerk of the authority originally competent to hear the dispute shall be in charge of all notifications and notices related to the arbitration proceedings.[61] Such notifications include the time and place of the hearings and all communications between the tribunal and the competent authority, witnesses, experts and all other individuals and entities.

Article 10 sets the time for the commencement of arbitral proceedings and illustrates some of the responsibilities of the secretary of the arbitral tribunal. The article requires the arbitral tribunal to fix the date for hearing the dispute within a period not exceeding five days from the date of its notification of the decision approving the arbitration agreement. Parties are notified through the clerk of the authority originally having jurisdiction over the dispute.[62] The responsibilities of the supervisory authority and the secretary of the arbitral tribunal will be illustrated in more detail below.

---

58 Article 8 of the Implementing Rules.

59 For further details see Appendix (Z) of the gas concession agreement between Saudi Arabia and Lukoil Overseas and the gas concession agreement between Saudi Arabia and Sinopec International Petroleum and Production Corporation *Umm Alqura Gazette*, issue No. 3990 dated 15/03/1425 H. 4/05/2004.

60 Article 9 of the Implementing Rules.

61 Article 8 of the Arbitration Act.

62 Article 10 of the Implementing Rules.

Notification of Parties, Appearance and Default, and Representation in the Arbitration

This part of the Implementing Rules can be divided into three: the first part illustrates issues related to notifying and communicating with the parties to the arbitration;[63] the second part specifies the competent persons to appear before the tribunal;[64] and the third part deals with appearing or failing to appear before the tribunal.[65]

Article 11 insists on the importance of the role of the secretary appointed by the supervisory authority. All the communication and notification relating to the dispute should be made by the clerk of the authority originally having jurisdiction over the dispute. These communications, whether carried out at the request of the parties or initiated by the arbitrators, should be assisted by the police and the local authority within the scope of their area of competence.[66]

Article 12 determines the official language for the content of all communications of the tribunal. A notification or communication shall be in Arabic in a number of copies according to the number of parties and should include all required information such as the timing of making the notification, the names, addresses of the parties and the server, the names of the arbitrators, the seat of the arbitral tribunal and the timing of the hearing.[67]

If the arbitration agreement provides for the settlement of the dispute by means of arbitration outside Saudi Arabia, the agreement is valid if the conflict of laws rules allow and one of the parties of the arbitration is of non-Saudi nationality. In decision number 155/T/4/ of 1415 H. (1995) the defendant, a foreign company, requested that arbitration should be held outside Saudi Arabia. The Committee decided that the defendant should be bound by Saudi arbitration law and therefore that the arbitration tribunal should be seated in Saudi Arabia, should apply Saudi substantive law and should be supervised by *Diwan Almazalim*.[68] However, if another law had been given applicability on the merit of the dispute, the *Diwan* would not have opposed the reference to arbitration outside Saudi Arabia, as in decision number 43/T/4 of 1416 H. (1996). In this case the parties to the dispute, a Saudi company against an American company, entered into a distribution agreement and agreed in the arbitration clause to refer their disputes to arbitration in Iowa in the United States. The *Diwan* rejected the claim that the dispute should

63 Articles 11–16 of the Implementing Rules.

64 Article 17 of the Implementing Rules.

65 Articles 18 and 19 of the Implementing Rules.

66 Article 11 of the Implementing Rules and see also article 15 of the Law of Procedure before Shari'a Courts, which determines the persons competent to assist in delivering notifications and communications as follows: the Umdah or chief of the quarter, the police station, to the head of the 'centre', or the chief of the tribe.

67 See article 12 of the Implementing Rules.

68 *Diwan Almazalim* decision No. 155/T/4 of 1415 H. (1995).

be settled restrictedly in Saudi Arabia on the ground of the applicability of other foreign laws on the dispute – when the American party insisted on its rights under the arbitration clause, the *Diwan* asked the parties to refer the dispute to the chosen forum.[69]

If all the parties to the arbitration are Saudis and the dispute is subject to Saudi law, they have no right to arbitrate outside Saudi Arabia and under any other laws, as that would be against public policy. In case number 143/T/4 of 1412 H. (1992) the Saudi disputants agreed to refer their dispute to arbitration in Zurich under the ICC rules. The dispute was a Saudi dispute in all its elements, which made the arbitration clause for arbitration outside Saudi Arabia null and void for contradicting public policy. The Committee stated that the dispute was subject to Saudi law and that the arbitration clause providing for the settlement of the dispute by means of arbitration in Zurich under the rules of the ICC was null and void. Regardless of its contradiction of Saudi arbitration law and its implementing rules, it was seen as an attempt to eliminate the jurisdiction of the Saudi judiciary over the dispute, which is against the public policy of Saudi Arabia. The Committee obliged the parties to refer the dispute to *Diwan Almazalim* to decide on the dispute.[70] To sum up in the issue of applicable law, if there is a foreign element in the dispute Saudi courts will look at the place of characteristic performance but will not apply foreign law. In cases in which a foreign law is applicable, Saudi courts will give the parties the choice of settling the dispute before the court or through arbitration in the given jurisdiction. However, if both parties to the dispute are of Saudi nationality, Saudi law will apply.

Notification

Articles 13 and 14 deal with the ways of notifying individual parties and determine the place and means of delivering the notifications.[71] Article 15 deals with the same issue but in the case of having legal persons as one of the parties to the arbitration. It determines the related issues of notifying the state, public persons and companies, organizations and private establishments. Notification to the state should be delivered to the competent minister, regional governor and head of the government authority concerned with the dispute, or to their deputies. In matters relating to public persons, notifications and communications should be delivered to the representative authorized by regulations, or his substitute. Finally, in matters relating to companies, associations and private establishments, the notifications and communications should be delivered to the head office as set forth in the commercial register, to the chairman of the board of directors or to the general manager, or to any employee substituting for such person; with respect to foreign

69 *Diwan Almazalim* decision No. 43/T/4 of 1416 H. (1996).

70 *Diwan Almazalim* decision No. 143/T/4 of 1412 H. (1992).

71 See articles 13 and 14 of the Implementing Rules.

companies having a branch or agent in Saudi Arabia, to such branch or agent. The Law of Procedure before Shari'a Courts explains the issue of the notification of parties to the dispute in greater detail. Article 18 of the Law reads as follows:

> With respect to government agencies, to their heads or those acting for them; With respect to public corporate persons, to their managers or those acting for them or representing them; With respect to companies, societies, and private establishments, to their managers or those acting for them or representing them; With respect to foreign companies and establishments which have a branch or an agent in the Kingdom, to the branch manager or the one acting for him or to the agent; or the one acting for him; With respect to armed forces personnel and those of similar status, to the immediate superior of the person to be served; With respect to sailors and ship personnel, to the captain; With respect to interdicted persons, to their trustees or guardians as the case may be; With respect to prisoners or detainees, to the warden of the prison or detention centre; With respect to persons who have no known place of residence or designated place of residence in the Kingdom, to the Ministry of Interior in the regular administrative ways for notification by appropriate means.[72]

Procedure

Under article 16 the secretary of the arbitral tribunal has to bear the duty of submitting the arbitration file to the supervisory authority and notifying the parties and arbitrators of the decision issued approving the arbitration agreement within one week from the date of the approval.[73]

Article 17 determines the capable persons for representing the parties before the arbitral tribunal. On the day fixed for hearing the arbitration, the parties should appear either in person or through a representative pursuant to a power of attorney, called *wakalah* in Arabic, issued by a notary public[74] or through any official authority or authority certified by a Chamber of Commerce and Industry. The option of appearance through a representative should not prejudice the right of the tribunal to require the personal appearance of a party if circumstances so require.[75] Wakalah can be translated as 'proxy' but under Shari'a wakalah is more than an agreement between two people to act on behalf of one another; it involves, in the case of general wakalah, the right to act absolutely as the principal party. In Islamic law, wakalah is a non-binding contract on both parties; it is dissolved

72 See article 15 of the Implementing Rules and Article 18 of the Law of Procedure before Shari'a Courts.

73 See article 16 of the Implementing Rules.

74 The body responsible for issuing powers of attorney in Saudi Arabia is known as *ketabat alad'l*.

75 Article 17 of the Implementing Rules.

by the death of the agent or the principal regardless of whether the other party is aware of the death. It can be dissolved by resignation, recession or any other ground of dissolving any contract. In the case of limited wakalah, the contract terminates by the time of executing the contract. In the case of a dispute, the power of attorney terminates on the time of rendering the final award.[76] Any agent to a party to an arbitration should be qualified to accept a power of attorney according to the law of Saudi Arabia.[77]

Article 18 deals with default in appearance before the arbitral tribunal. If one of the parties fails to appear and the tribunal is satisfied that he was notified properly, the tribunal may decide the dispute in the party's absence, provided the parties have both deposited in the arbitration file a record of their claim, defence, answers and documents. The award in such cases shall be deemed made as though all parties were presented. If the party was not duly summoned, the tribunal will be postponed to a subsequent hearing to be notified to the defaulting party. If there is more than one defendant party, some of whom were duly summoned while others were not, and either they all fail to appear or the party who was not duly summoned fails to appear, the tribunal shall, except in urgent cases, adjourn hearing the matter to a subsequent hearing to be notified to the non-appearing parties who were not duly summoned. The award in the matter shall be deemed made as if all parties failing to appear at the subsequent hearing were present. In addition, an award shall be deemed made as if a party were present if the party or his representative makes an appearance at any hearing and submits a case defence or related document. If a defaulting party makes an appearance before the end of the hearing, any award made therein shall be deemed null and void. There are strict conditions for issuing a judgment *in absentia* under the Hanbali teachings. Article 18 codifies the exceptional cases in which the tribunal can render an award without the physical presence of the parties to the dispute. Under Hanbali teaching, an award issued *in absentia* requires a judicial review before its execution because the defendant might have a defence against the claim; nonetheless, as a general rule, the tribunal is not allowed to issue a judgment *in absentia* except in the cases mentioned above.[78]

Article 19 provides for the re-notification of the party that has not been notified in the proper manner. According to the article, if a party fails to appear and it seems to the tribunal that his summons by publication was invalid, it shall suspend hearing the claim to a later hearing to be validly re-notified to such party.[79]

---

76 Supra n. 46, Alatasi, Vol. 5, articles 1521–1530.

77 There are a few persons who are unable to act as agents or accept the power of attorney before the judicial bodies in Saudi Arabia such as minors, women and non-Saudis. See the Code of Law Practice of Saudi Arabia, Royal Decree No. M/38 dated 28/06/1422 H. (2001) *Umm Alqura Gazette*, issue No. 3867 dated 17/08/1422 H. (2001).

78 See, in general, supra n. 5, Ibn Qodamah, Vol. 14, p. 96.

79 Article 19 of the Implementing Rules.

Hearings, Procedure and Recording of the Case

Confidentiality of Proceedings

Under article 20 the case shall be publicly heard before the arbitral tribunal unless the tribunal decides otherwise on its own initiative or on the request of one of the parties for reasons evaluated by the tribunal.[80] Accordingly, any member of the public is allowed to attend the hearings without restrictions.[81] Under this article the option of having a private hearing cannot be extended to the issuance of the final award, which must be in public.[82] This article seems to contradict one of the main purposes of arbitration, as confidentiality is deemed to be one of its advantages as a method. Some commentators claim that the objective behind the publicity of arbitral proceedings is to enhance transparency and impartiality, but this view does not match the reality in Saudi Arabia nowadays. As a general rule, court proceedings are to be held in public; however, in Saudi Arabia individuals who are not involved in the dispute cannot even enter the courtroom. In addition to the negative attitude of some judges, the infrastructure of most of the courts in Saudi Arabia does not enable members of the public to attend court proceedings. Saudi law should not impose publicity on the arbitral tribunal when state courts do not apply it to their own proceedings. Article 20 is supported by article 61 of the Law of Procedure before Shari'a Courts, which states that the judge on his own or at the request of one of the litigants can close the hearing in order to maintain order, observe public morality, or for the privacy of the family.[83] Although this article does not contradict the Hanbali law of arbitration, it does contradicts one of the objectives of the resort to arbitration as a private dispute settlement mechanism.

Traditionally, disputes used to be settled in public places. The judge or regional governor sat either in the mosque or in his *Diwan* to hear and settle disputes between members of the public. With reference to the Islamic law of arbitration, this article is in compliance with traditional rules; however, in the light of modern custom and trade practice, the application of this article can be harmful to the parties, especially in terms of their business reputation and credibility.

Article 21 requires there to be a satisfactory excuse for suspending the hearing of a case.[84] Article 22 upholds some of the rights of the parties to have a fair trail. The arbitral tribunal shall enable each party to represent his comments, defences

80 Article 20 of the Implementing Rules.

81 A. Aldar'an, *Alqawa'ed Al ijrae'iyah fe Al morafa'at Alshar'iyah* (1st edn., Altawbah Publications, 1993), p. 67.

82 Ibid.

83 Article 61 of the Law of Procedure before Shari'a Courts, Royal Decree No. M/21 dated 20/05/1421 H. (2000). *Umm Alqura Gazette*, issue No. 3811 dated 17/06/1421 H. (2000).

84 See article 21 of the Implementing Rules.

and answers orally or in writing to an appropriate extent on the date of the hearing.[85] As a general rule, the tribunal is not allowed to decide the dispute without hearing all the parties and giving them an equal chance to represent all their evidence.[86] Moreover, giving a judgment on the basis of the arbitrator's personal knowledge is prohibited, because it might create the suspicion of bias and constitute grounds for challenging the award. Even if the arbitrator feels certain of his own knowledge of the facts, he is not allowed to rely on it in rendering the award without clear evidence.[87] The article adds that the defendant shall be the final speaker, which is the normal end of any typical dispute before a Shari'a court.

The typical procedure before any Shari'a court consists of three stages. First, the plaintiff raises the claim, which should be precise in all its details. The claim can be in writing or verbal at the time of the trial. Second, the judge invites the defendant to answer the plaintiff's claim. At this stage, the defendant will either admit the claim (*iqrar*) or deny it (*nokoul*). If the defendant denies the claim, the judge will ask the plaintiff to adduce evidence (*baiyenah*), which can be anything like documents or oral testimony of witnesses. The final stage starts if the plaintiff fails to provide the court with sufficient testimonial evidence; he may then administer the oath (*yameen* or *qasam*). If the defendant swears that the claim is groundless, the claim will be dismissed; however, if the defendant refuses to take the oath, the case will be decided in favour of the plaintiff.[88]

Article 23 specifies some of the chairman's responsibilities toward managing proceedings. The responsibilities stated in this article are similar to those of a court judge; however, the chairman has no right to imprison anyone for any misbehaviour before the tribunal. In the case of such misbehaviour, the chairman can only expel the person from the place of the hearing and report him to the competent authority. Each arbitrator has the right to direct questions and interrogate parties or witnesses through the chairman of the tribunal.[89] The responsibilities of court judges toward managing proceedings are stated in articles 69 and 70 of the Law of Procedure before Shari'a Courts. The only difference is that the judge can imprison anyone disturbing order for up to 24 hours.[90] In accordance with the Law of Procedure before Shari'a Courts, the expelled persons might be referred to the authority after the 24-hour sentence in case of committing an offence against the judge or anyone at the trial; however, such misbehaviour cannot be decided by the same judge because he would be himself a party to the case.[91]

85 Article 22 of the Implementing Rules.

86 Supra n. 5, Ibn Qodamah, Vol. 14, p. 96.

87 Ibid.

88 See, in general, B. Ibn Farhoun, *Tabsirat Alhokkam Fe Usul Alaqdiyah Wa Manahej Alahkam*, ed. Taha Abdulraouf Sa'ad (1st edn., Maktabat Alkolliyat Alazhariyah, 1986).

89 Article 23 of the Implementing Rules.

90 See articles 69 and 70 of the Law of Procedure before Shari'a Courts.

91 This information was given by an official in the Ministry of Justice who preferred his name to be confidential.

Article 24 provides for what the tribunal might do in case parties reach an extrajudicial settlement. The parties can request the tribunal at any stage of the case to record their agreement as to an admission, settlement and waiver or otherwise in the record of the hearing and the tribunal shall make an award based on the parties' agreement.[92] Article 67 of the Law of Procedure before Shari'a Courts supports this article and provides for the same steps to be taken by the court in the case of reaching a settlement for the dispute outside court to give it a binding nature, instead of being a mere statement from the parties without enforceability.[93]

Article 25 provides for the official language for arbitration proceedings. Arabic is the official language before the arbitral tribunal, whether in oral discussions or in writing. The tribunal, the parties and other persons should, exclusively, speak Arabic. A foreigner who does not speak Arabic should be accompanied by an accredited translator who should sign with him the record of the hearing as to the oral statement he translated.

Arabic language is the official language in Saudi Arabia; therefore all communications and contracts before any governmental entity must be in Arabic. Contracts with the Saudi Government can be signed in an additional language but in the case of a dispute relating to the execution of such a contract the disputants should refer to the Arabic version of the contract.[94] This principle was established by article 1 of the Basic Law.[95] It is also supported by article 1 of the Law of Procedure before Shari'a Courts, which states that Arabic is the official language for all hearings and communications, and that if circumstances require the use of another language the documents or statements must be translated into Arabic.[96] In Hanbali law, if one of the parties to a dispute does not speak Arabic and the arbitrator does not know the party's language, an accredited translator must attend the hearing to translate between him and the arbitrator and between him and the other parties to the dispute. The translators should possess the characters of adalah, or full legal capacity.[97]

Article 26 gives the arbitral tribunal discretionary power to postpone the hearing of a case if the parties request it in order to represent their documents, papers or comments material.[98] Article 27 provides for the writing of the facts and proceedings of the hearing in a record prepared by the secretary of the tribunal

92 Article 24 of the Implementing Rules.

93 See article 67 of the Law of Procedure before Shari'a Courts.

94 See, for example, articles 9–31 of the gas concession agreement between Saudi Arabia and Lukoil Overseas. *Umm Alqura Gazette*, issue No. 3990 dated 15/03/1425 H. 4/05/2004.

95 The Basic Law of Saudi Arabia. Alnezam Alasasi Lelhokm. Royal Decree No. (90/A) dated 28/06/1412 H. (1992).

96 See article 1 of the Law of Procedure before Shari'a Courts.

97 Supra n. 5, Ibn Qodamah, Vol. 14, p. 84.

98 Article 26 of the Implementing Rules. See also article 65 of the Law of Procedure before Shari'a Courts.

under its supervision.[99] The principle of the writing of contracts and other similar documents related to arbitration agreements and clauses was established by the Quran in the following verse: 'When you deal with each other, in transactions involving future obligations in a fixed period of time reduce them to writing. Let a scribe write down faithfully as between the parties.'[100] The Sunna also supports the writing of commercial agreements, as do Islamic teachings, current laws and practices.[101]

Article 28 sets the conditions in which the arbitral tribunal can ask one of the parties to present any document material to the case.[102] *The Diwan* allows the use of foreign arbitral awards as precedent provided that it does not violate Shari'a rules or public policy in Saudi Arabia. Any foreign arbitral award as precedent should be used only to support a party's argument and not to claim enforcement of the foreign award, because enforcement is not under the competence of the arbitration tribunal.[103]

Article 29 deals with the conditions in which the arbitral tribunal can order the establishment of investigation measures having a material effect on the case if the facts sought to be established are relevant, admissible and material to the dispute. Article 30 deals with departing from the evidentiary procedure provided that the tribunal states the reasons for the departure in the record of the hearing and in the final award.[104] The issue of investigations and evidence has been dealt with in greater detail in other regulations, especially in the Law of Procedure before Shari'a Courts of 2000.[105]

Article 31 states certain rules for the oral statements of witnesses, which should be proved in writing or orally at the hearing and should accompany the witnesses. The hearing of such statements of witnesses should be in accordance with Shari'a principles. In addition, the article gives the other party the right to disprove the facts in a similar manner.[106] The article sets that the statements of witnesses should be in accordance with Shari'a rules, which require certain qualities to be possessed by persons giving statements. As a general rule, a witness should be a Muslim who has reached the age of puberty and who is not subject to any incapacity; he should also be a trustworthy person. The witness of non-Muslims is accepted in all subjects except hodoud. Shari'a requires a thorough investigation of witness trustworthiness because if there is any doubt about a witness he will not be heard. The oral testimony is to be made at the request of one of the parties.

---

99 Article 27 of the Implementing Rules.
100 The Quran 1: 282.
101 See article 69 of the Law of Procedure before Shari'a Courts.
102 See article 28 of the Implementing Rules.
103 *Diwan Almazalim* decision No. 29/T/4 of 1413 H. (1993).
104 See articles 29 and 30 of the Implementing Rules.
105 See articles 154, 155, 211 and 261 of the Law of Procedure before Shari'a Courts.
106 See article 31 of the Implementing Rules.

Some witnesses can be disqualified – such people are not allowed to participate as arbitrators in a dispute.[107]

Article 32 set the rules of interrogation at hearings; and article 33 deals with the rules of expert assistance. Experts are considered witnesses under this article – they can be challenged on the same grounds as witnesses and arbitrators.[108]

Article 34 regulates some related aspects to the expert witness such as requiring a supplementary report; however, the tribunal is not bound to take it into consideration when rendering the arbitral award.[109] Under the Hanbali teachings, such a report cannot be classified as evidence.[110]

Article 35 gives the arbitral tribunal the option to relocate the seat of the hearing. The arbitral tribunal may relocate in order to inspect disputed facts or any matter affecting the case. The tribunal should also prepare a record of the inspection procedure that complies with article 112 of the Law of Procedure before Shari'a Courts of 2000.[111]

The Implementing Rules provide that the arbitral tribunal should comply with the litigation principles of Shari'a.[112] The Implementing Rules were issued in 1985 prior to the enactment of the Law of Procedure before Shari'a Courts. Prior to the enactment of the Law, arbitrators used to rely on Shari'a principles in order to find governing rules for arbitral proceedings but after the enactment of the Law in 2000, it become applicable to all litigations and arbitration proceedings within the kingdom.[113]

One of the main differences between arbitration and litigation is that the arbitrators do not have the judicial and enforcement power of the court judge. Therefore, if the arbitral tribunal faces an issue that is not under its competence, such as forgery or other criminal offences, the issue should be referred to the competent authority having jurisdiction over the dispute. The tribunal should wait until the case has been investigated and should suspend issuing the award until a final judgment is rendered by the competent authority.[114]

Making, Challenging and Enforcing Arbitral Awards

When a case is ready for decision, the arbitral tribunal should declare the proceedings closed, fix a date for making the award and bring the case under

107 Supra n. 5, Ibn Qodamah, Vol. 14, p. 262.
108 See article 33 of the Implementing Rules.
109 See article 34 of the Implementing Rules.
110 Supra n. 5, Ibn Qodamah, Vol. 14, p. 262.
111 See article 35 of the Implementing Rules and article 112 of the Law of Procedure before Shari'a Courts of 2000.
112 See article 36 of the Implementing Rules.
113 See, in general, the Law of Procedure before Shari'a Courts.
114 See article 37 of the Implementing Rules.

review and discussion. Such a review should be held in private, with attendance restricted to the members of the arbitral tribunal only. When the arbitral tribunal fixes the date for making the award it should take into consideration the relevant provisions of the Arbitration Act and other relevant laws – in other words the Law of Procedure before Shari'a Courts of 2000.[115] With regard to the Arbitration Act the relevant articles are:

- article 9, which provides for an extension in the time before the issuance of the arbitral award subject to the mutual agreement of the parties or under the discretion of the arbitral tribunal;
- article 13, which states that in case of the death of one of the arbitrators the time for the award shall be extended by 30 days unless the other arbitrators decide on a longer period;
- article 14, which states that where an arbitrator is appointed in place of a dismissed or withdrawing arbitrator the date fixed for the award shall be extended by 30 days; and
- article 15, which gives the arbitral tribunal a discretionary power to extend the deadline of rendering the award.[116]

Article 39 exempts arbitrators from being bound by regulatory procedures except as provided in the Arbitration Act and the Implementing Rules. The article also adds that the award should be made in accordance with Shari'a principles and regulations in effect.[117] Prior to the issuance of the Law of Procedure before Shari'a Courts, arbitrators relied on Shari'a principles to govern arbitral procedure. This depends to a great degree on the arbitrator's individual understanding of Shari'a texts, which resulted in variations in practice from one arbitrator to another. The Law of Procedure before Shari'a Courts of 2000 codifies Shari'a principles in the light of common practice; it provides a set of rules to be followed by arbitral tribunal in case of the silence of arbitration regulations. As a general principle, when 'man-made' law says nothing, the tribunal should go back to Shari'a principles, because they serve as a safety measure for ensuring compliance with Islamic law in all cases.

Article 40 regulates some aspects of equality between parties to the arbitration and the procedure of reopening arbitral proceedings. The arbitral tribunal may not, during the review of the case and deliberation, hear explanations of one of the parties without the presence of the other party; nor may it receive documents unless the other party examines the same. However, if the arbitral tribunal considers such explanations and/or documents to be material it may extend the date for pronouncing the award and reopen the proceedings, taking care to record

115 See article 38 of the Implementing Rules; see also article 162 of the Law of Procedure before Shari'a Courts.

116 See articles 9, 13, 14 and 15 of the Arbitration Act of 1983.

117 See article 39 of the Implementing Rules.

the reasons and justifications and to notify the parties of the new date fixed for hearing the case.[118] The same content is provided by articles 66, 159 and 160 of the Law of Procedure before Shari'a Courts.[119]

The arbitral award should be made by majority except in the case of a sole arbitrator, and it should contain all the information relevant to the parties, the dispute and the arbitral tribunal.[120] Under classical Shari'a literature, the award should comply with the opinion of the majority of the arbitrators. There are four methods for issuing an arbitral award if unanimity cannot be reached: First, when forming the arbitration agreement the number of arbitrators should be odd. Second, arbitrators can seek the assistance of an external arbitrator and decide the case according to his opinion. The external arbitrator is not allowed to come up with a new judgement; his job is to choose one of the available decisions only.[121] Third, if the arbitrators fail to issue the award the dispute can be decided by another tribunal or by a sole arbitrator.[122] However, this option may lengthen the dispute, which contradicts the objective of arbitration as a swift dispute settlement mechanism. Fourth, if unanimity still cannot be reached and the parties to the dispute have exhausted the above-mentioned methods, they can refer to litigation as a last resort.[123] In practice, if the arbitral tribunal fails to issue its decision within 90 days of the supervisory authority approving the arbitration agreement the whole case is referred to the *Diwan*, which will perform the role of external arbitrator and choose one of the available opinions, decide the case anew or give the arbitral tribunal a time extension.[124]

When making the award, the arbitral tribunal should not exceed its terms of reference and look at issues that are not included in the arbitration agreement. In decision number 33/T/4 of 1414 H. (1994) the arbitration agreement had given the arbitration tribunal jurisdiction to decide the amount of damages for late performance of the contract. The tribunal decided in the same award on the claim for the initial cost of the contract, which was rejected by the *Diwan* for unconformity with the arbitration agreement.[125]

The arbitral tribunal is responsible for correcting technical, typographic and mathematical errors.[126] It is also in charge of issuing a supplementary award to explain ambiguity and uncertainty in the text of the arbitral award, which should be issued at the request of the parties to the arbitration.[127]

118 See article 40 of the Implementing Rules.
119 See articles 66, 159 and 160 of the Law of Procedure before Shari'a Courts.
120 See article 41 of the Implementing Rules.
121 Supra n. 31, Al Kenain, p. 124.
122 Supra n. 5, Ibn Qodamah, Vol. 10, p. 546.
123 Ibid.
124 *Diwan Almazalim* decision No. 35/T/4 of 1418 H. (1998).
125 *Diwan Almazalim* decision No. 33/T/4 of 1414 H. (1994).
126 See article 42 of the Implementing Rules.
127 See article 43 of the Implementing Rules.

If parties to the arbitration do not prevail in some claims, a judgment may be made apportioning the fee between them, according to the determination of the supervisory authority, or allocating the whole fee to one of the parties.[128] Any party may object to an order assessing arbitrator fees to the authority; however, the authority's decision on the objection is final.[129]

The arbitral award shall become an enforceable instrument upon the issuance of the enforcement order, which is the responsibility of the supervisory authority.[130] The supervisory authority should deliver to the prevailing party the enforcement copy of the arbitral award. This sets forth the enforcement order, ending with the following statement: 'All government departments and agencies concerned are hereby requested to execute this judgment by all available legal means even if it may require the use of coercive force by the police.'[131] The supervisory authority cannot issue the enforcement order unless requested to do so by the winning party or by third parties with interest in the enforcement of the arbitral award. Requests for the enforcement of arbitral awards should be accepted from third parties provided that they have interest in the enforcement of the award, such as guarantors and creditors, and that the argument of their not being party to the arbitration agreement has been rejected by the *Diwan*.[132] In addition, the competent authority should ensure that the party requesting enforcement has interest in the enforcement of the award. It should also review the award and ensure that it does not violate the public policies of the kingdom.[133]

Enforcement and Recognition of Foreign Arbitral Awards in Saudi Arabia

Recognition and enforcement are the most important steps after the issuance of the final award. Although Saudi Arabia only started to cooperate with the international legal community at a late stage, it has been in cooperation with its neighbouring countries since the 1950s. Saudi law does not have a clear answer for the conflict that arises when there is more than one application for the enforcement of different arbitral awards issued against the same person on the same specific issue. Some judges give priority to the application that is submitted first, whereas other judges give priority to the award that is issued first. Another opinion prefers that judges should look at the conflict of laws rules to decide which jurisdiction has the most connections with the arbitration and which law is more competent to govern the

128 See article 45 of the Implementing Rules.

129 See article 46 of the Implementing Rules.

130 See article 44 of the Implementing Rules.

131 Ibid., article 44 and see also article 196 of the Law of Procedure before Shari'a Courts.

132 *Diwan Almazalim* decision No. 136/T/4 of 1409 H. (1989).

133 Supra n. 6, Albejad, p. 240.

arbitration.[134] There are two important multilateral conventions of which Saudi Arabia is a member. These are the Riyadh Convention for Judicial Cooperation of 1983 (Riyadh Convention) and the New York Convention for the Enforcement and Recognition of Foreign Arbitral Awards of 1958 (New York Convention).

Riyadh Convention for Judicial Cooperation of 1983

The Riyadh Convention came into effect in order to replace the old Arab League Convention of 1952 in a way that mixed the spirit of the New York Convention of 1958 with Shari'a principles. In its preamble the Convention states that reaching a degree of legal harmony between the parties to the Convention is the main objective of the Convention, for the reason that these countries share many legal principles and fundamentals.[135] The Convention borrowed certain basic rules from the New York Convention and from Western bilateral agreements. Of the principles borrowed from Western conventions the one of most benefit is the rule restricting the courts in the place of enforcement from re-examining the merits of the dispute.[136] This principle was demonstrated in article 37 of the Riyadh Convention, which prohibited the judicial authority in the place of enforcement from looking again at the merits of the dispute. However, it seems that the judicial bodies in Saudi Arabia do not comply with this article of the agreement; they claim that the interpretation of the principle of public policy in Saudi Arabia differs even from most of the neighbouring countries. Actually, this claim is partly true, especially in cases involving prohibited or disputed issues under Shari'a such as banking interest and the sale of musical instruments and tobacco products. The same article provides that an arbitral award issued and recognized in one of the member states of the Convention cannot be set aside except in the following circumstances:

- if the dispute at issue is not arbitrable under the law of the place of arbitration;
- if the party against whom the award is invoked was not given proper notice of the appointment of the arbitrator or of the arbitration proceedings;
- if the award deals with a dispute not contemplated by or not falling within the terms of the submission to arbitration, or it contains decisions on matters beyond the scope of the submission to arbitration; or
- if the recognition of the award would be contrary to the principles of Islamic Shari'a, relevant laws and regulations or public order.

---

134 This piece of information was provided by one of the judges of the Shari'a Supreme Court of Jeddah who preferred his name to remain confidential.

135 The member states of the Conventions are: Jordan, the UAE, Bahrain, Tunisia, Algeria, Djibouti, Saudi Arabia, Sudan, Somalia, Iraq, Oman, Palestine, Qatar, Kuwait, Lebanon, Libya, Morocco, Mauritania and Yemen.

136 Supra n. 3, Saleh, p. 151.

When reading article 37 in conjunction with article 30 of the same agreement, a foreign arbitral award cannot be recognized or enforced if the award is issued *in absentia* unless:

- the losing party was duly informed of the arbitration;
- the dispute was referred to litigation in the place of the issuance of the award;
- one of the parties lacks the legal capacity under the law of the place of the issuance of the award; or
- the law of the place where the enforcement is sought has no connection with the dispute at issue.

According to the Convention, a party seeking the enforcement of an arbitral award in a place other than the place of the issuance of the award should provide, with the arbitration agreement, a certificate from the court of the place of the issuance of the award stating that the award is enforceable. In contrast with the New York Convention of 1958, which requires the arbitral award to be binding on the parties, the Riyadh Convention called back the condition of double exequatur, which requires the award to be final and operative in the place of the issuance.[137] It can be said that for the load of official procedure required by the Riyadh Convention, the Convention seems to be ineffective – enforcing a foreign arbitral award under the New York Convention might be more practical for the party seeking the enforcement of the award.

New York Convention for the Enforcement and Recognition of Foreign Arbitral Awards of 1958

The Convention on the Recognition and Enforcement of Foreign Arbitral Awards, hereinafter New York Convention, came into effect to overcome some of the impracticalities of the Geneva Convention of 1927 and to make the enforcement and recognition of foreign arbitral awards easier. It set arbitration as an effective dispute settlement mechanism. According to the first article of the Convention, the scope of the application of the Convention should include:

> the recognition and enforcement of arbitral awards made in the territory of a State other than the State where the recognition and enforcement of such awards are sought, and arising out of differences between persons, whether physical or legal. It shall also apply to arbitral awards not considered as domestic awards in the State where their recognition and enforcement are sought.[138]

137 See article 4.1 of the Convention on the Execution of Foreign Arbitral Awards (Geneva Convention) (26 September 1927) and article 5.1.e of the New York Convention of 1958.

138 Article 1 of the New York Convention of 1958.

In relation to Saudi Arabia, an arbitral award issued in a territory other than Saudi Arabia relating to a non-domestic dispute will be considered foreign. Moreover, if the arbitral award relating to a domestic dispute is issued outside Saudi Arabia it will also be considered foreign, meaning that the provisions of the New York Convention will apply. Parties seeking enforcement should apply to *Diwan Almazalim*, which will consider the enforcement after reviewing the award.

The New York Convention provides general guidance on the procedure of enforcing foreign arbitral awards and sets the documents that are required from the place of the enforcement of the award. The parties seeking the enforcement of an arbitral award should accompany their application with the following documents: the duly authenticated original award or a duly certified copy; and the original arbitration agreement or arbitration clause or a duly certified copy. The same article of the agreement adds that in cases where the award is made in a language other than the official language of the place where the parties are seeking the enforcement, the documents should be translated into the official language of the place of enforcement. The translation should be certified by an official or sworn translator or by a diplomatic or consular agent.[139] Furthermore, parties seeking the enforcement should be bound by the internal procedure of the place of enforcement of the award. Most of the jurisdictions in the world make their rules of procedure clear to everyone seeking the enforcement of an award, whereas in Saudi Arabia the rules of procedure rely heavily on royal decrees and ministerial circulars. However, this is not the problem. The problem arises when such royal decrees, ministerial circulars and internal regulations contradict each other and one has to search through hundreds of royal decrees, orders and circulars issued over a period of 40 years and mostly unavailable to the public. Royal Decree No. 51/M dated 17/02/1402 H. (1981) held *Diwan Almazalim* responsible for the recognition and enforcement of foreign arbitral awards in Saudi Arabia as well as judgments issued in the courts of the Arab League countries. The new law of *Diwan Almazalim* upholds the latter decree and provides that the administrative department of *Diwan Almazalim* is the competent authority for the enforcement and recognition of foreign arbitral awards in the kingdom.[140]

Diwan Almazalim's Circular No. 7 dated 15/05/1405 H. (1985) determines the procedure for filing an application for the enforcement of a foreign arbitral award in Saudi Arabia. According to the Circular, the party seeking the enforcement of a foreign arbitral award in Saudi Arabia should submit a request for the enforcement of the arbitral award in the same way as bringing a new claim before the *Diwan*. In order to commence the procedure, the party seeking the enforcement should submit certified copies of the relevant documents; however, in cases where the party does not have certified copies the *Diwan* may arrange for submission of the original documents. After receiving the request for enforcement, the *Diwan* will notify all the parties to the arbitration award. The person against whom the award has been

139 Article 4 of the New York Convention of 1958.

140 See article 13 of the law of *Diwan Almazalim*.

made has the right to see the application submitted against him and is allowed to defend himself before the *Diwan*.[141] This Circular is one of the main elements determining the credibility of arbitration as an alternative for litigation. The main problem here is that the *Diwan* re-examines all arbitration awards brought before it. Such practice is simply a waste of time, effort and resources; at the same time it indicates that arbitration is not a reliable dispute settlement mechanism.

Saudi law provides many remedies for cases in which the award is challenged before the *Diwan* and the *Diwan* accepts the challenge; however, foreign arbitral awards do not enjoy such treatment. The law is silent with regard to this issue; nonetheless, it can be understood that foreign arbitral awards are of no avail unless approved by the *Diwan*. It is unclear whether foreign arbitral awards or judgments can be used to establish facts before Saudi courts, as many judges have not yet reached the necessary level of understanding as to how legal systems really work. In addition, Saudi courts might enforce foreign arbitral awards or judgments on the basis of reciprocity; however, the application of this concept is still a matter of theoretical argument and no one knows how the *Diwan* applies it. The concept of reciprocity does not have a fundamental impact on the enforcement of foreign arbitral awards in Saudi Arabia nowadays as most of the country members of the United Nations have adopted the New York Conventions. For the countries that have not become members of the Conventions, Saudi Arabia has other instruments of enforcement of arbitral awards.[142]

Public Policy in Saudi Arabia

Public policy is of great importance to arbitration, especially when it comes to the enforcement of an arbitral award, irrespective of whether it is domestic or foreign. As a general rule, an arbitral award is unenforceable if it violates the public policy of the country in which the enforcement is sought.[143] This is also true in Saudi Arabia and is applicable to both foreign and domestic arbitral awards, despite the fact that the latter proceedings would have, by the time of the enforcement, already been very closely monitored by the supervisory authority. As a result, refusals to enforce are more common when setting aside foreign arbitral awards because public policy in Saudi Arabia covers a vast area of practice that might be unknown to foreign arbitrators sitting abroad and applying non-Saudi *lex arbitri*. The following section aims to provide an overview of Saudi public policy, its sources and how it is applied in practice.

141 *Diwan Almazalim*'s Circular No. 7 dated 15/05/1405 H. (1985).

142 There are five countries who are members of the Riyadh Convention but not yet of the New York Convention, which are: Iraq, Yemen, Somalia, Libya and Sudan.

143 See article 5 of the 1958 New York Convention on the Recognition and Enforcement of Foreign Arbitral Awards, 330 UNTS 538.

Public policy in the Saudi kingdom is derived from three principal sources: Shari'a; royal power, which is itself drawn from Shari'a with an emphasis on public customs and public interest within the framework of Shari'a's prescriptions; and public morals. At the outset, it should be noted that, historically, Muslim scholars have distinguished between Shari'a and Islamic jurisprudence, or fiqh. The concept of Islamic law was not in use at the time of the Muslim classical scholars – it began to develop as a reaction to Western influence. The concept of Shari'a is broader than jurisprudence – jurisprudence comes within, as along with other concepts of Islam such as Islamic creed and Quranic sciences, the umbrella of Shari'a. Shari'a, or Ash-Shari'a, literally means 'the pathway' or a way to be followed, the way that a Muslim has to walk in life. In its original usage, the term Shari'a meant the road to the watering place or the path leading to the water, i.e., the way to the source of life.[144] Arab lexicographers developed this to mean 'the law of water' and in time it has extended to cover all aspects of Muslim life, both spiritual and those pertaining to the exigencies of everyday life.[145] Shari'a is best translated as the 'way of life' and Ash-Shari'a as the 'way of the Muslim life' which is wider than the mere formal rites and legal provisions. Islamic law may be defined as the entire system of law and jurisprudence associated with the religion of Islam.

The primary sources of Shari'a are the Quran and the Sunna and there exist a number of other secondary sources or methods for adducing appropriate normative behaviour in response to new incidents and unregulated circumstances. These secondary sources are ijma', ijtihad, qiyas and urf (public interest and custom). The methods of ijma', ijtihad and qiyas are employed in the light of current circumstances in order to shed light on and analyse the Quran and the Sunna. The sustained use of these secondary sources led to the creation of a body of law known as fiqh. Western scholars tend to use 'fiqh' to describe Shari'a and Islamic jurisprudence interchangeably. The aforementioned distinction between the two should become clear and receive scholarly attention, given that Shari'a is the foundation of all doctrines formulated and developed under fiqh, whereas fiqh represents a human understanding and analysis of Shari'a sources. The term 'Saudi law' is more comprehensive than Shari'a and encompasses Islamic law and the codes and regulations adapted from other laws within the general framework of Shari'a principles. There are a few exceptions to this rule, particularly as regards Saudi legislation that is unrelated to Islamic teachings and principles. One example is the Banking Control Law, because it regulates some activities that are clearly prohibited under Islamic Law.

In Saudi Arabia, the primary sources of Shari'a – the Quran and the Sunna – have supremacy over all laws and man-made regulations or normative instruments. In the 1920s, King Abdul-Aziz attempted to codify the teachings of the four Islamic

144 Ibid.

145 See, generally, the Quran 45: 18 and 5: 48. See also C. Mallat, 'From Islamic to Middle Eastern Law: A Restatement of the Field (Part 1)', *American Journal of Comparative Law*, 51 (2003), pp. 699–719.

schools in a manner similar to that by which the Majalla codified Hanafi fiqh. Despite his best efforts, this project was vociferously opposed by certain radical scholars and did not materialize. In combination with his codification project, the King ordered Shari'a judges not to be bound by the rules of one school of fiqh, with the aim that the prevalence of one school should not have the result of abrogating another.[146] At the same time, however, some Ulama had their own agendas; they not only opposed the King's reform plans, but also sought to exert pressure on judges in all Saudi courts with a view to applying exclusively Hanbali fiqh under the teachings of the late scholar Ibn Taymiyyah. The main reason for their opposition rested in their fear that the expansion of civil codes could eventually culminate at the expense of Shari'a and ultimately lead to the promulgation of secular laws with little or no connection to Shari'a. In practice, although the Saudi legal system is premised on Shari'a on the basis of Hanbali teachings, judges have the freedom to apply any of the four schools of fiqh. This judicial latitude granted to Saudi judges is the direct result of the aforementioned order of King Abdul-Aziz to Shari'a judges.[147] Saudi judges currently rely on a number of legal commentaries – authored by recognized Islamic legal scholars – in the delivery of their judgments, but it should be noted that a codification of these dispersed commentaries is expected in the foreseeable future. Apart from Ibn Qodamah, the majority of scholars who authored these commentaries follow the teachings of the Hanbali scholar Ibn Taymiyyah.[148]

According to article 7 of the Saudi Basic Law, the ruling regime derives its power from the Holy Quran and the Prophet's Sunna, which have supremacy over all state laws.[149] Accordingly, the imposition of public policy restrictions within the kingdom cannot be relied upon to violate Shari'a principles under any circumstances. The Basic Law even emphasizes that even a temporary state of emergency during turmoil cannot violate article 7, which renders Shari'a the only source of regulation in the kingdom.[150]

Just like Saudi law, the kingdom itself as a political entity is inseparable from religion.[151] Regardless of his considerable regulatory authority, the King lacks the power to legislate in the very extensive field that has already been regulated by Shari'a, in respect of which he is bound by the same duty of obedience as are all

---

146 G. Sfeir, 'The Saudi Approach to Law Reform', *American Journal of Comparative Law*, 36 (1988), pp. 729–44.

147 Ibid., p. 732.

148 These books are: *Almoghni* by Ibn Qodamah; *Asharh Alkabeer* by Ibn Qodamah; *Sharh Zad Almustaqna'* by Albahouti and Alhajjawi; *Sharh Montaha Al Eradat* by Alfoutohi and Albahouti and; *Manar Assabeel* by Meri'e Alhabnali and Ibn Douawan.

149 See article 7 of the Saudi Basic Law, Royal Decree No. (90/A) dated 28/06/1412 H. (1992).

150 Ibid., articles 1 and 7.

151 D. Karl, 'Islamic Law in Saudi Arabia: What Foreign Attorneys Should Know', *Geo Wash J Intl Law & Economics*, 25 (1991), p. 131.

of his subjects.[152] Consequently, it can be said that the separation of law from religion is impossible in most aspects affecting public life in Saudi Arabia. Given the kingdom's political structure as an absolute monarchy, the King is endowed with authority to promulgate regulations by issuing such royal decrees that supplement existing Shari'a rules with a view to adapting to new circumstances, especially in relation to trade and commerce. 'In doing so, the Government tries to balance traditional prospects against modern needs.'[153] Royal decrees can also be considered a codification of some aspects of Shari'a law. This codification is achieved with the assistance of foreign laws and international practices that do not necessarily violate Shari'a principles. The decisions of judicial bodies have little impact on public policy because in Islamic legal practice they merely offer an interpretation of Shari'a and relevant royal decrees and are, moreover, subordinate to these.

What exactly constitutes public morals, interests and customs is not clearly delineated in Saudi law. What is abundantly precise, however, is that anything that is deemed as violating Shari'a would certainly fall outside acceptable public policy constraints. When discussing Saudi society in search of public morals and interests, it should be noted that the terms '*deen*', which means religion, and '*adat*', meaning custom, have been used interchangeably. The reason for this lies in the fact that some customs and traditions have been either derived from religion or upheld by it. This observation, however, may produce the result of restricting the enforcement of foreign arbitral awards in cases where the outcome of an arbitral award is contrary to Saudi public customs. The determination of the concept of public interest under Shari'a is derived through the use of the method of istihsan. The term '*istihsan*' may be translated as 'juristic preference'.[154] Another scholar preferred to translate it as 'public interest'. Conceptually, istihsan may be defined as the process of selecting one acceptable alternative over another, on the grounds that the first appears more suitable for the situation at hand, even though the selected solution may be technically weaker than the rejected one. Equally, istihsan has been viewed as a process for selecting the best solution for the general public interest as a form of ijtihad.[155] Istihsan allows judges and scholars some flexibility when interpreting the law to allow for the infusion of elements deemed useful. In other words, istihsan constitutes a permit for the spirit of the law to prevail over its letter.[156] Slight divergences exist between the various schools. Hanbali scholars call it '*istislah*', which may be translated as 'equity' or 'public

---

152 J. Schacht, 'Problems of Modern Islamic Legislation', *Studia Islamica*, 12 (1960), p. 133–36.

153 Supra n. 150, Karl, p. 142.

154 H. Fadel, 'The Islamic Viewpoint on New Assisted Reproductive Technology', *Fordham Urban Law Journal*, 30 (2002), pp. 148–50.

155 J. Makdisi, 'Legal Logic and Equity in Islamic Law', *American Journal of Comparative Law*, 33 (1985), pp. 63–66.

156 Supra n. 153, Fadel, p. 150.

interest', whereas Maliki scholars refer to it as 'almasaleh almursalah', which denotes a departure from strict textual adherence in favour of public welfare.[157] The principal precondition for the validity of istihsan is its compliance with the principles of Shari'a. Nonetheless, there are situations where the non-application of a Shari'a rule is more beneficial for public interest than strict textual application. For instance, in the field of finance and commerce the application of Shari'a may obfuscate socio-economic development, as is the case with the so-called '*istisna'*' contracts.[158] As a general rule, the object of the contract must exist at the time when the contract becomes binding upon the parties. The requirement of the existence of the object at the moment of the conclusion of the contract was made to protect the parties from assuming any risk through a hazard or uncertainty likely to harm party interests.[159] Public interest, therefore, required a relaxation of strict contract rules. This was done by Prophet Muhammad himself when he allowed Muslims to conclude contracts with future objectives under certain circumstances, even though the general rule required otherwise. At present, public interest is determined by reference to specific suitable options within the framework of the main principles of Shari'a.

The kingdom maintains a negative list of activities excluded from foreign investment. This is a fine example of activities prohibited for the benefit of public interest.[160] When it comes to the protection of public interest, Saudi authorities consider Shari'a at first instance, as well as the will of its population. King Abdullah ben Abdul-Aziz, in one of his speeches to the Shura Council, underlined the fundamental tenets of Saudi policy, stating that 'we will work in the interest of the religion, homeland, our citizens and our traditions'.[161]

In assessing a legal system that is fundamentally different to the types of legal system Western lawyers are used to, one must necessarily examine the underlying

157 Supra n. 154, Makdisi, p. 73.

158 Istisna' contracts are derived originally from slam contracts, wherein one party paid a year in advance for crops of a particular weight at the time of harvest. Istisna', or sale by manufacture, is a contract to manufacture a particular good not yet in existence, for an agreed price. The buyer need not pay for the goods until its acceptance and both parties may revoke their agreement at any time before delivery. Some scholars distinguish between the slam and istisna' contracts, but both seem to be based on the same theory; however, the slam is used mainly in respect of crops and carries a greater risk of a future discounted price. Istisna' contracts, on the other hand, are more common in construction and manufacturing and are more flexible in that they serve as financing and hedging tools.

159 N. Comair-Obeid, 'Particularity of the Contract's Subject-Matter in the Laws of the Arab Middle East', *Arab Law Quarterly*, 11 (1996), pp. 331–36.

160 The Saudi Arabia General Investment Agency (SAGIA), 'Negative List: Activities Excluded from Foreign Investment'. Available online at <http://www.sagia.gov.sa/en/business-environment/investment-laws/negative-list.html> [accessed 14 November 2008].

161 King Abdullah ben Abdul-Aziz, speech to the Shura Council in Riyadh, 14 April 2007.

reasons for such diversity. In the case of Saudi arbitration law, it is evident that two reasons are particularly prevalent. The first concerns the kingdom's troubled past, during which some of the arbitral tribunals that determined cases to which it was party rejected Islamic law as the law governing its contractual relations with third parties, even though this law was clearly stipulated in the relevant contracts. The frustration and embarrassment caused as a result had an impact far greater than merely downgrading the law of a particular country under the pretext that it was undeveloped and backward. Given that Islamic law pervades not only all aspects of normative conduct, but also all other social and public conduct within Muslim societies, those arbitral awards were perceived as having broader implications about Islam and Muslim states. Moreover, Saudi Arabia is a very conservative country in every respect, whose official policy strives to strike a balance between tradition and modernization.[162]

The result in the kingdom's contemporary arbitral law and judicial practice is hardly surprising. Disputes conducted in Saudi Arabia, or containing Saudi elements, are governed by the kingdom's *lex arbitri*, which requires not only that the arbitration clause and *compromis* be submitted to a designated competent authority for approval, but also that the proceedings be supervised by the said competent authority throughout their duration, save where conflict of laws rules permit the parties to refer to a foreign jurisdiction. Western lawyers may at first glance find these restrictions unduly compromising in terms of the benefits of arbitration, but closer examination reveals that equivalent procedures exist in developed arbitral fora. For one thing, both in Europe and in North America the arbitration clause may be subject to scrutiny, either by the tribunal itself or by reference to the courts of the *lex arbitri*. Equally, the parties are not generally free to turn to the civil courts during the course of the arbitral proceedings; institutional arbitration is to some degree monitored by relevant institutions, and, where significant improprieties occur, whether in terms of corruption or other, the parties may approach the courts of the *lex arbitri*. Finally, some Western arbitral legislation provides that the award requires ratification by the courts before enforcement proceedings can be undertaken.[163] As with Western public policy dictated by reference to local laws and perhaps social customs, so it is with Saudi Arabia that Shari'a is the benchmark in respect of public policy. In light of this, Saudi arbitration law does not seem to differ much from that of its Western contemporaries. Why, then, is it deemed problematic? The primary reason is obvious; where a Saudi element is involved, the parties cannot escape being subject to Saudi *lex arbitri*. They can,

162 'Some countries have sacrificed the soul of their culture in order to acquire the tools of Western technology. We want the tools but not at the price of annihilating our religion and cultural values'. Statement made by Bakr Abdullah Bakr, the Head of King Fahd University of Petroleum and Minerals Cited by W. Ochsenwald, 'Saudi Arabia and the Islamic Revival', *International Journal for Middle East Studies*, 13 (1981), pp. 271–72.

163 See, generally, A. Redfern and M. Hunter, *Law and Practice of International Commercial Arbitration* (3rd edn., Sweet and Maxwell, 2003), especially Chapters 9 and 10.

of course, choose to arbitrate outside the kingdom and avoid the difficulties, but their award would be unenforceable subsequently in Saudi Arabia. Furthermore, although in most countries there exists a consistent judicial practice that embraces the supervisory authority of civil courts over arbitral proceedings, in Saudi Arabia the situation is problematic. Despite the fact that the Saudi competent authorities (particularly the *Diwan*) do offer some jurisprudence as to their reasoning for either accepting or rejecting arbitration clauses – and the validity of the proceedings and compliance with public policy – there is no sense of precedent.[164] The judges decide on the basis of their personal opinions and are not obliged to adhere to any precedent, even if a decision of the Review Committee of the *Diwan* exists on a particular matter. Moreover, these cases are not generally accessible and it is telling that this is only the first instance in which a compilation has been made with a view to their examination. As a result, arbitration remains a very speculative business since the parties and their lawyers navigate through legal uncertainty. From an international law point of view, it may be argued that the decisions of all competent authorities are an expression of state practice on the basis that they are organs of the state. Thus, even if their decisions carry no binding precedent within the Saudi legal system, at least the said decisions reflect the will of the kingdom and bind it in its international relations. In any event, there is no doubt that a Hanbali arbitration law does exist, which itself informs Saudi arbitral law. The analysis in this chapter has demonstrated that this Hanbali corpus of law is in fact more flexible than Saudi law, particularly on the grounds of interpretative techniques. This finding should dismiss the notion that Shari'a is an archaic and backward-looking institution.

Parties intending to draft arbitration clauses and undertake arbitral proceedings in Saudi Arabia, or elsewhere in cases where a Saudi element is involved, should ensure that they are fully compliant with Shari'a law and Saudi public policy. Given the requirements regarding the status of arbitrators, foreign lawyers dealing with such disputes must constantly be alert as to reliable arbitrators that fulfil these exact criteria.

The New Arbitration Act

Among the set of legal reforms in Saudi Arabia, there is a foreseeable redrafting for the Arbitration Act and the Implementing Rules. The long-awaited law is expected to be a mixture of the Egyptian arbitration law and the arbitration rules of Dubai International Arbitration Centre which are heavily inspired by the similar rules of the London Court of International Arbitration. The prospective law should benefit from legal precedents and judicial practices and should, as a result, restrict the

---

164 Nonetheless, as has been demonstrated, the *Diwan* is not opposed to the parties themselves introducing foreign judgments or arbitral awards as evidence backing up their particular claims.

scope of judicial review exercised by the *Diwan*. However, public policy issues might not be touched upon – women, for instance, might still not be welcomed as arbitrators and Shari'a will remain the sole applicable law in domestic arbitration. It can be assumed that even a new act might not facilitate the enforcement of foreign arbitral awards owing to the vast scope of public policy restrictions but it is likely that the practice will experience more relaxation and flexibility. Nonetheless, bureaucracy, lack of clear procedural rules and lack of manpower in the *Diwan* are the real elements that impair arbitration in Saudi Arabia. The enactment of a new law will not necessarily mean the end for these existing problems.

Chapter 6
Arbitration for the Settlement of Banking Disputes in Saudi Arabia

In all legal systems around the world, contradiction of public policy is a great threat to the arbitral process. The banking and general legal systems of Saudi Arabia are structured in quite a strange manner owing to the obvious conflict between Shari'a principles and the way in which conventional banks function. This conflict has created a gap between Shari'a and the statutes within the Saudi legal system in various fields, especially where the dispute involves an unacceptable element under Shari'a, such as the imposition of interest, hereinafter '*riba*', which is the primary motive of the conventional banking system.

As discussed in the previous chapter, this conflict has proved to be a fatal legal tactic against banks by those defaulting debtors trying to avoid serving their debts, at least in part, and to lengthen the time of the disputes, which render the loan practically 'interest free'. After examining arbitration as a general mechanism of settling commercial disputes, this chapter examines the issues related to arbitration as a mechanism for the settlement of banking disputes in Saudi Arabia and will discuss the following points: the arbitrability of banking disputes; the arbitration clause in financial transactions; the concept of duality in the Saudi legal system; and alternative remedies when arbitration fails to serve its objectives. The study will be conducted in a comparative way between Shari'a, the statutes and current practice, and in some parts will compare Saudi law with the laws of some of the countries neighbouring Saudi Arabia, such as Egypt and the UAE. The reason for comparing Saudi law with Egyptian law is that Egyptian law is practically one of the sources of Saudi legislation. On the other hand, the UAE is a growing economic power in the region with close business ties with Saudi Arabia.

Banking Disputes under the Law of Saudi Arabia

Before proceeding to discuss the nature of banking disputes in Saudi Arabia, the scope of the word 'banking' under Saudi law should be determined in order to give a clearer vision of banking activities. The Banking Control Law of 1966 defined 'banking' as:

> the business of receiving money on current or fixed deposit account, opening of current accounts, opening of letters of credit, issuance of letters of guarantee, payment and collection of cheques, payment orders, promissory notes and

> similar other papers of value, discounting of bills, bills of exchange and other commercial papers, foreign exchange transactions and other banking business.[1]

This latter definition may bring up a few questions regarding the scope of banking business and consequently banking disputes; however, the most important question relates to the reason behind the absence of money-lending operations in the definition of banking business under the Act, when it should be considered as the core of banking business. Saudi legislators broadened the scope of the definition by inserting the following sentence 'and other banking business', by which it can be assumed that the Saudi legislators wanted to allow the practice to encompass controversial matters under Shari'a. For instance, the drafters of the Act were unable to include explicitly the activity of money lending with interest, or '*fawaied*', in the Act because riba is clearly prohibited under the constitution of the country, bearing in mind that the Act was drafted in 1966, at a time when the concept of banking and the imposition of interest was totally unacceptable to the majority of Saudis owing to its obvious violation of Shari'a. In a similar way to other GCC countries, Saudi society has been experiencing rapid changes following the first oil boom of the 1970s, when the business sector began to accept what it formerly used to reject, as well as transforming its attitude toward banking interest. One may expect that if Saudi Arabia were to redraft its Banking Act, the law would not differ from any banking statute anywhere in the world and interest might not be the dilemma that it used to be.

The banking activities quoted in the above definition, in addition to money lending, which has constituted an accepted practice of the commercial banks under the supervision of the Government, are the primary subject matters of banking disputes in Saudi Arabia. The question of which competent authority should settle banking disputes in Saudi Arabia carries an even greater deal of ambiguity. Despite the recent law reform, Saudi Arabia does not possess proper commercial courts. The competence of settling commercial disputes in general is therefore devolved among several semi-judicial committees, making it understandable that in many cases a great conflict of authority is manifested.[2] In any event, even the creation of specialized courts entrusted with the settlement of commercial disputes would not solve the problem, especially if the disputed case related to 'banking business', as these prospective courts would work under the supervision of the Ministry of Justice, which itself would never tolerate any violation of Shari'a.[3]

---

1 See article 1.b of the Banking Control Act of Saudi Arabia. Royal Decree No. M/5 dated 22/02/1386 H. (1966). *Umm Alqura Gazette*, issue No. 2126 dated 05/03/1386 H. (1966).

2 Examples for such cases can be found in the cases of cheques and negotiable instruments disputes involving the payment of interest.

3 See, in general, the Law of Judiciary and the Law of the Board of Grievances of Saudi Arabia. Issued by Royal Decree No. M/78 dated 19/09/1428 H. *Umm Alqura Gazette*, issue No. 4170 dated 30/09/1428 H. (12/10/2007).

In addition to arbitration, disputes relating to banking business can be settled through one of the following two committees in accordance with the subject matter of the dispute, irrespective of whether it relates to negotiable instruments or concerns other banking activities:

- the Committee for the Settlement of Banking Disputes under the Saudi Arabian Monetary Agency (SAMA), which is competent to settle disputes arising as a result of pure banking activities only, such as the opening of current and deposit accounts, letters of credit, money exchange, foreign transfer, money lending, etc;[4]
- the Committee for the Settlement of Disputes Involving Negotiable Instruments, which functions under the auspices of the Ministry of Commerce and Industry and possesses the jurisdiction to settle disputes related to cheques and other negotiable papers only. The Committee for Negotiable Instruments is also known as the Negotiable Instruments Office.

Arbitrability of Banking Disputes

The doctrine of arbitrability generally relates to the question of whether the applicable law allows a matter to be resolved by arbitration. All legal systems exclude some matters from the scope of arbitration and the non-arbitrable matter is referred to litigation even if the parties to the dispute agree to arbitrate.[5] As in other areas of Saudi commercial law, arbitration in general has not received sufficient attention from legislators, who prefer to rely on the classical Shari'a teachings and, in some cases, oppose modernizing the legal system even if the said modernization proffers to exist within the scope of Shari'a. This attitude has resulted in a great deal of ambiguity in Saudi day-to-day affairs, especially when a prohibited or disputed element is the subject matter of a dispute. Saudi law is relatively vague when providing an answer to the question of arbitrability. Under Saudi law, whether a dispute is arbitrable is answered by reference to the Arbitration Act and its Implementing Rules. According to article 2 of the Arbitration Act, arbitration is permitted in disputes where conciliation is permitted.[6] Therefore, the Act excludes some criminal disputes, as will be seen below, and disputes concerning public policy, which themselves are encompassed under the jurisdiction of Shari'a courts and the *Diwan Almazalim*, in addition to disputes relating to national sovereignty.

With regard to banking disputes, a few opinions exist under Shari'a as to whether to allow the use of conciliation. The reason for the difference in opinions

4 See Royal Order No. 4/110 of 1409 H. (1989) and Ministry of Finance Circular No. 17/5583 dated 19/09/1409 H. (1989).

5 M. Paul, 'Arbitrability of Copyright Disputes: *Desputeaux v. Les Editions Choutte* (comments)', *Canadian Business Law Journal*, 38 (2003), pp. 125–49.

6 Article 2 of the Arbitration Act of 1983.

is owing to the legal status of banking business under Shari'a law, given that Shari'a prohibits particular banking transactions. The question here is whether conciliation should be permitted where prohibited contracts are concerned. As a general rule, none of the Shari'a courts in Saudi Arabia or the Board of Grievances would decide on a dispute concerning a prohibited subject matter or, likewise, issue a decision entitling one of the parties to perform an unlawful act under Shari'a.[7] In order to determine the issue of arbitrability of a dispute in general, one needs to examine Shari'a law on conciliation as the fundamental basis for deciding the arbitrability of a dispute, especially when the process of conciliation concerns riba.

The Law on Conciliation in Saudi Arabia

Having said that disputes should be amenable to conciliation in order to be arbitrable, there are no specific rules on conciliation in the law of Saudi Arabia and the procedure depends wholly on Shari'a teachings. In the Arabic language, there is no semantic difference between conciliation and mediation – both terms can be translated as '*sulh*'. The doctrine of conciliation, or sulh, was established by the Quran, the Sunna, the teachings of the various schools of fiqh, as well as by common practice and customs. The Quranic verses recommend conciliation as a means of settlement of disputes in general and as the main mechanism for the settlement of family disputes in particular, stating that: 'If a woman senses oppression or desertion from her husband, the couple shall try to reconcile their differences and conciliation is best for them.'[8] The Quran also recommends conciliation in inheritance matters, as in the case of an unfair will, stating that: 'If anyone fears partiality or prejudice on the part of the testator, and conciliates between the parties concerned, there is no wrong in him.'[9] Moreover, the Quran regards conciliation as the best practice in the settlement of disputes generally, as the following verse recommends: 'If a person forgives and makes conciliation, his reward is due from Allah as Allah loves conciliators.'[10]

With regard to the Sunna, it was reported that the Prophet Muhammad conciliated between disputants or deferred deciding on a dispute in order to give the parties some time to reach an amiable settlement outside the court. In support of his practice, Prophet Muhammad also said that conciliation is permitted

7 This information was given by a senior judge in the Shari'a Supreme Court of Makkah, Saudi Arabia, who preferred his name to be confidential. He added that, as a general rule, Shari'a courts assume jurisdiction over all claims brought before them. They do not decide on cases that entitle a violation of Shari'a law.

8 The Quran 4: 128.

9 The Quran 2: 182.

10 The Quran 42: 40.

except if it legalizes a prohibited matter or prohibits a lawful matter.[11] After that, conciliation became a customary practice under Islamic law and an essential part of procedure before any Shari'a judge.

Under Hanbali law, the conciliation agreement is a valid contract, similar to the arbitration agreement, and all the rules applicable to the arbitration agreement should apply to the conciliation agreement *mutatis mutandis* in accordance with the general principles of contract under Shari'a.[12] Despite the latter similarities, there are some fundamental differences between conciliation and arbitration under Saudi law and Shari'a law in general. In arbitration, the arbitrators are chosen on the basis of the mutual agreement of the parties to the dispute, whereas in conciliation the entire process depends on the parties to the dispute or their representatives and the conciliators have no authority to impose their view on the parties. Unlike arbitration, there are no rules to regulate the conciliation procedure, as conciliation may be initiated by the parties to the dispute or by the judge as part of the common procedure. The issue of the predictability of the arbitral award makes conciliation less harmful to the parties, especially if one of them intends to waive some of his claims in order to end the dispute. This is because in conciliation both parties know the acceptable limits for their waiver, which are not known in arbitration. In addition, the conciliation results can be enforced in a way similar to enforcing arbitration awards provided that they take the form of an award after concluding a valid conciliation agreement or if done before the court. As with arbitration awards, a conciliation award is not enforceable without an enforcement order from the authority having original jurisdiction over the dispute, which will review the award to ensure its conformity with public policy. Judicial review is not required for the enforcement of conciliation awards concluded before the court and they carry the same strength as court decisions.[13]

Classical scholars emphasized the legality and importance of sulh as the primary basis for settling most kinds of dispute, but some scholars did not consider sulh, or the conciliation agreement, as an independent contract, as is the case with the arbitration agreement.[14] It has been argued that under Hanbali law, a conciliation agreement is not an independent agreement and cannot stand on its own. Scholars who support this view assume that there is nothing that can be called a conciliation agreement and that such agreements are to be attached to another type of contract such that the conciliation award possesses most of its features. For instance, the conciliation agreement in commercial disputes may be considered as sales contract, lease contract, gift agreement, termination of a contract agreement,

11 A. ben Gasim, *Hashiyat Alraoud Almourbi' Sharh Zad Almostaqna* (1st edn., Almatba'a Alahliyah Liloffset, 1976), Vol. 5, p. 128.

12 I. Alhamoud, *Conciliation in Commercial Disputes and its Applications*. A paper presented at the Conference on Arbitration and Conciliation, Taif, Saudi Arabia, 15-16/05/1424 H. (2004).

13 Ibid.

14 M. Ibn Qodamah, *Almoghni* (1st edn., Hajar Publications, 1992), Vol. 4, p. 322.

settlement agreement, loan agreement, etc.[15] In other words, Hanbali scholars claim that there is no conciliation in commercial disputes and what is thought to be conciliation is merely negotiation of a new contract or amendment of an existing contract. However, such an opinion seems to add even more ambiguity to the legal status of conciliation and also contradicts the contractual nature of the conciliation agreement, which is actually independent and should not be influenced by other contracts.

Conciliation Practice in Saudi Arabia

Conciliation in Criminal Disputes

Besides family disputes, conciliation is one of the primary methods for settling many kinds of criminal dispute in Saudi Arabia, especially those concerned with private injury, such as murder and personal criminal injury. Under Shari'a, any offence committed against a person is amenable to conciliation, i.e., arbitration. This issue requires a distinction between so-called 'hodoud' offences, which are those committed against society as a whole, such as terrorism, assassination and adultery; and crimes committed against individuals, such as murder and personal injury, which can be subject to conciliation proceedings. Moreover, there are some crimes that are of a mixed nature, but which are nonetheless classified under the category of hodoud, particularly theft and rape, which cannot be subject to any kind of settlement, even though they involve a private entitlement, because of their relation to state power and society and whose punishment has already been determined by the Quran. Consequently, hodoud crimes cannot be subject to any kind of extrajudicial settlement.[16]

It is obvious from case law that criminal disputes can be subject to conciliation as long as they do not concern a hodoud crime. In a case before the Shari'a Supreme Court of Riyadh, the Court ordered the execution of a murderer by beheading him in a public place; however, following a process of conciliation, a settlement was reached between the defendant and the plaintiffs, i.e., the family of the victim, which entitled the defendant to pay the amount of 1.7 million riyals in exchange for a direct waiver of the claim of execution of the defendant.[17] In order to encourage conciliation and other types of alternative dispute resolution

15 Muhammad ben Moflih, *Kitab Alforou'* (1st edn., Dar Alkotoub Alilmiyah, 2003), Vol. 4, p. 268.

16 M. Ibn Taymiyyah, *Majmou' Alfatawa* (2nd edn., The Ministry of Islamic Affairs of Saudi Arabia, 1995), Vol. 3, p. 139. If an offence is not reported to an authority, i.e., the court or the police, the persons who are concerned with the offence have the right not to report it; nonetheless, the settlement is of no value if the claim reaches the authority.

17 See A. Aloraini, 'Conciliation in Criminal Matters', *Al-Adl Journal*, 8 (2001), pp. 1–23.

in general, Saudi courts prefer to delay the execution of particular sentences in order to give third parties the chance to intervene between disputants and thus save the guilty party from the death penalty. This tendency has its roots in the practice of the companions of the Prophet, as Omar ben Alkhattab, the second Caliph after the Prophet, said: 'Defer the issuance of your judgments; let the disputants conciliate.'[18] In another case where conciliation was involved, the parties reached a settlement requiring the defendant to pay double the amount of the actual compensation in exchange for a prompt waiver of the plaintiff's right. In this case, the plaintiff was shot by the defendant and, as a result, the plaintiff was rendered paralysed, which, according to the law, entitled him to receive damages of 500,000 riyals. The defendant preferred to pay the amount of one million riyals and get released from prison promptly.[19] No statistics exist concerning the exact number of criminal cases in which conciliation has been involved, but it may be said that conciliation has been a great influence on the finality of decisions in criminal matters in Saudi Arabia.

Conciliation in Commercial Disputes

Conciliation in commercial disputes has been divided into two main types according to the characteristics of the conciliation award: the first is '*sulh moua'wadah*' and the other is '*sulh isqat*'.[20] The second type of sulh, i.e. sulh isqat, is the one that is most related to banking disputes nowadays because such disputes mainly involve financial claims – settlement may be reached through reducing the amount of the claim or rescheduling the remainder of the claim.[21] In a claim brought before the Shari'a Supreme Court in Taif, Saudi Arabia, a conciliation award was approved by the Court in order to reduce the amount claimed by the plaintiff from 840,000 riyals to 700,000 riyals, subject to immediate payment.[22] The conciliation award can also assist in rescheduling a claim, as was achieved in another case brought before the Board of Grievances, where the plaintiff agreed to reschedule his claim against the defendant if the defendant paid the instalments on time; otherwise, the payment of the full amount was due on demand at any time.[23] The same kind of sulh may also result in rescheduling the payment of outstanding claims, which is accepted by Shari'a as long as the deferral of the payment itself does not bring

18 T. Alonaizan, 'Conciliation Before and After the Death of the Victim', *Al-Adl Journal*, 7 (2000), pp. 1–29.

19 Ibid.

20 Sulh moua'wadah results usually in a barter deal between the parties to the dispute, whereas in sulh isqat, one of the parties waivers or discounts part of the claim.

21 Supra n. 11, ben Gasim, Vol. 5, p. 141.

22 See sulh document No. 51 dated 26/06/1421 H. (2001) from the Supreme Shari'a Court of Taif (Saudi Arabia).

23 The Board of Grievances decision No. 369/2/Q of 1421 H. (2001).

any benefit to the claimant; otherwise, such deferral would be considered as riba or usury.[24]

Sulh can also result in a total waiver of a part of the claim, while also simultaneously discounting another part of the same claim, as occurred in the following case. A company claimed a payment of 192,084 riyals as damages for some defective goods, in addition to an amount of 300,000 riyals as compensation for certain direct and indirect losses as a result of faulty goods. The Board of Grievances approved a conciliation award entitling the defendant to pay only the amount of SR 120,000 out of the SR 492,084 initially claimed by the plaintiff. In this case, the parties agreed to reduce the amount of the claim from SR 492,084 to SR 120,000 and omit the payment of the compensation.[25]

The above-quoted cases constitute examples for claims arising out of normal commerce and not from banking activities. If the claim relates to banking business, Shari'a courts and the Board of Grievances will not approve the conciliation award unless the conciliation award discards the interest and requires payment of the capital initially received from the bank without any additional cost. Nonetheless, the voluntary payment of interest can still be an effective extrajudicial method for the settlement of banking interest disputes, although the enforcement of the conciliation award is totally dependent on the good faith of the parties to the dispute, as well as on the business relationship established between them.[26]

Despite the argument that conciliation is inapplicable in prohibited subject matters, common practice nowadays clearly suggests that banking disputes can be subject to conciliation in accordance with the main principles of Shari'a and the general Quranic verses, as well as the tradition of the Prophet, which did not specify the scope of conciliation. Moreover, the following Quranic verse encourages people to give more flexibility in terms of rescheduling repayment of a debt if the borrower is facing hardship and is unable to pay the sum owed on time: 'If the debtor is in hardship, let him have respite until it is easier, but if you forego out of charity, it is better for you if you realize.'[27] Although, the latter Quranic verse does not include the word conciliation, the conciliatory spirit can be felt within its teachings.

Theoretically, banking disputes are arbitrable in Saudi Arabia because they can be subject to conciliation, whereas, in reality, banks are faced with a great deal of discrimination when it comes to the ratification of arbitration agreements and the execution of arbitral awards. This discriminatory treatment may have negative effects on many aspects of Saudi Arabia's commercial and social life. Banks may restrict the provision of conventional banking facilities, on the basis that the settlement of disputes arising out of related transactions may not be fair for

---

24 The Board of Grievances decisions 'Makkah branch' No. 992/2/Q of 1421 H. (2001).

25 The Board of Grievances decision No. 651/1/Q of 1423 H. (2003).

26 This piece of information was given by Mr. Ahmad Mazhar, in an informal visit to his law firm in Jeddah Saudi Arabia on 20 December 2007.

27 The Quran 1: 280.

the bank. For the same reason, the restriction in the provision of banking facilities might slow economic growth, especially when the alternative is more costly for customers.[28] Another direct effect of the unfair treatment of banking disputes can be seen in attempts to avoid choosing Saudi Arabia as the applicable forum, where it would otherwise be the most convenient forum for the particular conventional banking dispute. For the sake of public interest, banking disputes should receive more attention both in arbitration and in litigation, because any discrimination against the banks has the potential to undermine the credibility of Saudi Arabia as a potential financial centre and may slow the flow of foreign investment to the kingdom.

The Arbitration Clause and Arbitration Agreement in Financial Transactions in Saudi Arabia

As a general principle of Shari'a contract law, parties to the contract are free to stipulate whatever they want. According to some schools of fiqh, there are restrictions on this principle and conformity with the general principles of Shari'a is required.[29] Following the principle of freedom of contract as established in Ibn Taymiyyah's treatises, arbitration clauses or agreements of this nature (*compromis*) are permissible even if the subject matter of the dispute at issue is prohibited.[30] This opinion enhances the autonomy of the arbitration agreement as an agreement separate from the underlying transaction and drives us to regard arbitration agreements related to banking transactions as lawful independent agreements of their own accord, regardless of the subject matter of the dispute. The following few paragraphs will not discuss the legality of arbitration agreements concerned with banking transactions, this being the subject of a long-contested debate in the field of contract law. It will instead discuss the use of arbitration clauses in banking transactions in Saudi Arabia.

In the light of common practice, financial transactions in Saudi Arabia can be classified as either Islamic or conventional. The classification is undertaken in accordance with the nature of the transaction as a whole and whether it is Shari'a compliant. Nonetheless, the law treats each class of disputes differently, as disputes relating to Islamic banking are settled like any other normal commercial

28 When considering Islamic banking as an alternative to the conventional banking system, the Islamic banking system has not been developed to attract large-scale businesses and the cost of Islamic facilities is almost the same as the conventional ones, if it not higher. For more details see M. El-Gamal, *Islamic Finance, Law, Economics and Practice* (1st edn., Cambridge University Press, 2006), pp. 77–78.

29 N. Hammad, 'Adhesion Contracts in the Islamic Jurisprudence', *Al-Adl Journal*, 24 (2005), pp. 51–78.

30 See, generally, F. Vogel and S. Hayes, *Islamic Law and Finance: Religion, Risk and Return* (1st edn., Kluwer Law International, 1998), Chapter 5, pp. 97–128.

dispute, given that Islamic banks theoretically function in a manner similar to normal commerce. In such transactions, the arbitration clause usually provides for the settlement of disputes by means of domestic arbitration in accordance with the Arbitration Act of 1983 of Saudi Arabia and under the supervision of the *Diwan Almazalim*.[31] In these cases, the arbitration is performed normally without any impediment and the award is enforced in a way similar to that of the enforcement of any ordinary arbitral award. This is owing to the nature of Islamic banking transactions, which repackages the underlying transaction from a loan agreement with interest to a sales transaction in order to avoid riba.[32]

Domestic conventional banking transactions are arbitrable in principle; however, when it comes to the ratification of an arbitration agreement or the enforcement of an arbitral award, arbitration might encounter some obstacles from *Diwan Almazalim*, it being the supervisory body for arbitration proceedings in Saudi Arabia.[33] The *Diwan*'s attitude does not seem to serve the main objectives behind resorting to arbitration as a fast, cheap and reliable dispute settlement mechanism; moreover, some of the decisions of the *Diwan* can be considered as a great waste of time and resources that undermines the credibility of arbitration in general. Nowadays, arbitration for the settlement of domestic conventional banking disputes has proved to be ineffective, as will be seen below.

As a general rule, if both parties to the contract are of Saudi nationality, their choices for adopting a method of dispute settlement are very limited. Saudi parties have to resort either to the Committee for the Settlement of Banking Disputes or to arbitration in Saudi Arabia, which excludes all those elements that are deemed to violate Shari'a, i.e., interest accruing from the enforcement order.[34] On the other hand, the existence of a foreign element to the arbitration agreement can offer more choices to the disputants and the resort to international arbitration anywhere in the world can become a possible option provided that, for the purpose of enforcement in Saudi Arabia, the arbitral award is in conformity with Shari'a rules.[35] It has been noted that the *Diwan* upholds the parties' right to arbitrate wherever they stipulate, as long as a foreign element exists in the dispute. In a former dispute between a Saudi bank and a foreign company, the arbitration agreement provided for the settlement of disputes arising out of the contract by means of arbitration in Zurich, subject to the rules of the International Chamber of Commerce. The foreign party insisted that Saudi Arabia be the seat of the arbitration proceeding

31 This piece of information has been provided by the Shari'a Compliance Officer at the Islamic Retail Banking Division of one of the commercial banks in Saudi Arabia (12 January 2008).

32 For more details on this kind of transaction, please see A. Saeed, *Islamic Banking and Interest* (2nd edn., Brill Publishers, 1999). See also T. El Diwany, *The Problem with Interest* (2nd edn., Kreatoc Ltd, 2003), pp. 135–92.

33 See *Diwan Almazalim* decision No. 50/1418 dated 24/01/1409 H. (1988).

34 See *Diwan Almazalim* decision No. 59/1419 dated 28/10/1419 H. (1999).

35 This information was provided by an official in the Saudi Arabian Monetary Agency, who prefers his name to be confidential (7 January 2008).

and that Shari'a be the substantive law applicable to the dispute. It was obvious that the foreign party was trying to escape the payment of interest as provided in the loan agreement between the parties to the dispute. However, the *Diwan* issued a decision denying the jurisdiction over the dispute on the grounds of the existence of an arbitration agreement with which the parties had an obligation to comply and resort to arbitration in Zurich and under the rules of the ICC. The Review Committee stated:

> [T]he *Diwan* has no jurisdiction over this dispute for two reasons; first, the existence of the arbitration agreement. The parties should resort to arbitration in Zurich as they stipulated. Secondly, the *Diwan* is not the authority with original jurisdiction over the dispute and the parties. We conclude that the parties to the dispute should either resort to arbitration in accordance with the arbitration agreement or refer the case to the Committee for the Settlement of Banking Disputes of the Saudi Arabian Monetary Agency.[36]

It can be said that having a foreign party involved in a dispute is the only way to enforce the full payment of interest. This method has been upheld by the *Diwan*, but on what grounds? There are two main arguments surrounding this issue and one of them suggests that the *Diwan* allows resorting to international arbitration on the grounds of the principle of Alaqd Shari' at Almouta'qedeen, which is the Islamic equivalent for *Pacta Sunt Servanda*. It may be understood from this view that the parties to the arbitration agreement are obliged to respect the terms of the said agreement as long as they are allowed to. Another argument suggests, however, that the *Diwan* does not rely on the principles of contract law, not because it wants to enhance the freedom of contracts generally, but because it is instead forced to uphold original arbitration clauses because it lacks competence over disputes. There is then no possible defence against the insistence on the right to arbitrate outside Saudi Arabia. This issue will be elaborated in more detail below.

Duality in the Saudi Legal System: Banking Interest as an Example

In Saudi Arabia, the existence of two governing bodies of law with regard to banking business has created a great deal of uncertainty. The uncertainty has not been caused by the existence of the two bodies themselves; rather, it has been created because both bodies of law contradict each other in some very sensitive matters. Interest payment is one of the main points of conflict between Shari'a and existing banking regulations and practices because, despite the fact that it represents the main motive for the conventional banking system, it is prohibited

36 The author was given access to the archive of a Saudi commercial bank on the condition that all the relevant information about the parties and the dispute remain confidential.

under Shari'a. In Saudi Arabia, judicial review will lead to an indirect application of Shari'a law if the arbitration is governed by a law other than Shari'a or Saudi law, or is granted in a non-Muslim country. When *Diwan Almazalim* reviews an arbitral award, it searches for any contradiction of the main Shari'a principles as well as contradictions of other areas of public order. If contradictions are found, the party seeking the enforcement of the award will have two options: enforce the award after excluding the part contradicting public policy; or refer the entire dispute to the competent authority to decide the case anew.

In the second scenario, the competent authority is the *Diwan* itself, one of the Committees of the Ministry of Commerce and Industry or the Committee for the Settlement of Banking Disputes of SAMA. Disputes relating to conventional banking are a clear example of the duality in the Saudi legal system for the reason that the *Diwan*, as the competent authority for the enforcement of arbitral awards, will not enforce the parts that contradict Shari'a, whereas someone else would. Despite the willingness of the Committee for the Settlement of Banking Disputes to enforce interest payment, it is unable to impose its decisions and force the losing parties to comply fully with its judgments. The weakness in the enforceability of the Committee's decisions is owing to its nature, which does not give it the power to act as a judicial committee – if it were considered so, it would have to comply with Shari'a rules, which is not the reason for its existence.

Another face of this duality can be found even in the existence of the Committee for the Settlement of Banking Disputes itself. The function of the Committee contradicts article 1 of the Basic Law, which states that '[t]he Kingdom of Saudi Arabia is a sovereign Arab Islamic state with Islam as its religion; the Quran and the Sunnah are its constitution', and article 7, which states that 'the Government in Saudi Arabia derives power from the Holy Quran and the Prophet's tradition'.[37] Although the Committee for the Settlement of Banking Disputes works under the supervision of SAMA, the function of the Committee violates article 6 of the Charter of the Saudi Arabian Monetary Agency, which does not allow SAMA to act in any manner which contradicts the teachings of Islamic law. What the Committee does can be considered as support of a prohibited activity under Shari'a.[38] The argument for the prohibition of the function of the Committee comes from a well-known principle under Shari'a that provides for the prohibition of all activities associated with riba, as will be seen below. The legal status of interest under Shari'a and under the statute law of Saudi Arabia as a sign of contradicting duality within the legal system, as well as the methods of settling banking disputes, will be examined in the next part of this chapter.

---

37 The Basic Law of Saudi Arabia, issued by Royal Decree No. A/90 dated 27/08/1412 H. (1992). *Umm Alqura Gazette*, issue No. 3397 dated 02/09/1412 H. (1992).

38 See, generally, article 6 of the Charter of the Saudi Arabian Monetary Agency. Issued by Royal Decree No. 23 dated 23/05/1377 H. (1957). *Umm Alqura Gazette*, issue No. 1698 dated 06/06/1377 H. (1957).

Interest under Shari'a

The issue of interest has been a religious and ethical dilemma for many Muslim businessmen since the early years of Islam for many reasons. First, usury, or riba, is very similar to some kinds of sales contracts, especially futures contracts for the sale of not-yet-existing subject matters, known as 'bay' al salam'. The argument for riba in the Quran can be seen in the following verse: 'They said "Trade is like interest" while Allah has permitted trade and forbidden interest.'[39] Second, interest is the main motive for modern banking business and can be considered as the cornerstone of any modern economy.

Islam came to abolish some of the pre-Islamic practices in order to protect the whole society from their negative effects. In the pre-Islamic era, charging interest was a standard condition for any loan agreement; however, the total prohibition went through different stages and took a long time during the life of Prophet Muhammad to become final. When looking at the religious basis of the prohibition of riba, the complete ban has gone through four stages, starting with showing that riba is not recommended for Muslims and that they should avoid it as much as they can, and ending up with a definite prohibition.

The first stage discouraged people from charging interest over loans given to other people, a discouragement that can be understood through the following verse: 'That which you give as interest to increase within other people's wealth increases not with Allah; but that which you give in charity, seeking the goodwill of Allah, multiplies manifold.'[40]

In the second stage, the prohibition took the form of reminding Muslims what previous nations had done before the Quran showed that their practices were not the right thing to do. The following verse might indicate that Muslims should stop charging interest over loans: 'And for their taking interest even though it was forbidden for them, and their wrongful appropriation of other peoples' property, we have prepared for those among them who reject faith a grievous punishment.'[41]

The third stage clearly demonstrated that riba was prohibited and therefore a sin. It can be seen in the following verse that riba had not yet quite reached the level of being one of the major sins that Muslims must not even get close to: 'O believers, take not doubled and redoubled interest, and fear Allah so that you may prosper. Fear the fire which has been prepared for those who reject faith, and obey Allah and the Prophet so that you may receive mercy.'[42]

In the fourth and final stages, the prohibition of riba became final – since then it has been considered as one of the major sins, i.e., very close to murder, worse than adultery and similar in guilt to terrorism, which can be understood through the following verses of the Quran:

39 The Quran 1: 275.
40 The Quran 30: 39.
41 The Quran 4: 161.
42 The Quran 2: 130.

> O believers, fear Allah, and give up the interest that remains outstanding if you are believers;[43]

> Those who charge interest shall be raised like those who have been driven to madness by the touch of the Devil; this is because they say: "Trade is like interest" while Allah has permitted trade and forbidden interest. Hence those who have received the admonition from their Lord and gave up may have what has already passed, their case being entrusted to Allah; but those who revert shall be the inhabitants of the fire and abide therein for ever.[44]

This latter Quranic verse determines the legal basis for settling disputes involving interest or riba. Judges in Shari'a courts and *Diwan Almazalim* apply the principle established by this verse when deciding on any disputes or when reviewing arbitral awards: 'If you do not do so, then be sure of being at war with Allah and His Messenger. But, if you repent, you can have your principal. Neither should you commit injustice nor should you be subjected to it.'[45] In accordance with the teachings of this verse, interest must be avoided; however, if a person is involved in a usurious transaction he must not take more than the principal amount that he lent and interest must be excluded from any Shari'a-compliant judgment. The prohibition of riba in the Sunna was not just a restricted prohibition like the prohibition of many unlawful actions. The prohibition of interest followed the doctrine of extended prohibition, i.e., the prohibition covers all activities related to the prohibited subject matter and all the people involved in it are sinners on an equal basis.

The doctrine of extended prohibition of interest was established by the following Hadeeth: 'Prophet Muhammad cursed the receiver and the payer of riba, the one who records it and the witnesses to the transaction and said: they are all alike [in the sin].'[46] This Hadeeth can also be the legal basis for arguing for the prohibition of the functions of the Committee for the Settlement of Banking Disputes, as when the Committee upholds a riba transaction, it is considered to be involved in it, if not as the one who records it then as witness to the transaction. Moreover, another Hadeeth establishing a general rule for detecting unlawful transactions reads as follows: '[A]ny loan attract[ing] a benefit is riba.'[47] This rule is a very important safety measure against certain practices employed by some 'Islamic banks', which take advantage of differences in legal opinion among scholars with regard to the scope of the prohibition of riba. Riba is generally classified as unlawful

43 The Quran 1: 278.

44 The Quran 1: 275.

45 The Quran 1: 279.

46 Al-Imam Alzaylai'e, *Tabeen Alhaqaiq Sharh Kanz Aldaqaiq* (1st edn., Dar Alkotoub Alilmiyah, 2000), Vol. 4, p. 84.

47 Supra n. 30, Vogel, p. 77.

advantage by way of excess, as in '*riba alfadl*', and rescheduling of debt, as in '*riba alnasi'ah*'.[48]

The issue of riba alfadl arises in contracts of sale where there is an increase in the terms of exchange and the subject matter of the contract and consideration are identical. For instance, the exchange of a certain amount of US dollars for a higher amount of US dollars can be considered as riba, but if the consideration is different from the subject matter, as in the case of exchanging US dollars for Saudi riyals, there is no riba as long as the exchange is made on the spot.[49] There are some similarities between this class of riba and the practices of some Islamic banks nowadays, as some of them avoid riba alnasi'ah to get involved in riba alfadl. The law on riba alfadl was established by the following Hadeeth:

> [T]he selling of gold for gold is riba (usury) except if the exchange is from hand to hand and equal in amount and similarly, the selling of silver for silver is riba (usury) unless it is from hand to hand and equal in amount.[50]

Riba alnasi'ah, mostly referred to as riba aljahiliyah or, sometimes, the obvious riba, literally means 'the riba of the pre-Islamic era', because it was a very common practice among Arabs before Islam. This type of riba is similar to charging interest over loans and to delaying damages. It has been reported that Prophet Muhammad described all pre-Islam riba contracts as and cancelled his own uncle's Moreover, in the treaty of the Prophet with the Christians of Najran,[51] the Prophet cancelled the interest accrued on their debts, which had originated in the pre-Islamic period.[52]

For the sake of representing some of their practices as Shari'a compliant, some of the pioneers of modern Islamic banking have adopted the narrowest sense available for determining riba. They recognize the latter type only, i.e., riba alnasi'ah, arguing that it is the only prohibited practice mentioned in the Quran. They also rely on the reasoning of some of the companions of Prophet Muhammad, who said: '[T]here is no riba except riba alnasi'ah.'[53]

Having said that interest is prohibited under Shari'a, we should explore the reason behind this prohibition. There are many social, ethical and economic factors supporting the prohibition of riba, which have been summarized by Kula as follows:

---

48 H. Ramadan, *Understanding Islamic Law from Classical to Contemporary* (1st edn., Alta Mira Press, 2006), p. 117.

49 Ibid.

50 Supra n. 28, El-Gamal, p. 68.

51 Najran is a city in the south of Saudi Arabia.

52 A. Saeed, *Islamic Banking and Interest: A Study of the Prohibition of Riba and its Contemporary Interpretation* (2nd edn., Brill Publisher, 1999), p. 30.

53 Ibid.

> The reason why usury is prohibited in Islam is manifold. First, the taking of interest, in the main, implies appropriating another person's property without giving him/her anything in exchange, because one who lends one pound for two pounds gets an extra pound for "no real effort". Second, dependence on interest prevents some people from working for a living, since the person with money can earn much more through interest without working for it. In this way individuals with money who will not bother to take the trouble of running a business will inevitably undermine the worth of work in the community. This will not only deprive the individuals with wealth of justly earned benefits, but it will also depreciate the wellbeing of the Islamic community for it is not possible to sustain the flow of goods and services by simply borrowing and lending money alone. The third and perhaps the most important aspect of riba is that it is, essentially, a transfer of money from the "poor" to the "rich", which is contrary to Islamic teaching.[54]

The financial crisis of 2008/09 showed a collapse in the value of banking assets which the Quran uses different terms to describe such as shrink and crunch.[55] The prohibition of riba can be considered as one of the main principles in Islamic economics nowadays. Modern economists have defined riba in the new contexts as any unjustifiable increase in capital, whether through loans or sales. More precisely, any positive, fixed, predetermined rate tied to the maturity and amount of the principal (i.e., guaranteed regardless of the performance of the investment).[56] The distinction should be made between riba and the rate of return or profit on capital, as Islam encourages the earning and sharing of profits, because profits represent a successful entrepreneurship and the creation of additional wealth. Interest, however, is considered as a cost that is accrued regardless of the outcome of the business operations and that may not create wealth if there are business losses.[57]

To sum up, all forms of interest charged over loans are totally prohibited under Shari'a and contradict the public policy of Saudi Arabia. A contract involving such terms is null and void in the part including the prohibited action. This view has been upheld by the teachings of all fiqh schools, the fatawa of the Ulama, and the judgments of Shari'a courts and the Board of Grievances. For instance, the Minister of Justice ordered all Shari'a courts and kitabat aladl, or 'notaries', not to authenticate the mortgages of commercial bank loans on which such banks take interest from the debtor by a certain percentage. The order covers any agreement or contract involving the payment of interest because it is prohibited by Shari'a.[58]

---

54 E. Kula, 'Is Contemporary Interest Rate in Conflict with Islamic Ethics?', *Kyklos International Review for Social Sciences*, 61/1 (2008), pp. 45–49.

55 The Quran 1: 276.

56 Z. Iqbal and H. Tsubota, *Emerging Islamic Capital Markets: A Quickening Pace and New Potential* (World Bank Publications, 2006), p. 6.

57 Ibid.

58 See the Minister of Justice Circular No. 107/2/T dated 25/08/1389 H. (1969).

The Minister of Justice's order was upheld by the Supreme Judicial Council, which prohibited borrowing from commercial banks because they charge interest. The same decision exempts judges from deciding on disputes that involve the payment of any form of interest or loans associated with benefits.[59] It can be said that when kitabat aladl refuse to authenticate loan agreements, they might go against the injunction provided in one of the verses of the Quran that obliges them to authenticate any agreement, as they are not held responsible for their content. That verse reads as follows:

> O you who believe! When you contract a debt for a fixed term, record it in writing. Let a scribe record it in writing between you in (terms of) equity. No scribe should refuse to write as Allah hath taught him, so let him write, and let him who incurred the debt dictate, and let him observe his duty to Allah his Lord, and diminish naught thereof.[60]

Interest is prohibited under Shari'a as applied in Saudi Arabia, but the overall status is not really clear and a great deal of ambiguity surrounds the issue as a whole. This might be owing to the fact that the two bodies of law, i.e., Shari'a and the statute, are applied in parallel with the theoretical supremacy of Shari'a ruling. Current practice in Saudi Arabia has not identified whether riba is prohibited; however, it can be observed that even if riba is prohibited the prohibition is unenforceable in the sense that a person or a bank can charge interest as long as no dispute reaches the authority.

Arbitral awards entitling one of the parties to perform any unacceptable act under Shari'a, such as paying interest, will be set aside and the Board of Grievances will not enforce the parts contradicting Shari'a. A typical case in which a party seeks the enforcement of an arbitral award including interest can be seen in the following. An application for the enforcement of an arbitral award made in Bahrain was refused because it entitled one of the parties to pay interest. The Board allowed the enforcement of the part that complied with Shari'a only and the losing party was forced to repay the principal but without interest.[61]

Although banks claiming interest is against Shari'a, a client refusing the performance of a binding contract is against Shari'a as well, because it contradicts one of the main principles of Shari'a contract law, which is Alaqd Shari' at Almouta'qedeen, Arabic for *Pacta Sunt Servanda.* The non-performance of a contract may contradict some of the Quranic texts such as: 'O ye who believe! Fulfil (all) obligations.'[62] Nonetheless, these principles can be easily challenged by

59 See the decision of the Supreme Judicial Council No. 291 dated 25/10/1401 H. (1980).

60 The Quran 1: 282.

61 *Diwan Almazalim* decision No. 19/28 of 1399 H. (1979).

62 The Quran 5: 1.

the assumption that Shari'a prevails over the terms of any contract if the contract provides for a breach of one of the established principles of Shari'a.[63]

Interest under the Banking Regulations

The banking system is the heart of any modern economy and a strong economy cannot exist without a sound banking system.[64] From this fact, Saudi Arabia had to allow the establishment of commercial banks and the first Saudi bank was established in the 1930s. Banks started, from that time, to provide services and charge interest – the banking network soon expanded, especially in the 1960s and 1970s. The oil boom of the 1970s resulted in the establishment of some public funds that started lending to individuals and certain kinds of business with zero interest and on very flexible terms.[65] The oil boom also resulted in an accumulation of a huge amount of cash and liquid assets in a very short period of time, which led commercial banks to be more generous in providing their facilities without thorough consideration of the creditworthiness of their clients. Following that, banks started to suffer from a major legal problem represented in the refusal of Shari'a courts and the Committee for the Settlement of Commercial Disputes to recognize the validity of interest in banking transactions. The official position was not clear as the Government allowed Saudi banks to charge interest as long as it was necessary for the financial system and served the public interest, but it refused to recognize it in the case of disputes.

Despite article 149 of the Code of Commercial Courts of 1931, there is no mention of interest in Saudi regulations.[66] Financial regulations in Saudi Arabia do not give a clear answer to the question of whether charging interest on loans or awarding interest in arbitral awards is a permitted action. Even the Banking Control Act and its implementing rules did not mention the word interest, or fawaied, in its text. The situation is truly vague and confusing to the extent that nobody is able to determine whether interest is legal or illegal. There are different reasons for this, such as that riba was practised for many decades even though such practices contradict the main principles of Shari'a and that the Government

63 Supra n. 46, Al Imam Alzaylai'e, Vol. 4, p. 98.

64 R. Sylla, 'Financial Systems and Economic Modernization', *Journal of Economic History*, 62 (2002), pp. 277–92.

65 These funds were established by the Government, and they work under its direct supervision: The Saudi Arabian Agricultural Fund established in 1963; The Saudi Credit Bank founded in 1971; The Public Investment Fund created in 1973; The Saudi Industrial Development Fund established in 1974; The Real Estate Development Fund established in 1974.

66 Article 149 of the Code of Commercial Court does not really deal with interest charged over loans; it deals with one of the tricks applied by the Islamic bank to circumvent the prohibited riba. The example given in that article describes exactly the Tawarrouq transactions applied by Islamic banks nowadays.

itself deals with it in some of its contracts. Having said that riba violates Shari'a, there is no punishment for riba dealing – all that the judicial bodies do is annul the contradicting part of the contract.

It is appropriate to quote a conversation between King Faisal ben Abdul-Aziz (1903–1975) and a businessman, which shows that some regulatory bodies were more or less impartial with regard to banking interest. A bank customer complained to King Faisal that his bank was claiming interest, which he refused to pay because it is against Shari'a. The businessman expected the King to abolish the payment of interest but the King said that, since the bank granted the complainant a certain facility for a specified period, and he refused to pay interest, the complainant must return this favour to the bank and give the bank an equal amount for an identical period, after which time the bank is to repay it to him without interest. The complainant is said to have settled the interest to his bank without further objection.[67] By the early 1980s, banks complained to the authorities, arguing that they were losing too much and that the risk was too high. This complaint led to the establishment of the Committee for the Settlement of Banking Disputes in 1987.[68] The establishment of the Committee as a last resort for banks did not serve the banks' objectives in full and interest remained an avoidable obligation.

As a general rule, Saudi law is applicable to all governmental contracts. This choice of law may indicate that whatever the Government stipulates is not against the law or public policy. The practice of the Saudi Government adds more ambiguity, however, as charging interest became a valid practice in most of the former governmental contracts, both domestically and internationally. For instance, the recent gas concession agreements concluded in 2004 have a specific clause for interest charged on the amount of the financial guarantee in case of late payment. Article 18 in all three gas concession agreements provides for interest to be charged for late payment at the rate of LIBOR plus 1 per cent, which is exactly the prohibited riba under Shari'a.[69] Moreover, and contrary to its Charter, the Saudi Arabian Monetary Agency, 'SAMA', receives interest on assets deposited or invested with international financial institutions.[70] For one reason or another, the Saudi Government has been investing in US Treasury securities, which are simply debt certificates with interest charged over them.[71] In addition, the Government of Saudi Arabia has been financing its budget deficit through internal borrowing where the major lenders are the General Organization for Social Insurance and the Pension and Retirement Fund. Both organizations work under the supervision of

---

67 M. Alameldin, 'Banking Disputes in Saudi Arabia', *International Financial Law Review*, 10 (1991), pp. 36–38.

68 Ibid.

69 See article 18 of the concession agreement between Saudi Arabia and Lukoil Saudi Arabia Ltd. *Umm Alqura Gazette*, issue No. 3990 dated 15/03/1425 H. (04/05/2005).

70 *Saudi Arabian Monetary Agency v. Dresnder Bank AG* (2003), WL 23145143.

71 See, generally, D. Spiro, *The Hidden Hand of American Hegemony: Petrodollar Recycling and International Markets* (1st edn., Cornell University Publication, 1999).

the Ministry of Finance and the Government has been serving the debt owed to those funds since the mid-1980s with a total interest accounting for SR 30 billion in the year 2000.[72] It can be said that charging interest is a governmental practice, but it does not usually apply to domestic transactions, i.e., contracts within the private sector other than banks, for the reason that *Diwan Almazalim* is the applicable forum for settling disputes arising out of the execution of such contracts and the *Diwan* does not recognize interest. It can be said again that interest payment is prohibited under Saudi law, but the prohibition is unenforceable as long as the parties voluntarily comply with their agreement.

The clash on this very specific legal issue represents a bigger point of controversy between two schools of thought within the Saudi authorities, and even within the society as a whole. A conservative party who rejects any attempt at reform or development and insists on leaving this vague situation against a larger group who seeks the modernization of the system without prejudice to the established principles and moral values of the society and arbitration in such an economically, religiously sensitive issue is one example of this clash.[73]

The Settlement of Banking Disputes in Saudi Arabia

Having said that interest is partly contrary to the public policy of Saudi Arabia and that arbitral awards should not include interest to render them enforceable, this section will examine the ways of settling such disputes in Saudi Arabia. First of all, Shari'a courts and *Diwan Almazalim* are not competent for the settlement of disputes relating to banking activities.[74] In addition, if a claim for interest is brought before Shari'a courts or *Diwan Almazalim*, the contract will be considered null and void in the part that violates Shari'a law. Therefore, the available remedies refer the dispute to arbitration, the Committee for the Settlement of Banking Disputes, or the Committee for the Settlement of Negotiable Instruments Disputes.

Arbitration

The previous chapter examined arbitration law and practice in the case of normal commercial dealings that do not violate the principles of Shari'a or public policy. The following part of this chapter will examine arbitration in disputes related to

---

72 A. Shoult, *Doing Business with Saudi Arabia* (3rd edn., GMB Publishing Ltd, 2006), p. 42.

73 The Chairman *of Diwan Almazalim*, Sheik Muhammad Alissa. *Okaz Newspaper*, issue No. 2459 dated 11/03/2008. The Sheik added that some judges even oppose computerizing the archive system in addition to the reform of some existing regulations and procedures.

74 Royal Order No. 729/8 dated 10/07/1407 H. (1987).

domestic conventional banking in Saudi Arabia. As concluded above, arbitral awards violating Shari'a law are of no effect and cannot be enforced in Saudi Arabia, either wholly or at least in the contradicting part of the award. Even though arbitration is an independent dispute resolution method, arbitration is found to be attached to the domestic legal system and the public order of the place of the issuance and enforcement, for the reason that arbitral awards cannot be enforced unless they are judicially approved in the place of enforcement. They should be, at the same time, valid at the place of issuance. It can be said that, unlike other neighbouring states, there is no way whatsoever to enforce an arbitral award concerning domestic conventional banking in Saudi Arabia if it provides for the performance of a prohibited act under Shari'a. Prior to the establishment of the Committee for the Settlement of Banking Disputes, arbitration was the only available remedy for banks; nonetheless, the enforcement of the award was totally dependent on the good faith of the parties to the dispute. For instance, in a loan agreement concluded in 1985, a Saudi bank agreed to settle a dispute that arose between it and a Saudi businessman, who refused to serve his debt by means of arbitration in Saudi Arabia subject to the ICC arbitration rules and under the supervision of the Jeddah Chamber of Commerce and Industry. The final award upheld the bank's right to receive interest on the principal amount in addition to the immediate repayment of the principal amount in cash. The arbitration panel applied the principle of Alaqd Shari' at Almouta'qedeen, where the terms of the contract prevail over the law and arbitrators should rely on it when issuing their decisions without prejudice to the public order. When the bank filed a request for the enforcement of the award, the *Diwan* rejected the enforcement of the part contradicting Shari'a and gave the bank a choice between executing the award in the part compliant with Shari'a or referring the whole dispute to the competent authority of that time, i.e., the Committee for the Settlement of Commercial Disputes, to decide it anew. In another case, the *Diwan* blocked all possible solutions, rejected the whole award on the grounds of the prohibition of the subject matter of the dispute and denied jurisdiction on the case. The bank had to settle the dispute through conciliation with the debtor, who had the upper hand at that time and asked for rescheduling of the principal only, which the bank had to agree upon as the very last resort. In a number of arbitration cases concluded before the establishment of the Committee for the Settlement of Banking Disputes the *Diwan* gave the party seeking the enforcement of the arbitral award a choice between executing the Shari'a-compliant part of the award or referring the case to the Committee for the Settlement of Commercial Disputes under the Ministry of Commerce and Industry. However, on most occasions the *Diwan* rejects the enforcement of an arbitral award, leaving no room for alternative remedies. In such cases, the parties to the dispute have to initiate a new claim before the competent authority, which is very costly and time-consuming.

After the establishment of the Committee for the Settlement of Banking Disputes, arbitration became less attractive to banks as a method for settling domestic disputes, as resorting to the Committee for the Settlement of Banking

Disputes under SAMA gives banks a better chance of recovering the outstanding claims for interest. Moreover, in some circumstances, arbitration is a useless dispute settlement mechanism for banks owing to the *Diwan*'s inflexibility or even hostility against banks, as the *Diwan* considers all banking activities to be violations of Shari'a. The legal doctrine of 'ma boniya ala batil fahowa batil' applied by the *Diwan* provides for the illegality of all actions and practices if they are based on illegal principles, which might be one of the legal basis for denying the enforcement of arbitral awards providing for interest.[75] It can be assumed that the *Diwan* regards arbitration agreements and awards as illegal because of the nature of the underlying contract, which is a void contract under Shari'a.

As a result, the number of arbitration cases in which banks are involved has become very limited and, practically, banks in Saudi Arabia do not resort to arbitration any more in disputes relating to domestic conventional banking. The banks refrain from resorting to arbitration in domestic conventional contracts because the Committee for the Settlement of Banking Disputes of SAMA gives better solutions, as it looks at the dispute from a contractual point of view without the strict adherence to Shari'a rules applied by the *Diwan*. Therefore, arbitration remains a very speculative business while disputing parties and their lawyers navigate through legal uncertainty.

It has been noticed that the *Diwan* denies jurisdiction over any claim involving banks, even if the case falls within the *Diwan*'s general jurisdiction as the competent authority for the enforcement of arbitral awards in the kingdom. In the following case, the *Diwan* rejected the whole application for the enforcement of a domestic award on the grounds of having banks as parties to the dispute. The application for the enforcement of an arbitral award in relation to a dispute involving a Saudi company and two national banks was filed but rejected by the *Diwan* on the grounds of lacking jurisdiction to hear disputes in which a bank is involved.[76] In its decision, the *Diwan* quoted Royal Order No. 8/729 of 1407 H. (1987) as the basis for its refusal; however, the previous royal order determines the competent authority for the settlement of a banking dispute. The *Diwan*, when reviewing the arbitral award, is not settling the dispute; it is merely enforcing the decision of the arbitration committee with regard to the dispute after a general review of the award. It was a disappointment when the *Diwan* exceeded its terms of reference and tried to decide on the case anew. Accordingly, the presence of a bank as a party to the dispute can be grounds for setting aside an arbitral award without looking at the merit of the award itself, which can be considered as discrimination against banks. On the other hand, it can be said that there was a misunderstanding by the *Diwan* because the *Diwan* treated the enforcement application in a manner similar to treating an initial claim where, if it were the case, the reasoning of the *Diwan*

75 See *Diwan Almazalim* decision No. 11/D/F/2 of 1417 H. (1997). The legal doctrine of 'ma boniya ala batil fahowa batil' can be translated as 'anything based on something illegal is illegal'.

76 *Diwan Almazalim* decision No. 50/1418 dated 24/01/1409 H. (1988).

would be accurate. However, as the application was for the enforcement of a final arbitral award, the *Diwan* should not have intervened in such a discriminatory way. In a case where the party seeking the enforcement of the arbitral award insisted on the full enforcement of the award, the *Diwan* gave the option of referring the whole case to the competent authority, i.e., the Committee for the Settlement of Banking Disputes, which was supposed to be the second option after looking at the award. The *Diwan* declined to look at the award in the first stage on the grounds of having banks as parties to the arbitration. In another case, after the parties to the dispute spent a great deal of time and money, the award was set aside by the *Diwan* even though none of the parties challenged it. This last case shows the main difference between arbitration under the *Diwan* and the judgments of the Committee for the Settlement of Banking Disputes, which are binding on the parties if they are not opposed by the parties before issuing the award, as will be seen below.

It can be assumed that the *Diwan* follows one of the opinions under the Hanbali school, which considers contracts related to prohibited subject matters as null and void – there is therefore no real dispute because the whole transaction is of no value at all.[77] Nonetheless, the *Diwan*'s practices led to a movement among banks to avoid the jurisdiction of the Saudi authorities over their transactions, as will be discussed below. Yet, the high level of legal risk also encouraged banks to move toward Islamic banking, which seems to be ethically acceptable for customers and judges and has proved to be more profitable and less risky for banks in Saudi Arabia.

In international banking transactions where at least one of the parties to the dispute is considered to be a foreign party, even though it is not, parties to the contract can stipulate to arbitrate anywhere outside Saudi Arabia, which is usually their first preference. In any scenario, Shari'a secures its position by not allowing the enforcement of arbitral awards contradicting it, as the enforcement order must be filtered by the *Diwan* in the light of Shari'a ruling. However, arbitration is not the favourite dispute settlement mechanism, as in most cases the parties to the contract stipulate that English law or the law of New York is the proper law of the contract and therefore that London or New York is the appropriate forum. This tactic is mainly preferred by banks because there are no impediments to the enforcement of interest and other prohibited or disputed sale contracts like in Saudi Arabia. By doing so, the Saudi court will not be involved in the dispute by any means; however, if the arbitration award is brought to Saudi Arabia for the sake of enforcement, it will be regarded as invalid and the *Diwan* will consider it a circumvention to avoid the jurisdiction of the Saudi judiciary. In most cases, the parties to the dispute are wholly Saudis but the legal entity is incorporated somewhere outside Saudi Arabia, so they would be considered as foreign parties, as in the following example. The case of *Islamic Investment Company of the Gulf (Bahamas) Ltd v Symphony Gems NV and others* is a clear example of such tactics of circumvention to avoid the application of Shari'a law on transactions where the

---

77 Supra n. 46, Alzaylai'e, Vol. 4, p. 101.

application of Shari'a could affect the parties' right to receive interest. In this case, the English court quoted: 'The fact that the claimant was based in Saudi Arabia, and the offer made in that country was insufficient to bring into play the illegality principle, on the assumption that the agreement was contrary to Saudi law.'[78]
It was noted that a great deal of care was put into the drafting agreements concerning international conventional banking. They tried to find a way to render the law of Saudi Arabia inapplicable to the transaction, even though the actual parties to the contract were of Saudi nationality and Saudi Arabia was the place of characteristic performance and conclusion of the contract. Some Saudi businessmen adopted this attitude because of the pressure put on them by foreign parties, as adjudication under any law other than Saudi law is more convenient for both of them.

In *Midland International Trade Services Ltd and Others v. Al-Sudairy and Others* the English court decided on a case related to their actions in Saudi Arabia. The agreement provided for the Saudi company to pay interest on the sums advanced and to repay the third plaintiff by honouring bills of exchange payable in Riyadh. The agreement was expressly to be governed by, and construed in accordance with, English law and the parties to it agreed to submit their disputes to the jurisdiction of the English courts without prejudice to the right of the third plaintiff to sue the Saudi company in Saudi Arabia. The case was first brought to the Committee for the Settlement of Negotiable Instruments Disputes in Riyadh, where interest was not awarded. Then a claim was initiated in London, where the English court concluded by awarding interest to the second and third plaintiffs.[79]

From current practice it can be noted that, in the absence of good faith, there are a few ways to avoid the intervention of the courts of Saudi Arabia in arbitration, which can be summarized as follows:

- The party benefiting from the banking facilities should incorporate a business entity outside the kingdom of Saudi Arabia with total independence from other Saudi corporations, as in the above case of *Islamic Investment Company of the Gulf (Bahamas) Ltd v. Symphony Gems NV and Others.* By doing so, the Saudi authorities would have no way to intervene in the arbitral process and there would be no need to resort to the *Diwan* for enforcing the award, as everything would be done outside Saudi Arabia provided that the parties have enough assets outside the jurisdiction of the Saudi court.
- Foreign banks can deal with Saudi parties safely by having a well-drafted agreement wherein the foreign bank is assured that Saudi Arabia is not the applicable forum for the settlement of any dispute. Such assurance can be obtained through the following steps:

78 See *Islamic Investment Company of the Gulf (Bahamas) Ltd v. Symphony Gems NV and Others* [2002] All ER (D) 171 (Feb.).

79 *Midland International Trade Services Ltd v. Al-Sudairy* (QBD, 11 April 1990), *The Financial Times*, 2 May 1990.

- The Saudi party establishes a branch in the home country of the bank to carry out business activities and have a permanent address.
- The place of the characteristic performance should be that of the home country of the bank, which means that if there is a dispute it will be outside Saudi Arabia and therefore out of the reach of the Saudi judiciary. The Saudi judiciary would not be competent to decide on it unless both parties were of Saudi nationality. In this case, arbitral awards should be enforced in the place where the contract was executed.
- Finally, the bank providing the facilities should retain sufficient collateral against the debt within its own legal system to avoid forum shopping in case the debtor defaults. If that happened, the bank would have to resort to the Saudi judiciary to recover its claims and would encounter the problem of interest being contrary to public policy.

Banking Disputes in Neighbouring Countries

Neighbouring states that have laws based on principles similar to those of Saudi Arabia, such as Egypt and the United Arab Emirates, still have a different approach to the issue of banking interest in general.[80] It should be noted that the Constitution of the UAE followed the Kuwaiti model and that both constitutions were drafted by Egyptian scholars and inspired by the Egyptian Constitutions, especially the Constitution of 1971.[81] The approaches adopted by neighbouring countries reflects their tolerance of interest in arbitral awards, as in some cases interest has been treated as being totally compliant with public policy, for example, in the UAE; and in other cases interest is allowed with certain restrictions, such as in Egypt. In Egypt, the law has recently been hesitant with regard to banking interest. Apart from the UAE and Oman, other GCC states do not have a clear answer to the question of whether interest is contrary to public policy. The uncertainty is owing to the fact that interest contradicts the constitutions of all these countries, including the UAE itself; however, they do allow interest to be charged either on loans or as delay damages in commercial transactions.

In Egypt, as the pioneer of modern statute law in Arab countries, the issue of interest in general and in arbitral awards in particular has become theoretically vague in the last two decades as a result of the 1980 amendment of the constitution

80 W. Ballantyne, 'The States of the GCC: Sources of Law, the Shari'a and the Extent to which it Applies', *Arab Law Quarterly*, 3 (1986), pp. 1–18.

81 See, generally, Butti, Al-Muhairi, 'The Position of Shari'a within the UAE Constitution and the Federal Supreme Court's Application of the Constitutional Clause concerning Shari'a', *Arab Law Quarterly*, 11 (1996), pp. 219–44. The Kuwaiti Constitution was drafted by Abdulrazzaq Al-Sanhuri and the UAE Constitution was drafted by Professor Wahid Ra'fat; both are well-known Egyptian jurists.

and because the decisions of the commercial court contradict each other.[82] For instance, article 227 of the Civil Code of 1949 stipulated that contracting parties could agree on interest rates of up to 7 per cent. Based on the amended constitution of 1980 identifying Shari'a as the principal source of legislation, the Sheik of Alazhar brought a claim before the Supreme Constitutional Court pleading against a lower court judgment obliging Alazhar to pay a debt and the 4 per cent interest on it according to the relevant article of the Civil Code of 1949. The court dismissed the case, arguing that 'the Shari'a rulings cannot be applicable to the already existing legislation retroactively without creating confusion and instability for the commercial and judicial process'.[83] However, the Sheik of Alazhar himself, in his well-known fatwa, allowed interest on banking deposits, as he said: 'riba is haram but banking interest is halal'. Sheik Alazhar Muhammad Sayed Tantawi was the first respectful figure in the Islamic world to give such an opinion. The fatwa itself can also be regarded as a shift in the attitude of many Muslims toward banking interest, even though the Sheik himself put restrictions on the application of interest in various contracts where the main condition is not to take advantage of the hardship of debtors and also not to enhance the difference between the classes of society.[84]

The Sheik of Alazhar's fatwa encouraged Islamic banks to adopt various methods for calculating interest charged on loans, covering it with different names – a practice that resulted in a similar interest rate to conventional loans or even a higher rate on some occasions.[85] Another opinion of Egyptian scholars with regard to banking interest reveals a misunderstanding of the mechanism of interest. This opinion suggests that a fixed interest rate is prohibited but that a variable interest rate is permissible. It might be thought that the two rates cannot differ substantially as interest is charged in both cases, albeit calculated differently, but instead of determining the rate at the beginning of the agreement, the interest would be reviewed at the beginning of each sub-period into which the loan is divided.[86] The decisions of the Egyptian courts, even after the claim of the Sheik

82 S. Habachy, 'Commentary on the Decision of the Supreme Court of Egypt Given on 4 May 1985 Concerning the Legitimacy of Interest and the Constitutionality of Article 226 of the New Egyptian Civil Code of 1948', *Arab Law Quarterly*, 1 (1985), pp. 239–41.

83 F. Nomani, 'The Problem of Interest and Islamic Banking in a Comparative Perspective: The Case of Egypt, Iran and Pakistan', *Review of Middle East Economics and Finance*, 1/1 (2003), pp. 37–70.

84 See the fatwa of *Majma' Albohouth Al Islamiya Bil Azhar*, 'the Islamic Research Committee of Alazhar', concerning banking interest dated 23/09/1423 H. 28/11/2002, Cairo, Egypt.

85 One of the methods is called 'cost plus profit', where the bank estimates the real value of the principal on the maturity date and adds what it considers as administrative fees, which sometimes result in a rate that is higher than the conventional rate; however, according to this method, banks are not allowed to charge any additional fees after the maturity date.

86 Supra n. 32, El Diwany, p. 137.

of Alazhar, did not pay any consideration to the argument that interest violates the Constitution. The court of first instance at the south of Cairo decided that the Egyptian Government, representing the Ministry of Finance and the Taxation Department, should pay an operator of a hotel the amount of 33,320.13 Egyptian pounds as compensatory interest for late payment of three years.[87] The confusion created by the amendment of the Constitution did not apply to the legal system, as courts continued to regard charging interest as part of the public policy of Egypt.

Conversely, the legality of the practice of charging interest in the UAE is not disputed. The law has integrated it as a fundamental practice to the extent that charging interest is not a matter of conflict; if there is a dispute, it will only be about when to charge interest and how much the rate will be. For instance, article 76 of Federal Law No. 18 of 1993, known as the Commercial Transactions Law, emphasizes the right of a commercial debtor to charge interest, stating:

> A creditor is entitled to receive interest on a commercial loan as per the rate of interest stipulated in the contract. If such rate is not stated in the contract, it shall be calculated according to the rate of interest current in the market at the time of dealing, provided that it shall not exceed 12% until full settlement.[88]

The structures of the economy and the ruling system have contributed to the relaxed regulatory attitude toward many traditionally controversial issues and have caused riba to be represented as a normal and even necessary practice in the economic life of the UAE.[89] As a result, interest has become an established principle within UAE law; it is not considered as a religious dilemma and is not even faced with opposition, as it is in Saudi Arabia or Egypt.[90] Furthermore, it has been argued that the Dubai International Financial Centre enjoys actual independence in the fields of civil and commercial law, with the express authorization of the amended UAE Constitution, which introduced common law-based regulations. The legislators did that hoping to attract foreign investment, even at the expense of the established principles of the society. Some commentators added that Law No. 18 of 1993 concerning commercial transactions is an attempt to circumvent the application of Shari'a in commercial matters.[91]

---

87 The Court of First Instance at the South of Cairo, decision No. 4615 of 1992. See also, The Supreme Court of Egypt decisions No. 93/6/7 of 1996 and decision No. 26/16/8 of 1996.

88 The UAE Federal No. 18 of 1993, Commercial Transactions Law, article 76.

89 H. Tamimi, 'Interest under the UAE Law and as applied by the Courts of Abu Dhabi', *Arab Law Quarterly*, 17 (2002), pp. 50–52.

90 This is owing to the various degrees of influence of the religious institutions on the regulatory bodies and on the public. It can be said that Shari'a has no influence on the commercial law of the UAE.

91 A. Carballo, 'The Law of the Dubai International Financial Centre: Common Law Oasis or Mirage within the UAE?', *Arab Law Quarterly*, 21 (2007), pp. 91–104.

One of the similarities between the mechanisms banks employ in paying interest on deposits in the UAE and Saudi Arabia is the way of stipulating. As a general rule, banks in Saudi Arabia and the UAE do not pay interest unless the client requests it; however, the main difference is that in Saudi Arabia there are no certain rules for regulating interest – everything is based on market practice and the terms of the contract. Regarding loan agreements in the UAE, the law provides for the interest rate to be determined by agreement between parties – in the case of not specifying the interest rate, the rate would be determined by the common interest rate in the market provided that it did not exceed 12 per cent.[92]

Bearing in mind that the UAE is a Muslim state with Shari'a as a principal source of legislation, it has been noted that economic necessity led it to change its view of interest, which in turn led to its first allowing interest in commercial loans and then allowing interest as an ordinary practice in all areas of commercial activity. As an obvious violation of Shari'a, UAE law allowed for what some scholars call 'obvious riba', or 'riba aljahiliyah', which is the 'riba alnasi'ah' discussed above. This kind of riba cannot be circumvented and the law allowing it reads as follows: 'Where the contract stipulates the rate of interest and the debtor delays payment, the delay interest shall be calculated on the basis of the agreed rate until full settlement.'[93] Another article in the same law states clearly that the debtor is obliged to pay interest over the debt to the creditor subject to their agreement.[94] Consequently, charging interest is not disputed at all and the latter ceiling for the interest rate is upheld by case law. In the absence of an agreement between parties as to the interest rate, UAE law allows simple interest to be charged on all financial transactions within the limit of 12 per cent per annum. The same rule also applies to delay interest as a means of compensation, known in Shari'a as 'riba aljahiliyah'.

In a case decided in 1980, the Federal Supreme Court considered certain provisions of the Abu Dhabi Code of Civil Procedure that expressly allowed interest. The statutory language under review in 1980 provided that the rate of interest determined by the court may not exceed the rate of interest agreed upon by the parties, or upon the basis of which they transacted, and that in the absence of an agreement the court may determine the rate provided that it does not exceed 12 per cent with respect to commercial transactions and 9 per cent with respect to non-commercial transactions. In its 1980 judgment, the Federal Supreme Court held that these statutory provisions were constitutional, but that banks would not be permitted to charge rates of interest in excess of 12 per cent and that only simple interest would be allowed. In this particular case, the Federal Supreme Court first considered an objection by the borrower that all interest-bearing transactions were void pursuant to article 714 of the Civil Code (promulgated pursuant to Federal Law No. 5 of 1985). Article 714 provides that if a contract of loan provides for

92 Commercial Transactions Law of the UAE article 399.1.a.

93 Ibid., article 77. See also article 7 of the Federal Constitution of the United Arab Emirates of 1971.

94 Ibid., article 409.3.

a benefit in excess of the essence of the contract, then such a provision will be void. However, the Federal Supreme Court held that the Civil Code did not apply to banking transactions, which were commercial by nature and were therefore governed by the Commercial Code. The Federal Supreme Court therefore held that the borrower's challenge to the entirety of the interest owed to the bank could not be sustained. However, the Federal Supreme Court agreed with the borrower's challenge to the bank's attempt to collect interest in excess of 12 per cent and held that the interest rate ceiling established by the 1980 judgment would continue to apply.[95] In the decision of the Federal Supreme Court of Abu Dhabi No. 245/20 dated 7 May 2000, the Court established that charging interest in excess of the statutory ceiling of 12 per cent per annum is permitted as long as all parties agree to it. In accordance with article 76 of the Commercial Transactions Law of 1993, the Court did not distinguish between interests charged before or after the maturity date and the Court argued that the statutory limit should apply in the absence of such an agreement.[96] The scope of judicial review under UAE law is very limited compared to that of Saudi Arabia. Apart from the general grounds provided in article 5 of the New York Convention of 1958, no obvious obstacles for the enforcement of arbitral awards can be found in Saudi Arabia, which might be owing to the fact that the economic situation in that country forces the legal regime to be more tolerant in this respect.[97]

To sum up, interest is not considered as an impediment to arbitration at all in the UAE as it has become an essential element of both the economy and the legal system. Some may argue that arbitral awards providing for interest can be challenged in Egypt on the grounds of their contradiction of the Constitution, i.e., Islamic Shari'a. This argument is still only theoretical, however, and setting aside an arbitral award in Egypt on the grounds of interest is unlikely to happen, as Egyptian courts have their own rules of determining and enforcing interest obligations.[98]

The Committee for the Settlement of Banking Disputes

The Committee for the Settlement of Banking Disputes is the only authority in Saudi Arabia that recognizes charging interest as a valid practice. The Committee is competent to settle disputes arising out of the conduct of banking business

95 Ibid.

96 Supra n. 91, Tamimi. See also the UAE Supreme Federal Court decision dated 6 September 1983.

97 N. Angell and G. Feulner, 'Arbitration of Disputes in the United Arab Emirates', *Arab Law Quarterly*, 3 (1988), pp. 19–32.

98 See *Southern Pacific Properties (Middle East) Limited [SPP(ME)] v. Arab Republic of Egypt*, Case No. ARB/84/3. ICSID report (1st edn., Cambridge University Press, 1995), p. 242.

between banks and customers, and disputes between commercial banks in Saudi Arabia. Settlement of cheques and negotiable instruments disputes were excluded from the jurisdiction of the Committee as they fall under the jurisdiction of the Committee for the Settlement of Negotiable Instruments Disputes and, in some cases, Shari'a courts. If *Diwan Almazalim* finds an arbitral award to be contrary to public policy and the dispute relates to banking business, the *Diwan* will refer the whole case to the Committee to be decided anew as one of the remedies available to the parties to the dispute. In the following paragraphs, the procedure of the Committee will be described with reference to the available cases and materials.

First of all, it should be noted that the Committee was established as a compromise between Shari'a and economic interest in order to remove the burden from judges who faced a religious dilemma when deciding on disputes related to banking business. The dilemma occurred because of the gap between the legal right of the bank to collect the amount of interest in full, as stipulated in the agreement between the parties following the principle of *Pacta Sunt Servanda*, on the one hand and the fact that the whole transaction is unacceptable under Shari'a on the other. It should also be noted that there are no statutory rules of procedure for the Committee and proceedings rely fully on practice.[99]

In Saudi Arabia, legal prosecution concerning banking disputes or financial claims in general may be brought initially to one of the departments of the Ministry of Interior, known as Alhoqooq Almadaniyah, which in its turn will refer the case to the Committee for the Settlement of Banking Disputes. The claim can be initiated directly to the Committee or raised through the Regional Governorate, called Al Imarah. Any of these bodies will refer the case to the Committee. In the case of bringing the claim before the Alhoqooq Almadaniyah, the Department has the right to take action against the debtor to force him to pay off the debt if it finds the claim to be genuine. If the debtor challenges the claim either in full or in part, the whole case is sent to the competent authority, which would be the Committee for the Settlement of Banking Disputes in the case of banking disputes.

After obtaining approval to look at the dispute, the secretary of the Committee will then notify the respondent of the claim, attaching a copy of the claim and asking him to respond to it within one month. All claim notifications must be in writing and in full detail. Such details include the names of the parties, the nature of the relief or order applied for or the directions sought from the Committee, the names and addresses of the persons on whom it is intended to serve the application and the applicant's address for service, in addition to the signature of the applicant or his representative. The applicant may state the amount of his claim in foreign currency. Notifications of claims, hearings and decisions are sent through the claimant's bank to the respondent if he is a customer; in the case of having another bank as a respondent, the secretary will notify him directly. The secretariat prepares a report about the suit and in some cases an accountant is called by the Committee to check the amount of the claim. The Committee may also order a deposit by

99 Supra n. 67, Alameldin.

way of security for the administrative fees. It has been noted that accountants mainly admit banking service charges, as a substitute term for interest, until the end of the facility agreement between the parties. In this way, no tacit renewal of the facility can be claimed unless it is proved that an amount was withdrawn by the customer after the end of the facility agreement. In such cases interest can be granted up to the date of the later withdrawal. The Committee used to consider such an accountancy report as final and binding on parties without giving parties the chance to challenge it or even to know its content; the Committee gave the parties notice of it during the hearing only. The Committee appoints a venue for the hearing, which is usually the headquarters of the Saudi Arabian Monetary Agency in Riyadh. The hearings are held in private and the attendance is restricted to the parties to the disputes or their authorized lawyers; however, any power of attorney must contain the right to settle and transact on behalf of the principal. The Committee looks at the case as it was on the day of its presentation to the Alhoqooq Almadaniyah or to the Committee, but the amount of the claim can be amended. A written record of the examination is made and signed by both plaintiff and defendant, which is considered as evidence against any statement that the debtor makes during the examination.

According to the royal decree providing for the establishment of the Committee, the Committee was formed in order to find solutions for banking disputes. In the case of not reaching a fair settlement between the parties, the Committee should refer the case to the competent authority because the Committee is not a judicial body.[100] In practice, the Committee does not follow the instructions of the royal decree and tries to impose its own view on parties even if all parties or any one of them rejects the proposed solution. If the parties accept the proposed, or sometimes imposed, settlement and the parties conclude a transaction agreement, the Committee will add the following statement to the award: 'This decision is considered an injunction enforceable by the authorities legally competent.' Nonetheless, if the parties or one of them refuses the proposed solution, the award will not include the latter statement, which shows the conciliatory nature of the Committee's decisions. In other words, the Committee's decisions are treated in the same way as conciliation awards, which are non-binding on the party that rejects it. As a general rule, the decisions of the Committee are binding and enforceable; however, it has been noticed that the Alhoqooq Almadaniyah found difficulties executing the decisions of the Committee either because of a lack of clear instructions or because of the unwillingness of debtors to pay off their debts. All of this might be owing to the fact that the Committee is not a judicial body. Another reason for the weakness in the decisions of the Committee is the possibility that the decisions of the Committee can be challenged before *Diwan Almazalim* on the grounds of contradicting public policy. In one of the *Diwan*'s cases, the losing party, i.e., the debtor to the bank, argued that SAMA, when instructing the losing party to pay interest, did not violate only Shari'a but even its own charter that prohibits SAMA from acting in

100 See the Circular of the Minster of Interior No. 10207 of 07/02/1407 H. (1987).

any manner contradictory to Shari'a. The *Diwan* did not issue a decision for this dispute as the plaintiff requested a stay of proceedings – the plaintiff then reached a settlement with the bank outside the *Diwan*.

As an attempt to add strength to the decisions of the Committee, the Minister of Finance advised the Ministry of the Interior that the decisions of the Committee are final, enforceable and unchallengeable, asking the Minister of the Interior to put on more pressure to oblige debtors to pay off their debts, because the delay in the payment would have a negative effect on local banks and on the economy as a whole. Nonetheless, the enforcement of the Committee's decisions through the Ministry of the Interior faced many obstacles, which led the Ministry of Finance to impose its own measures to ensure the enforcement of the decisions of the Committee. As a remedy, a plaintiff can ask the Committee to place a defendant's name on a blacklist in order to prevent him from travelling abroad and thereby obtaining new facilities from banks. Moreover, the Committee can freeze or seize the defendant's banking assets, although it is disputed whether the Committee can freeze or seize all the moveable and immovable property of a defendant. In most cases the Committee cannot order a seizure of the defendant's non-banking assets unless it is pledged as a security against the debt, for the reason that such orders must be made through one of the bodies of the Ministry of Justice or *Diwan Almazalim*, and these bodies will not usually approve such actions if the seizure is to be made to recover a claim of banking interest. However, if the claim is brought to recover the principal only, the *Diwan* or Shari'a court will usually approve it. Appeals can be made through the Governor of the Saudi Arabian Monetary Agency, the Minster of Finance or to the Committee directly.

Since it was founded in 1987, the Committee has been facing some problems, making it unable to serve the objectives of its establishment. First is the absence of clear procedural rules – there are no procedural rules for the working of the Committee and all the proceedings are done in a vague manner. Second is the lack of enforceability of the Committee's decisions, which is the biggest problem. This issue makes the Committee totally dependent on other governmental bodies such as the Ministry of the Interior, the Ministry of Justice and *Diwan Almazalim*. Dependence on other governmental bodies for enforcing the judgments of the Committee is not a problem on its own as all other judicial bodies rely on other authorities to enforce their decisions; the problem occurs as a result of the contradiction between the principles applied by the other bodies, i.e., the Ministry of Justice and the *Diwan*, and the principles applied by the Committee. For instance, in cases where a real property is pledged to the debt, the enforcement of the agreement will face great difficulties when authenticating the agreement at kitabat aladl and when reaching *Diwan Almazalim* to obtain the order to sell the pledged property, since the *Diwan* might not approve the selling of such property for the recovery of interest.[101] Moreover, banks have some problems with securities

101 See for details the Commercial Mortgage Act, Royal Decree No. M/75 dated 21/11/1424 H. (2004). *Umm Alqura Gazette*, issue No. 3981 dated 07/01/1425 H. (2004).

other than real property, especially in the case of guarantees. Guarantees under Saudi law can be classified into two types: presence guarantee, called 'kafalah hodouriya', is where the guarantor guarantees the presence of the debtor before the official authorities only; and full guarantee, 'Kafalat Ghorm wa Ada'', gives the bank the option of claiming the debt from the guarantor directly. The main problem associated with such guarantees arises when the amount of the claim is not stated in the letter of guarantee provided by the guarantor. The guarantee will be considered void and of no effect or the amount claimed by the guarantor will be considered as the correct amount.

Third, as with conciliation, acceptance of the award by the parties is an essential condition for the enforcement of any award, showing the conciliatory nature of the Committee's decisions. Fourth, in addition to the absence of clear procedural and substantive rules and owing to the fact that none of the members of the Committee have a legal background, the Committee cannot function as a judicial body. Some of its decisions even seem to be impractical and harmful to parties, as in the case of rescheduling a debt in annual instalments for 20 years with a fixed interest. In this case, a debtor refused to pay his instalments because of financial difficulties. The defendant presented an official document issued from the Shari'a court stating that he was unable to pay off his debt and that he should enjoy very flexible terms of repayment.[102] The Committee calculated the amounts claimed by the bank and divided it by 20 years instead of five years. The decision was accepted by both parties as being the last resort for the bank.[103] In another case, the Committee totally cancelled the interest in exchange of the repayment of the principal in cash. The decision is seen to be reasonable in normal circumstances, but in this case the bank had to accept the decision after more than two years of not receiving any payment for the facilities granted to the defendant, which means that the defendant enjoyed an interest-free loan.

It has been noted that in many of its decisions the Committee rescheduled debt claims for various periods ranging from five years to up to 30 years. Nonetheless, the Committee can issue relaxed decisions if it finds the defendant willing to pay the full amount in cash. Such relaxations include discounting part of the interest as in the following example: a businessman borrowed an amount of SR 19,000,000 from one of the commercial banks in Jeddah. The parties stipulated on charging interest at the rate of 5.5 per cent per annum for five years. Following the market depression in the late 1990s, the businessman was unable to pay the instalments for 14 months owing to financial difficulties. The bank brought a claim before

102 This kind of document is known as Saq E'isar; one of the main advantages of obtaining such a deed can be the very relaxed repayment terms as such documents are issued for insolvent persons.

103 This case and the following cases have been provided by one of the commercial banks in Saudi Arabia and the author is not allowed to disclose any information that might give any assumption of the identity of the parties to the dispute, by either providing numbers, dates or names, etc.

the Committee asking for the payment of the principal plus the stipulated interest in full or a direct liquidation of the collateral in accordance with the terms of the contract. The Committee, during the hearing, proposed that the businessman could end the dispute if he paid the principal in cash and the bank should exclude 50 per cent of the outstanding claim of interest; the parties agreed on that.

Following the stock market crash in early 2006, the Committee has been experiencing some difficulties dealing with the large number of disputes between banks and their clients, vice versa with regard to banking facilities granted to buy shares with the guarantee of existing shares owned by debtors. This kind of dispute started to appear as a result of the common banking practice of liquidating securities placed as collaterals when the market value falls below a certain limit without notifying the clients, even though it is a violation of SAMA's regulations.[104] Until recently, commercial banks used to conduct stock brokerage directly, not through a specialized subsidiary, which raised the suspicion that banks were contributing to the crisis because of the conflict of interest between conducting stock brokerage, holding shares as debt security and managing speculative funds. This problem was also worsened by the ill supervision of the Capital Market Authority, which denied supervision of the practices of commercial banks because it fell under the competence of SAMA. SAMA in its turn denied the responsibility because such activities relate to the stock market and it was the responsibility of the Capital Market Authority to supervise such activities.[105] The settlement of such disputes would take a long time because the competence of this kind of dispute is still a matter of conflict between the Committee for the Settlement of Securities Disputes of the Capital Market Authority and the Committee for the Settlement of Banking Disputes, and also because of the large number of disputes. These disputes relate to banking business because they arose out of the execution of banking transactions, and they could also fall under the jurisdiction of the Committee for the Settlement of Securities Disputes of the Capital Market Authority because they relate to price manipulation and to the selling of securities without the owner's permission.

The Committee for the Settlement of Negotiable Instruments Disputes

Another competent body for the settlement of banking disputes is the Committee for the Settlement of Negotiable Instruments Disputes, which is competent to settle disputes arising out of negotiable instruments such as cheques, promissory notes and bills of exchange. Established by the Law of Negotiable Instruments, the Commercial Paper Committee is also known as the Office for the Settlement of Commercial Papers Disputes and has the jurisdiction to hear claims concerning bills

---

104 See Circular No. 333/BC/200 dated 22/08/1413 H. (1993).

105 A. Baamir, 'Issues of Disclosure and Transparency in the Saudi Stock Market', *Arab Law Quarterly*, 22 (2008), pp. 63–85.

of exchange, promissory notes and cheques only.[106] The Negotiable Instruments Law provides the substantive legal provisions applied by the Commercial Paper Committee. The law largely reproduces the provisions of the Geneva Convention Providing a Uniform Law for Bills of Exchange and Promissory Notes of 7 June 1930 and for Cheques of 9 March 1931, even though Saudi Arabia has not become a party to the conventions themselves. The Law of Commercial Papers can be considered as a mixture of the Code of Commercial Courts of 1931 and the above-mentioned Conventions, with some modifications to meet Shari'a requirements. For instance, as Shari'a forbids the payment and charging of interest, any provisions in the Conventions relating to prohibited practices under Shari'a were omitted from the Negotiable Instruments Law. In practice, this position has been applied by offsetting interest payments voluntarily made by the debtor against the principal of the debt. The procedure before the Committee is subject to the provisions of the Code of Commercial Courts of 1931 and decisions may be appealed to the Minister of Commerce or to the Committee itself.[107] It is planned for this committee to join the new commercial courts; however, up to the time of writing this book nothing much has been done in the merging process.

Unlike the Committee for the Settlement of Banking Disputes, wherein most of the submitted disputes occur between banks or between banks and customers, the majority of the disputes submitted to this Committee do not involve interest. The Committee for the Settlement of Negotiable Instruments Disputes applies Shari'a law and does not recognize the obligation to pay interest as a valid contract. At the same time, this Committee does not have the competence to award damages – all claims for damages should be directed to the appropriate authority.[108] With regard to riba, negotiable instruments related to usurious transactions are considered by the Committee to be void and of no value because the underlying contract is considered void.[109] Appeals against the Committee's decisions are made either to the Minister of Commerce and Industry or to the Committee itself. When the decisions of the Committee become final, they are enforced by the Alhoqooq Almadaniyah, which may detain the losing party until full payment is made. The Committee is not really a committee and, contrary to its name, it consists only of one of the legal advisers of the Ministry of Commerce and Industry, who is usually not a Shari'a-trained adviser. The legal adviser usually works as the secretary and arbitrator at the same time. The hearings of the Committee are held in the legal department of the Ministry of Commerce and Industry, where attendance is

106 See, in general, The Law of Commercial Papers, *Nizam Alawraq Altejariyah*. Issued by Royal Decree No. 37 dated 11/10/1383 H. (1963). *Umm Alqura Gazette*, issue No. 2010 dated 15/10/1383 H. (1963).

107 Ibid.

108 See the decision of the Committee for the Settlement of Negotiable Instruments Disputes No. 82/1405 dated 08/05/1405 H. (1985).

109 The Committee for the Settlement of Negotiable Instruments Disputes, decision No. 67/1404 dated 11/04/1404 H. (1984).

restricted to the parties to the dispute only. It has been noticed that the decisions of this Committee are easier to enforce than the decisions of the Committee for the Settlement of Banking Disputes for the reason that the decisions of this Committee do not contradict Shari'a. The decisions of this Committee are directly enforced by the Alhoqooq Almadaniyah, which will detain the respondent until full settlement of the claim is reached.

Unlike Saudi Arabia, the majority of the legal systems in the Muslim world have no problem with regard to arbitration in banking disputes, as it is treated in the same manner as other commercial disputes. In Saudi Arabia, the problem occurs because the principles of conventional banking contradict the principles of Shari'a, especially when it comes to sensitive issues such as interest. Nowadays, interest is the main motive behind the banking system, which can be considered as the core of modern economies; nonetheless, Saudi law does not give a clear answer to the question of the arbitrability of disputes in general and of banking disputes in particular, and refers the whole issue instead to the law on conciliation. The law on conciliation itself carries a great deal of ambiguity and conflict among the fiqh schools, especially when added to the fact that there were no rules on conciliation in Saudi Arabia until now. What is practised over there is no more than a personal effort to find pacific solutions to disputes or to avoid litigation. Another issue that worsens the situation is the duality within Saudi law. This duality is not a problem in itself, as two straight lines can go in parallel without clashing and two different schools of thought can complement each other, unless a fundamental point of conflict occurs between them, which is the case of interest in arbitral awards in Saudi Arabia. The contradiction between the two bodies of law with regard to interest is the main problem and it has caused a great deal of uncertainty in relation to arbitration, as Shari'a prohibits all forms of banking interest and Saudi law does not enforce this prohibition. After being the best solution for banking disputes, it can be concluded that arbitration becomes a less attractive method for the settlement of domestic conventional banking disputes for the reason that the Committee for the Settlement of Banking Disputes offers a better chance for recovering interest claims. Moreover, arbitration for banking disputes tends to be more risky, as the *Diwan* will consider arbitral awards providing for the payment of interest as contrary to public policy and will refuse the enforcement either in part or in full. In the latter case, the *Diwan* will either exclude the interest from the award or refer the whole dispute to the Committee for the Settlement of Banking Disputes to be decided anew, which is a waste of time and money and weakens the credibility of arbitration as a fast, cheap and effective dispute settlement mechanism. It has also been noted that banks attempt to avoid the jurisdiction of the Saudi judiciary in international banking contracts and try to apply a mechanism in which Saudi law has no influence on the transaction in general and on the settlement of disputes in particular.

The future of the semi-judicial committees is not yet clear as the new Law of Judiciary states that such committees will be incorporated in the new commercial courts.[110] The Law first calls for a reform in the procedural law before joining the specialized committees within the competence of the Ministry of Justice.[111] The new Law excludes some of the committees from this merger because it deals with sensitive issues on the one hand and on the other hand because Shari'a judges are not qualified enough to decide on them. The law excludes the Committee for the Settlement of Banking Disputes, the Committee for the Settlement of Securities Disputes and the Committee for the Settlement of Customs Disputes.[112] There are a few reasons behind excluding the Committee for the Settlement of Banking Disputes from the expected merger. First, the Ministry of Justice, when upholding the practice of riba, violates the Constitution of Saudi Arabia, especially articles 1 and 7 that regard the Quran and the Sunna as the main sources of legislation – these sources state clearly that riba, speculation on banking assets like shares and bonds, is forbidden. Second, recognizing riba contradicts the main objectives behind the establishment of the Ministry as a tool for applying Shari'a in daily life and also violates the Law of Judiciary, which states that Shari'a prevails over all man-made regulations.[113] Finally, the reason for excluding the Committee for the Settlement of Banking Disputes from the competent of the general judiciary is exactly the same reason for establishing it in the first place.

As an issue related to arbitration, the Saudi judiciary suffers from the lack of judges in general and judges specializing in commercial matters in particular. This is owing to the nature of the training received by judges, who do not receive enough training in modern commerce. Such training programmes as are available are neither efficient nor sufficient. The curriculum of Shari'a faculties and the High Institute of the Judiciary totally depend on the classical Shari'a treatises, which were written a few centuries ago before the creation of current business practice. Moreover, it is difficult to find people who are qualified equally well in Shari'a and commercial law. Even if such a person is found, as in the case of experienced lawyers, such a person must hold a Shari'a degree in order to be appointed as a judge, in addition to further hidden requirements. The old guard within the Ministry of Justice considers any attempt at reform as a threat to the application of Shari'a in Saudi Arabia – in their view Shari'a should be kept in the same way as applied by classical scholars. Such attitudes result in a conflict between the application of Shari'a and economic interest that is not a result of the application

---

110 These committees are: the Committee for the Settlement of Negotiable Instruments Disputes; the Committee for the Settlement of Commercial Disputes; the Committee for the Settlement of Labour Disputes; the Committee for the Settlement of Media Disputes; the Committee for the Settlement of Securities Disputes; the Committee for the Settlement of Customs Disputes; and the Commercial Departments of *Diwan Almazalim*.

111 See article 9.1 of the Law of Judiciary of Saudi Arabia.

112 See, generally, section 3, articles 1 and 2 of the Law of Judiciary of Saudi Arabia of 2007.

113 See the Law of Judiciary of Saudi Arabia, issued by Royal Decree No. M/78 dated 19/09/1428 H. (2007). *Umm Alqura Gazette*, issue No. 4170 dated 30/09/1428 H. 12/10/2007.

of Shari'a itself; it is a result of not adapting the application of Shari'a principles to modern commercial life. Failure to update Shari'a teachings in Saudi Arabia has many negative impacts, where the difficulties faced in arbitration in banking disputes reflect the wider scene of daily life in the continuous conflict between the different schools of thought, nepotism, slow procedures, etc.

The application of Saudi arbitration law to banking disputes contradicts the main objectives behind resorting to arbitration as a reliable, independent, swift and cheap dispute settlement mechanism. Unlike many arbitration rules, the arbitration agreement should be sent to the *Diwan* in order to obtain approval before the commencement of the arbitration. According to some officials at the *Diwan*, the ratification may take a period of between one and three months and in some cases may take years! Furthermore, the law does not give a clear answer to the question of whether banking interest is prohibited. However, as a final conclusion it can be said that interest is prohibited in Saudi Arabia but that the prohibition is unenforceable in the sense that the prohibition will only apply if there is a dispute before a Shari'a court. There are other alternative remedies in case arbitration fails to serve its objectives, such as resorting to the Committee for the Settlement of Banking Disputes of the Saudi Arabian Monetary Agency, which would be the best solution in a case where the party is claiming the payment of interest. Nonetheless, the decisions of this Committee are not binding on the party that rejects them. Avoidance of the jurisdiction of the Saudi judiciary has been proved to work on such occasions. Yet, if the enforcement is sought in Saudi Arabia, Shari'a rules will apply and such steps of jurisdiction avoidance will not work.

Bibliography

Books

Aghndies, Nicolas, *Islamic Theories of Finance: With an Introduction to Islamic Law and Bibliography* (1st edn., USA, Gorgias Press, 2005)

Al-Adl, *Modawanat Alahkam Alqada'iyah* (1st and 2nd edn., Saudi Arabia, Ministry of Justice of Saudi Arabia, 2007)

Alahdab, Abdulhameed, *Altahkeem Ahkamouh wa Masaderouh* (1st edn., Beirut, Naoufal Publications, 1990)

Alastal, Ismaeil, *Altahkeem fe AlShari'a Alislamiyah* (1st edn., Cairo, Maktabat Alnahdah Al Arabiyah, 1986)

Alatasi, Muhammad, *Sharh Almjallah* (1st edn., Pakistan, Maktabah Haqqaniyah, 1949)

Albejad, Muhammad, *Dirasah Li Nizam Altahkeem* (1st edn., Saudi Arabia, Institute of Public Administration, 1991)

Albejad, Muhammad, *Arbitration in Saudi Arabia* (1st edn., Saudi Arabia, Institute of Public Administration, 1999)

Aldar'an, Abdullah, *Alqawa'ed Al ijrae'iyah fe Al morafa'at Alshar'iyah* (1st edn., Saudi Arabia, Altawbah Publications, 1993)

Alfahal, Abdulrazzaq, *Qada' Almazalim wa Tatbiqatoh Fe Almamlakah Al Arabiya Al Saudiya* (2nd edn., Saudi Arabia, Dar Alnawabigh, 1994)

Ali, Jawad, *History of Arab before Islam* (3rd edn., Beirut, Dar Al elm lelmalayeen, 1970)

Aljaziri, Abdulrahman, *Ketab Al Fiqh Ala Almathahib Al Arba'a* (1st edn., Beirut, Dar Alkutob Alilmiyah, 2003)

Aljuhany, Uwaidah, *Najd before the Salafi Reform Movement: Social, Political and Religious Conditions during the Three Centuries Preceding the Rise of the Saudi State* (1st edn., Saudi Arabia, Ithaca Press in association with the King Abdul-Aziz Foundation for Research and Archives, 2002)

Al-Kenain, Abdullah, *Tasbeeb Alahkam Alqadaiyyah fe AlShari'a Alislamiyah* (1st edn., Saudi Arabia, Al Kenain, 1999)

Al-Kenain, Abdullah, *Altahkeem fe AlShari'a Alislamiyah: Altahkeem Al'am, wa Altahkeem fe Alshiqaq Alzaouji* (1st edn., Saudi Arabia, Dar Alasimah, 2000)

Almawardi, *Adab Alqadi* (4th edn., Baghdad, Dar Alani Liltiba'a Publishers, 1972)

Almithin, Wasil, *Procedural Defences in Shari'a* (1st edn., Saudi Arabia, Konoz Ashbilia Lil Nashr, 2005)

Alramly, Shamsaddin Muhammad, *Nihayat Almohtaj Ila Sharh Alminhaj* (3rd edn., Beirut, Dar Ihya' Altorath, 1993)
Al Razi, Fakhraddin, *Al Mahsul Fi 'Ilm Usul al Fiqh*, ed. Dr Taha Jabir al 'Alwani (1st edn., Saudi Arabia, Imam ibn Saud Islamic University, 1979)
Alsadlan, Saleh, *Alqawaid Alfiqhiyah Alkubra wa Matafarra' Minha* (1st edn., Saudi Arabia, Dar Balancia, 1997)
Al-Samaan, Yahiya, *The Legal Protection of Foreign Investment in The Kingdom of Saudi Arabia* (1st edn., Saudi Arabia, Dar Alandalus for Publication and Distribution, 2000)
Alsamnani, Ali, *Rawdat Alqodat wa Taouq Alnajat*, ed. Salahaddin Alnahi (2nd edn., Beirut, Moassasat Alrisalah, 1984)
Al-Sanhury, Abdulrazzq, *The Sources of Truth in the Muslim Fiqh* (1st edn., Beirut, Maktabat Alhalabi Alhoqouqiyah, 1998)
Alshafi'e, Muhammad, *Alrisalah* (1st edn., Beirut, Dar Alkotoub Al Ilmiyah, 2001)
Alwani, Taha, *Source Methodology in Islamic Jurisprudence* (3rd edn., USA, The International Institute of Islamic Thought, 2003)
Alzaylai'e, Al Imam, *Tabeen Alhaqaiq Sharh Kanz Aldaqaiq* (1st edn., Beirut, Dar Alkotoub Alilmiyah, 2000)
Amazu, Asouzu, *International Commercial Arbitration and African States: Practice, Participation, and Institutional Development* (1st edn., UK, Cambridge University Press, 2001)
Am-Na'im, Abdullah, *Toward an Islamic Reformation* (1st edn., USA, Syracuse University Press, 1996)
Ashoush, Ahmad, *The law of the Oil Concessions in the Arab Countries* (1st edn., Cairo, Alsharikah Almuttahidah Lelnashr wa Altawze', 1975)
Bakhashab, Omar, *The Application of the New York Convention for the Recognition and Enforcement of Foreign Arbitral Awards in Saudi Arabia* (1st edn., Saudi Arabia, King Saud University, 2004)
Bearman, Peri, Rudolph Peters and Frank E. Vogel, *The Islamic School of Law: Evolution, Development and Progress* (1st edn., USA, Harvard University Press, 2005)
ben Ahmad ben Hanbal, Salaah, *Sirat Alimam Ahmad ben Hanbal*, ed. Muhammad Alzali (1st edn., Beirut, Almaktab Alislami Lel Tiba'a wa Annashr, 1997)
ben Anas, Malik, *Almuwatt'a*, ed. Muhammad Fouad Abdulbaqi (1st edn., Beirut, Dar Alkotoub Alilmiyah, 2000)
ben Gasim, Abdulrahman, *Hashiyat Alraoud Almourbi' Sharh Zad Almostaqna* (1st edn., Saudi Arabia, Almatba'a Alahliyah Liloffset, 1976)
ben Ismael Albukhari, Abo Abdullah Muhammad, *Aljame' Alsaheeh "Saheeh Albukhari"* (1st edn., Beirut, Dar Aljeel, 2005)
ben Maza, Hossamaddin, *Sharh Adab Alqadi*, ed. Abilwafa Alafgani and Abibakur Alhashimi (1st edn., Beirut, Dar Alkotoub Al Ilmiyah, 1994)
ben Moflih, Muhammad, *Kitab Alforou'* (1st edn., Beirut, Dar Alkotoub Alilmiyah, 2003)

Buckles, Thomas, *Laws of Evidence* (1st edn., USA, Thomson Delmar Learning, 2003)

Carr, Indira and Richard Kinder, *Statutes and Conventions on International Trade Law* (4th edn., London, Cavendish Publishing Limited, 2003)

Collier, J.G., *Conflict of Laws* (3rd edn., Cambridge, Cambridge University Press, 2001)

Coulson, Noel, *Commercial Law in the Gulf States; The Islamic Legal Tradition* (1st edn., London, Graham & Trotman, 1984)

Cranston, Ross, *Principles of Banking Law* (2nd edn., Oxford, Oxford University Press, 2002)

Delong-Bas, Natana, *Wahhabi Islam from Revival and Reform to Global Jihad* (1st edn., USA, Oxford University Press, 2004)

Domenico, Di Pietro, *Enforcement of International Arbitration Awards: The New York Convention of 1958* (1st edn., London, Cameron May, 2001)

El-Dean, B., *Privatisation and the Creation of a Market-Based Legal System: The Case of Egypt* (1st edn., Netherland, Brill Publications, 2002)

El Diwany, Tarek, *The Problem with Interest* (2nd edn., London, Kreatoc Ltd, 2003)

El-Gamal, Mahmoud, *Islamic Finance, Law, Economics and Practice* (1st edn., Cambridge, Cambridge University Press, 2006)

El Sheikh, Fathelrahman, *The Legal Regime of Foreign Private Investment in the Sudan and Saudi Arabia: A Case Study of Developing Countries* (2nd edn., Cambridge, Cambridge University Press, 2003)

Esposito, John, *Islam: The Straight Path* (1st edn., Oxford, Oxford University Press, 1988)

Haddad, Yvonne and Barbara Stowasser, *Islamic Law and the Challenges of Modernity* (1st edn., USA, Altamira Press, 2004)

Hallaq, Wael, *Authority, Continuity, and Change in Islamic Law* (1st edn., Cambridge, Cambridge University Press, 2005)

Hallaq, Wael, *The Origins and Evolution of Islamic Law* (4th edn., Cambridge, Cambridge University Press, 2007)

Harold, J., *Bonaparte in Egypt* (1st edn., London, Hamish Hamilton Publications, 1963)

Hashim, Mahmoud M., *Alqada' wa Nizam Al Ithbat fe Alfiqh Al Islami wa Alnzimah Alwad'iyah* (1st edn., Saudi Arabia, King Saud University, 1988)

Heynman, Stephen, *Islam and Social Policy* (1st edn., USA, Vanderbilt University Press, 2004)

Hitti, Philip, *History of the Arabs* (10th edn., London, Macmillan, 2002)

Holden, David and Richard Johns, *The House of Saud* (1st edn., London, Sedgwick and Jackson, 1981)

Hourani, Albert, *A History of the Arab People* (1st edn., USA, Warner Books, 1991)

Ibn Farhoun, *Tabsirat Alhokkam Fe Usul Alaqdiyah Wa Manahej Alahkam*, ed. Taha Abdulraouf Sa'ad (1st edn., Cairo, Maktabat Alkolliyat Alazhariyah, 1986)

Ibn Nujaim, Zainalabeden, *Albahr Alraeq Sharh Kanz Aldaqaek* (2nd edn., Beirut, Dar Alma'refah, 1993)

Ibn Qayem Aljaoziyah, *Bada'I Alfawaid*, ed. Hisham Ata, Adil Adawi and Ashraf Ahmad (1st edn., Saudi Arabia, Nizar Mustafa Albaz Publishers, 1996)

Ibn Qodamah, M., Almaqdisi, *Almoghni* (1st edn., Cairo, Hajar Publications, 1992)

Ibn Taymiyyah, M., *Majmou' Alfatawa* (2nd edn., Saudi Arabia, The Ministry of Islamic Affairs of Saudi Arabia, 1995)

Ibrahim, Muhammad, *A Critical Analysis of Nizam Alta'n Biltamiz fe Almamlakah Alarabiya Alsaoudia* (1st edn., Saudi Arabia, Institute of Public Administration, 1998)

Iqbal, Zamir and Hirpshi Tsubota, *Emerging Islamic Capital Markets: A Quickening Pace and New Potential* (World Bank Publications, USA, 2006)

Kennett, L., *Suez: The Twice-Fought War* (1st edn., USA, McGraw Hill, 1969)

Lerrick, Alison and Q. Javed Mian, *Saudi Business and Labor Law* (2nd edn., London, Graham & Trotman, 1987)

Lew, J.D.M., L.A. Mistelis and S. Kröll, *Comparative International Commercial Arbitration* (1st edn., Netherland, Kluwer Law International, 2003)

Mahmood, Saiyed, *Arbitration Rules: A Comparative Study between Shari'a, Kuwaiti and Egyptian Law* (1st edn., Cairo, Aleman Publishers, 2000)

Mahmoud, Saiyed, *Arbitration Codes: Comparative Study between the Arbitration Codes of Saudi Arabia, Kuwait and Egypt* (2nd edn., Cairo, Dar Alkotob Alqanoniyah, 2007)

Maugeri, Leonardo, *The Age of Oil: The Methodology, History, and Future of the World's Most Controversial Resource* (1st edn., Greenwood Publishing Group, 2006)

Miller, David, *Search for Security: Saudi Arabian Oil and American Foreign Policy, 1939–1948* (1st edn., USA, University of North Carolina Press, 1980)

Ministry of Justice of Saudi Arabia, *Litigation in Saudi Arabia: History, Institutions and Principles* (1st edn., Saudi Arabia, Ministry of Justice, 1999)

Mitha, Farouk, *Algazali and the Ismailis: A Debate on Reasoning and Authority in Medieval Islam* (1st edn., London, Institute of Ismaili Studies, 2001)

Motki, Harold, *The Origins of Islamic Jurisprudence: Meccan Fiqh before the Classical Schools* (1st edn., Brill Publications, Netherland, 2002)

Nasir, Jamal, *The Islamic Law of Personal Status* (2nd edn., London, Graham & Trotman, 1990)

Pearl, David, *A Text Book on Muslim Law* (1st edn., London, Croom Helm, 1979)

Peters, Rudolph, *Crimes and Punishment in Islamic Law* (1st edn., Cambridge University Press, Cambridge, 2005)

Quandt, William, *Saudi Arabia in the 1980s: Foreign Policy, Security, and Oil* (1st edn., USA, Brookings Institution, 1981)

Ramadan, Hisham, *Understanding Islamic Law from Classical to Contemporary* (1st edn., USA, Alta Mira Press, 2006)
Ramadan, Saiyed, *Islamic Law, its Scope and Equity* (1st edn., London, Macmillan, 1960)
Redfern, Alan and Martin Hunter, *Law and Practice of International Commercial Arbitration* (3rd edn., London, Sweet and Maxwell, 2003)
Reed, Lucy, Jan Paulsson and Nigel Blackaby, *Guide to ICSID Arbitration* (1st edn., Netherland, Kluwer Law International, 2004)
Rosen, Lawrence, *The Justice of Islam: Comparative Perspectives on Islamic Law and Society* (1st edn., Oxford, Oxford University Press, 2000)
Saeed, Abdullah, *Islamic Banking and Interest* (2nd edn., Netherlands, Brill Publishers, 1999)
Saeed, Abdullah, *Islamic Banking and Interest: A Study of the Prohibition of Riba and its Contemporary Interpretation* (2nd edn., Netherland, Brill Publisher, 1999)
Sa'ied, Ameen, *The History of the Saudi State* (1st edn., Saudi Arabia, Darat Almalik Abdul-Aziz, 1973)
Sami, Fawzi, *International Commercial Arbitration in Arab Countries* (1st edn., Amman, Dar Althaqafa lil Nashr wa Altaouze', 2006)
Samir, Saleh, *Commercial Arbitration in the Arab Middle East: A Study in Shari'a and Statute Law* (1st edn., London, Graham & Trotman, 1984)
Samir, Saleh, *Commercial Arbitration in the Arab Middle East: Shari'a, Syria, Lebanon and Egypt* (2nd edn., Heart Publishing, 2006)
Samuel, Geoffrey, *Contract Law: Cases and Materials* (1st edn., London, Sweet and Maxwell, 2007)
Schabler, B., L. Stenberg and R. Mottahereh, *Globalization and the Muslim World* (1st edn., USA, Syracuse University Press, 2004)
Shoult, Anthony, *Doing Business with Saudi Arabia* (3rd edn., London, GMB Publishing Ltd, 2006)
Skovgaard-Petersen, Jakob, *Defining Islam for the Egyptian State: Mufti and Fatwas of the Dar al-Ifta* (1st edn., Netherland, Brill Publishers, 1997)
Spiro, David, *The Hidden Hand of American Hegemony: Petrodollar Recycling and International Markets* (1st edn., USA, Cornell University Publications, 1999)
Taher Kurdi, Muhammad, *Altareekh Alqaweem Le Mecca Wa Bait Allah Alkareem* (1st edn., Saudi Arabia, Albaz Publications, 1962)
Tweeddale, Andrew, *Arbitration of Commercial Disputes: International and English Law and Practice* (1st edn., Oxford, Oxford University Press, 2007)
Vitalis, Robert, *American's Kingdom: Mythmaking on the Saudi Oil Frontier* (1st edn., USA, Stamford University Press, 2007)
Vogel, Frank, *Islamic Law and Legal System* (1st edn., Netherland, Brill, 1999)
Vogel, Frank and Samuel Hayes, *Islamic Law and Finance: Religion, Risk and Return* (1st edn., Kluwer Law International, Netherlands, 1998)

Weiler, Todd, *International Investment Law and Arbitration: Leading Cases from ICSID, NAFTA, Bilateral Treaties and Customary International Law* (1st edn., London, Cameron May, 2005)

Journal Articles and Periodicals

Abd-Alhaqq, Irshad, 'Islamic Law; An Overview of its Origin and Elements', *Journal of Islamic Law*, 1/1 (1996), pp. 26–31

Abd-Alhaqq, Irshad, 'Legal Injunctions of the Quran', *Journal of Islamic Law*, 2 (1997), pp. 53–64

Abd-Alhaqq, Irshad, 'Islamic Law: An Overview of its Origin and Elements', *Journal of Islamic Law and Culture*, 7/1 (2002), pp. 27–54

Affaki, Bachir G., 'Demand Guarantees in the Arab Middle East', *Journal of International Banking Law*, 12 (1997), pp. 271–76

Aggarwal, Rajesh K. and Tarik Yousef, 'Islamic Banks and Investment Financing', *Journal of Money, Credit and Banking*, 32/1 (February 2000), pp. 93–120

Alameldin, Mohieldin I., 'Banking Disputes in Saudi Arabia', *International Financial Law Review*, 10 (1991), pp. 36–38

Al-Baharna, Husain M., 'International Commercial Arbitration in Perspective', *Arab Law Quarterly*, 3 (1988), pp. 3–18

Al-Bashir, Muhammad and Muhammad Al-Amine, 'Istisna' and its Application in Islamic Banking', *Arab Law Quarterly*, 16 (2001), pp. 22–48

Algari, Ibrahim H., 'The Formation of the Contract in Islamic Shari'a', *Ministry of Justice of Saudi Arabia Journal*, 11 (2001), pp. 1–13

Al-Ghadyan, Ahmed A., 'The Judiciary in Saudi Arabia', *Arab Law Quarterly*, 13 (1998), pp. 235–51

Alhammad, Hammad A., 'Wakalah Contract in Shari'a and its Applications in the Saudi Law', *Al-Adl Journal*, 23 (2005), pp. 129–66

Alhamoud, Ibrahim, 'Conciliation in Commercial Disputes and its Applications'. A paper represented at the Conference on arbitration and Conciliation, Taif, Saudi Arabia (15-16/05/1424 H. 2004)

Aljofan, Nasir M., 'Publicity of Court Proceedings in Saudi Arabia', *Al-Adl Journal*, 5 (2000), pp. 10–38

Aljuhani, Eid M., 'The New Saudi Arbitration Act', *Riyadh Chamber of Commerce and Industry Magazine*, 1 (1985), pp. 22–30

Al-Jumah, Khaled M., 'Arab State Contract Disputes: Lessons from the Past', *Arab Law Quarterly*, 17 (2002), pp. 215–40

Al-Kenain, Abdullah, 'Tadween Almorafa'a Alqadaiyah', *Al-Adl Journal*, 2 (1999), pp. 76–115

Alkhadimi, Nooraddin M., 'Makasid Altashree': Mafhomha, Daroratha, Thawabetoha', *Al-Adl Journal*, 6 (2000), pp. 1–27

Alkhenain, Abdullah M., 'Contracts Involving Uncertainty', *Al-Adl Journal*, 13 (2002), pp. 170–73

Al-Masri, Rafic Y., 'Are all Forms of Interest Prohibited?', *King Abdul-Aziz University Journal of Islamic Economics*, 17/1 (2004), pp. 37–41
Al-Muhairi, Butti, 'Islamisation and Modernisation within the UAE Penal Law: Shari'a in the Pre-modern Period', *Arab Law Quarterly*, 10 (1995), pp. 287–309
Al-Muhairi, Butti, 'The Position of Shari'a within the UAE Constitution and the Federal Supreme Court's Application of the Constitutional Clause concerning Shari'a', *Arab Law Quarterly*, 11 (1996), pp. 219–44
Alonaizan, Tameem, 'Conciliation Before and After the Death of the Victim', *Al-Adl Journal*, 7 (2000), pp. 1–29
Aloraini, Ahmad, 'Conciliation in Criminal Matters', *Al-Adl Journal*, 8 (2001), pp. 1–23
Alqurashi, Zeyad, 'Arbitration under the Islamic Shari'a', *Oil, Gas and Energy Intelligence*, 1/2 (March 2003), pp. 30–44
Alroshoud, Ksaled S., 'Altahkeem Altijari fe Almamlakah Alarabiya Alsaudia wa Tatbiqatoh fe Alqada'', *Al-Adl Journal*, 52 (2004), pp. 52–85
Al-Samman, Yahiya, 'The Settlement of Foreign Investment Disputes by Means of Domestic Arbitration in Saudi Arabia', *Arab Law Quarterly*, 9 (1994), pp. 217–20
Alwethainani, Khalid Z., 'Securities Pledging in Shari'a', *Al-Adl Journal*, 28 (2006), pp. 86–122
Ambrose, Clare, 'Arbitration and the Free Movement of Judgments', *Arbitration International*, 19/1 (2003), pp. 3–27
Amin, S.H., 'An Islamic Approach to International Commercial Arbitration', *Journal of Islamic Law*, 1 (1996), pp. 203–36
Angell, Nicholas B., and Gray R. Feulner, 'Arbitration of Disputes in the United Arab Emirates', *Arab Law Quarterly*, 3 (1988), pp. 19–32
Arab, Hassan, 'Execution of Foreign Judgments in the UAE', *Arab Law Quarterly*, 17 (2002), pp. 208–11
Arabi, Oussama, 'Contract Stipulations (Shurut) in Islamic Law: The Ottoman Majalla and Ibn Taymiyya', *International Journal of Middle East Studies*, 30/1 (February 1998), pp. 29–50
Arabi, Oussama, 'Orienting the Gaze: Marcel Morand and the Codification of Le Droit Musulman Algerien', *Journal of Islamic Studies*, 11/1 (2000), pp. 43–72
Arrawi, Abduljalil, 'Principles of the Islamic Law on Contracts', *George Washington Law Review*, 36 (1953), pp. 32–36
Baamir, Abdulrahman, 'Issues of Disclosure and Transparency in the Saudi Stock Market', *Arab Law Quarterly*, 22 (2008), pp. 63–87
Baamir, Abdulrahman and Ilias Bantekas, 'Saudi Law as *Lex Arbitri*: Evaluation of Saudi Arbitration Law and Judicial Practice', *Arbitration International*, 25/2 (2009), pp. 239–70
Bakhashab, Omar, 'Extraterritoriality in the Saudi Arbitration Act', *King Abdul-Aziz University Journal*, 14/1 (2000), pp. 152–64

Ballantyne, W.M., 'Arbitration in the Gulf States: "Delocalisation": A Short Comparative Study', *Arab Law Quarterly*, 1 (1985–1986), pp. 205–15

Ballantyne, W.M., 'The States of the GCC: Sources of Law. The Shari'a and the Extent to which it Applies', *Arab Law Quarterly*, 3 (1986), pp. 1–18

Ballantyne, W.M., 'Syndicated Loans', *Arab Law Quarterly*, 11 (1996), pp. 372–82

Berger, Klaus P., 'International Arbitral Practice and the UNIDROIT Principles of International Commercial Contracts', *American Journal of Comparative Law*, 46 (1998), pp. 129–50

Berger, Maurits S., 'Conflicts of Law and Public Policy in Egyptian Family Law: Islamic Law through the Backdoor', *American Journal of Comparative Law*, 50 (2002), pp. 555–94

Blanchard, Christopher M., 'The Islamic Tradition of Wahhabism and Salafiyya', *Congressional Research Service Report for Congress*, submitted on (17/01/2007). Available online at <http://www.fas.org/sgp/crs/misc/RS21695.pdf> [accessed 17 July 2009]

Boshoff, L.L., 'Saudi Arabia: Arbitration vs. Litigation', *Arab Law Quarterly*, 1 (1985–1986), pp. 299–311

Brand, Joseph L., 'Aspects of Saudi Arabian Law and Practice', *Boston College International and Comparative Law Review*, 9/1 (1986), pp. 1–46

Brower, Charles N. and Jeremy K. Sharpe, 'International Commercial Arbitration and the Islamic World: The Third Phase', *American Journal of International Law*, 97 (2003), pp. 643–56

Brown, Nathan J., 'Sharia and State in the Modern Muslim Middle East', *International Journal of Middle East Studies*, 29/3 (August 1997), pp. 359–76

Busse, Daniel, 'Privity to an Arbitration Agreement', *International Arbitration Law Review*, 8/3 (2005), pp. 95–102

Carballo, Alejandro, 'The Law of the Dubai International Financial Centre: Common Law Oasis or Mirage within the UAE?', *Arab Law Quarterly*, 21 (2007), pp. 91–104

Carbonneau, Thomas E., 'The Ballad of Transborder Arbitration', *University of Miami Law Review*, 56/4 (July 2002), pp. 773–830

Childress, Carol L., 'Saudi Arabian Contract Law: A Comparative Perspective', *St Thomas Law Forum*, 2 (1990), pp. 69–96

Chsenwald, W.O., 'Saudi Arabia and the Islamic Revival', *International Journal for Middle East Studies*, 13 (1981), pp. 271–72

Clinton, Robert L., 'Game Theory, Legal History, and the Origins of Judicial Review: A Revisionist Analysis of *Marbury v. Madison*', *American Journal of Political Science*, 38/2 (May 1994), pp. 285–302

Comair-Obeid, Nayla, 'Particularity of the Contract's Subject Matter in the Law of the Arab Middle East', *Arab Law Quarterly*, 11 (1996), pp. 331–49

Contini, Paolo, 'International Commercial Arbitration: The United Nations Convention on the Recognition and Enforcement of Foreign Arbitral Awards', *American Journal of Comparative Law*, 8 (1959), pp. 283–309

Delaume, George, 'State Contracts and Transnational Arbitration', *American Journal of International Law*, 75 (1981), pp. 784–819

Delaume, Georges R., 'ICSID Arbitration and the Courts', *American Journal of International Law*, 77/4 (1983), pp. 784–803

Dimitrakopoulos, Antonios, 'Arbitration Practice in the UAE', *Arab Law Quarterly*, 16 (2001), pp. 389–403

Diwan, Ricky H., 'Problems Associated with the Enforcement of Arbitral Awards', *Arbitration International*, 19/1 (2003), pp. 55–67

Duguid, Stephen, 'A Biographical Approach to the Study of Social Change in the Middle East: Abdullah Tariki as a New Man', *International Journal of Middle East Studies*, 1/3 (1970), pp. 195–220

El-Malik, El-Walied M., 'Minerals Investment under Shari'a Law', *Arab Law Quarterly*, 6 (1993), pp. 106–40

El Mallakh, R., 'Challenge of Affluence: Abu Dhabi', *Middle East Journal*, 24/2 (1970), pp. 135–38

Fadel, Hossam, 'The Islamic Viewpoint on New Assisted Reproductive Technology', *Fordham Urban Law Journal*, 30 (2002), pp. 148–50

Farhad, Noman, 'The Problem of Interest and Islamic Banking in a Comparative Perspective: The Case of Egypt, Iran and Pakistan', *Review of Middle East Economics and Finance*, 1/1 (2003), pp. 37–70

Ford, Christopher A., 'Siyar-ization and its Discontent: International Law and Islam's Constitutional Crisis', *Texas International Law Journal*, 30 (1995), pp. 499–533

Franck, Susan, 'The Liability of International Arbitrators: A Comparative Analysis and Proposal for Qualified Immunity', *New York Law School Journal of International and Comparative Law*, 20/1 (2000), pp. 1–59

Franck, Susan, 'The Legitimacy Crisis in Investment Treaty Arbitration: Privatizing Public International Law through Inconsistent Decisions', *Fordham Law Journal*, 73 (2005), pp. 1521–1625

Freeman Jalet, Frances T., 'Judicial Review of Arbitration: The Judicial Attitude', *Cornell Law Quarterly*, 45 (1959–1960), pp. 519–57

Gaupp, Dirk, 'A Brief Overview of Secular Turkey's Framework for Islamic Banking and Finance Transactions: Basis for Big Business or Negligible Side Issue?', *Journal of International Banking Law and Regulation*, 23/2 (2008), pp. 90–95

Gotanda, John Y., 'Awarding Interest in International Arbitration', *American Journal of International Law*, 90/1 (January 1996), pp. 40–63

Habachy, Saba, 'Property, Right, and Contract in Muslim Law', *Columbia Law Review*, 62 (1962), pp. 450–73

Habachy, Saba, 'Commentary on the Decision of the Supreme Court of Egypt given on 4 May 1985 Concerning the Legitimacy of Interest and the Constitutionality of Article 226 of the New Egyptian Civil Code of 1948', *Arab Law Quarterly*, 1 (1985), pp. 239–41

Haberbeck, Andreas, 'Risk Sharing in an Islamic Society', *Arab Law Quarterly*, 2 (1987), pp. 138–47.

Hallaq, Wael B., 'On the Origins of the Controversy about the Existence of Mujtahids and the Gate of Ijtihad', *Studia Islamica*, 63 (1986), pp. 129–44

Hamid, M.E., 'Islamic Law of Contract or Contracts', *Journal of Islamic and Comparative Law*, 3 (1969), pp. 1–11

Hammad, Nazeeh, 'Adhesion Contracts in the Islamic Jurisprudence', *Al-Adl Journal*, 24 (2005), pp. 51–78

Hammad, Nazeeh, 'The Law on the Case of More than Multi Obligations in the Contract', *Al-Adl Journal*, 27 (2006), pp. 74–108

Hanson, Maren, 'The Influence of French Law on the Legal Development of Saudi Arabia', *Arab Law Quarterly*, 2 (1987), pp. 272–91

Hassan, Hussein, 'Contracts In Islamic Law: The Principles of Commutative Justice and Liberality', *Journal of Islamic Studies*, 13/3 (2002), pp. 257–97

Hoyt, Mont P. and R. Doak Bishop, 'International Dispute Resolution: Drafting Mediation, Choice of Forum and Arbitration Clauses', *International Energy Law & Taxation Review*, 1 (2000), pp. 7–15

Hurvitz, Nimrod, 'Schools of Law and Historical Context: Re-Examining the Formation of the Hanbali Madhhab', *Journal of Islamic Law and Society*, 7/1 (2000), pp. 37–64

Jobst, Andreas A., 'Derivatives in Islamic Finance', *Journal of Islamic Economic Studies*, 15/1 (2007), pp. 1–32

Jobst, Andreas A., 'The Economics of Islamic Finance and Securitization', *Journal of Structured Finance*, 13/1 (2007), pp. 1–35

Kahn-Freund, O., 'On Uses and Misuses of Comparative Law', *Modern Law Review*, 37/1 (1974), 1–27

Karakayali, Nedim, 'The Uses of the Stranger: Circulation, Arbitration, Secrecy, and Dirt', *Sociological Theory*, 24/4 (December 2006), pp. 312–30

Karl, D.J., 'Islamic Law in Saudi Arabia: What Foreign Attorneys Should Know', *Geo Wash J Intl Law & Economics*, 25 (1991), pp. 131–70

Kelly, J.B., 'The Buraimi Oasis Dispute', *Journal of International Affairs*, 32/3 (July 1956), pp. 318–24

Khan, Hamid M., 'Nothing is Written: Fundamentalism, Revivalism, Reformism and the Fate of Islamic Law', *Michigan Journal of International Law*, 24 (2002–2003), pp. 273–345

Kissam, Leo T. and Edmond K. Leach, 'Sovereign Expropriation of Property and Abrogation of Concession Contracts', *Fordham Law Review*, 28 (1959–1960), pp. 177–200

Koraytem, Thabet, 'The Islamic Nature of the Saudi Regulations for Companies', *Arab Law Quarterly*, 15 (2000), pp. 63–69

Kreindler, Richard H., 'An Overview of the Arbitration Rules of the Recently Established GCC Commercial Arbitration Centre, Bahrain', *Arab Law Quarterly*, 12 (1997), pp. 3–25

Kula, Erhun, 'Is Contemporary Interest Rate in Conflict with Islamic Ethics?', *Kyklos International Review for Social Sciences*, 61/1 (2008), pp. 45–49

Kutty, Faisal, 'The Shari'a Factor in International Commercial Arbitration', *Loyola of Los Angeles International and Comparative Law Review*, 28 (2006), pp. 565–624

Kwan, James and Emma Teale, 'Arbitration in the United Arab Emirates: The Traps, the Tricks and Tips for the Unwary', *International Arbitration Law Review*, 9/4 (2006), pp. 95–99

Lalive, Jean-Flavien, 'Recent Version: Abrogation or Alteration of an Economic Development Agreement between a State and a Private Foreign Party', *The Business Lawyer*, 17 (1961–1962), pp. 434–68

Lalive, Jean-Flavien, 'Contracts between a State or a State Agency and a Foreign Company. Theory and Practice: Choice of Law and a New Arbitration Case', *International and Comparative Law Quarterly*, 18 (July 1964), pp. 987–1021

Layish, Aharon, 'Saudi Arabian Legal Reform as a Mechanism to Moderate Wahhabi Doctrine', *Journal of the American Oriental Society*, 107/2 (April–June 1987), pp. 279–92

Lombardi, Clark B. and Nathan J. Brown, 'Do Constitutions Requiring Adherence to Shari'a Threaten Human Rights? How Egypt's Constitutional Court Reconciles Islamic Law with the Liberal Rule of Law', *American University International Law Review*, 21 (2006), pp. 379–436

Looney, Robert, 'Development Strategies for Saudi Arabia: Escaping the Rentier State Syndrome', *Strategic Insights*, 3/3 (March 2004). Available online at <http://www.ccc.nps.navy.mil/si/2004/mar/looneyMar04.pdf> [accessed 10 May 2009]

Mahassni, Hassan, and Neal F. Grenley, 'Public Sector Dispute Resolution in Saudi Arabia: Procedures and Practices of Saudi Arabia's Administrative Court', *The International Lawyer*, 21/3 (1987), pp. 827–44

Makdisi, John, 'Legal Logic and Equity in Islamic Law', *American Journal of Comparative Law*, 33 (1985), pp. 63–78

Mallat, Chibli, 'Commercial Law in the Middle East: Between Classical Transactions and Modern Business', *American Journal of Comparative Law*, 48 (2000), pp. 81–142

Mallat, Chibli, 'From Islamic to Middle Eastern Law: A Restatement of the Field (part 1)', *American Journal of Comparative Law*, 51 (2003), pp. 699–719

Mallat, Chibli, 'From Islamic to Middle Eastern Law: A Restatement of the Field (part 2)', *American Journal of Comparative Law*, 52 (2004), pp. 209–86

McMillen, Michael J.T., 'Islamic Shari'ah-Compliant Project Finance: Collateral Security and Financing Structure Case Study', *Fordham International Law Journal*, 24 (2000–2001), pp. 1184–1263

Messick, Brinkley, 'The Mufti, the Text and the World: Legal Interpretation in Yemen', *Man, New Series*, 21/1 (1986), pp. 102–19

Meyer-Reumann, Rolf, 'The Banking System in Saudi Arabia', *Arab Law Quarterly*, 10 (1995), pp. 207–37

Mistelis, Loukas, 'Regulatory Aspects: Globalization, Harmonization, Legal Transplants, and Law Reform – Some Fundamental Observations', *The International Lawyer*, 34 (2000), pp. 1055–1070

Mohd, Habib and Sharif Al-Mulla, 'Conventions of Enforcement of Foreign Judgments in the Arab States', *Arab Law Quarterly*, 14 (1999), pp. 33–56.

Moore, Michael M., 'International Arbitration between States and Foreign Investors – The World Bank Convention', *Stanford Law Review*, 18 (1965–1966), pp. 1359–80

Nerz, Alexander, 'The Structuring of an Arbitration Clause in a Contract with a Saudi Party', *Arab Law Quarterly*, 1 (1985–1986), pp. 380–87

Noor, Mohammed, 'Principles of Islamic Contract Law', *Journal of Law and Religion*, 6 (1988), pp. 115–30

Noorzoy, M. Siddieq, 'Islamic Laws on Riba (Interest) and their Economic Implications', *International Journal of Middle East Studies*, 14/1 (February 1982), pp. 3–17

Obeid, Comair, 'Particularity of the Contract's Subject-Matter in the Laws of the Arab Middle East', *Arab Law Quarterly*, 11 (1996), pp. 331–36

Ochsenwald, William, 'Saudi Arabia and the Islamic Revival', *International Journal of Middle East Studies*, 13/3 (August 1981), pp. 271–86

Paul, Michell M., 'Arbitrability of Copyright Disputes: *Desputeaux v. Les Editions Choutte*. (Comments)', *Canadian Business Law Journal*, 38 (2003), pp. 125–49

Peters Hamlin, Kristan L., 'The Impact of Islamic Revivalism on Contract and Usury Law in Iran, Saudi Arabia, and Egypt', *Texas International Law Journal*, 22 (1987), pp. 352–79

Ragib, Wajdi, 'Is Arbitration a type of Litigation?', *University of Kuwait Law Journal*, 17/1 (1993), pp. 131–72

Roy, Kristin T., 'The New York Convention and Saudi Arabia: Can a Country use the Public Policy Defence to Refuse Enforcement of Non-Domestic Arbitral Awards?', *Fordham International Law Journal*, 18 (1994–1995), pp. 920–26

Rutledge, Peter B., 'Toward a Contractual Approach for Arbitral Immunity', *Georgian Law Review*, 39 (2004–2005), pp. 151–214

Saeed, Abdullah, 'Ijtihād and Innovation in Neo-Modernist Islamic Thought in Indonesia', *Islam and Christian-Muslim Relations*, 8/3 (1997), pp. 279–95

Saleh, Nabil, 'The Law Governing Contracts in Arabia', *International and Comparative Law Quarterly*, 38 (1989), pp. 761–87

Saleh, Nabil, 'Definition and Formation of Contract under Islamic and Arab Laws', *Arab Law Quarterly*, 5 (1990), pp. 101–16

Saleh, Samir, 'The Recognition and Enforcement of Foreign Arbitral Awards in the States of the Arab Middle East', *Arab Law Quarterly*, 1 (1985–1986), pp. 19–31

Sayen, George, 'Arbitration, Conciliation and the Islamic Legal Tradition in Saudi Arabia', *University of Pennsylvania Journal of International Business Law*, 9/2 (1987), pp. 211–27

Schacht, Joseph, 'Islamic Law in Contemporary States', *American Journal of Comparative Law*, 8 (1959), pp. 133–36

Schacht, Joseph, 'Problems of Modern Islamic Legislation', *Studia Islamica*, 12 (1960), pp. 99–129

Schwebel, Stephen M. and J. Gillis Wetter, 'Arbitration and the Exhaustion of the Local Remedies', *American Journal of International Law*, 60 (1966), pp. 484–501

Seriki, Hakeem, 'Substantive or Procedural: An Arbitration Perspective', *International Arbitration Law Review*, 9/1 (2006), pp. 24–32

Sfeir, George, 'The Saudi Approach to Law Reform', *American Journal of Comparative Law*, 36 (1988), pp. 729–44

Sfeir, George N., 'An Islamic Conseil D'Etat: Saudi Arabia Board of Grievances', *Arab Law Quarterly*, 4 (1989), pp. 128–37

Shackleton, Stewart R., 'Annual Review of English Judicial Decisions on Arbitration – 2000', *International Arbitration Law Review*, 4/6 (2001), pp. 178–201

Shackleton, Stewart R., 'Annual Review of English Judicial Decisions on Arbitration – 2002', *International Arbitration Law Review*, 6/6 (2003), pp. 220–36

Shepard, William E., 'Islam and Ideology: Towards a Typology', *International Journal of Middle East Studies*, 19/3 (August 1987), pp. 307–35

Shihata, Ibrahim F., 'Some Trends in Banking Law and their Relevance to the GCC States', *Arab Law Quarterly*, 13 (1998), pp. 303–35

Siddiqi, Mohammad N., 'Riba, Bank Interest and the Rationale of its Prohibition', Visiting Scholars' Research Series, No. 2, Islamic Development Bank, Jeddah, Saudi Arabia (2004)

Sole, Juan, 'Introducing Islamic Banking into Conventional Banking System', IMF Working Paper No. WP/07/175, International Monetary Fund (2007)

Sylla, Richard, 'Financial Systems and Economic Modernization', *Journal of Economic History*, 62 (2002), pp. 277–92

Tamimi, Hind, 'Interest under the UAE Law and as Applied by the Courts of Abu Dhabi', *Arab Law Quarterly*, 17 (2002), pp. 50–52

Tavender QC, E.D.D., 'Considerations of Fairness in the Context of International Commercial Arbitrations', *Alberta Law Review*, 34/3 (1996), pp. 509–45

Taylor, J. Michael, 'Islamic Commercial Banking – Moving into the Mainstream?', *The Transnational Lawyer*, 18 (2004–2005), pp. 417–30

Time Magazine, 'Time Clock', 15 February 1954

Truck, Nancy B., 'Resolution of Disputes in Saudi Arabia', *Arab Law Quarterly*, 6 (1991), pp. 6–32

Umm Alqura Gazette, issue No. 64 dated 5/9/1344 H (1926)

Umm Alqura Gazette, issue No. 140 dated 21/02/1346 H (1927)

Umm Alqura Gazette, issue No. 143 dated 13/03/1346(1927)

Umm Alqura Gazette, issue No. 144 dated 20/03/1346 (1927)

Umm Alqura Gazette, issue No. 374 dated 22/03/1350 H. (1931)

Umm Alqura Gazette, issue No. 375 dated 22/03/1350 H. (1931)
Umm Alqura Gazette, issue No. 376 dated 22/03/1350 H. (1931)
Umm Alqura Gazette, issue No. 1698 dated 06/06/1377 H. (1957)
Umm Alqura Gazette, issue No. 2010 dated 15/10/1383 H. (1963)
Umm Alqura Gazette, issue No. 2010 dated 15/10/1383 H. (1963)
Umm Alqura Gazette, issue No. 2126 dated 05/03/1386 H. (1966)
Umm Alqura Gazette, issue No. 2969 dated 22/08/1403 H (1983)
Umm Alqura Gazette, issue No. 3069 dated 10/10/1405 H (1985)
Umm Alqura Gazette, issue No. 3397 dated 02/09/1412 H. (1992)
Umm Alqura Gazette, issue No. 3811 dated 17/06/1421 (2000)
Umm Alqura Gazette, issue No. 3867 dated 17/08/1422 H. (2001)
Umm Alqura Gazette, issue No. 3981 dated 07/01/1425 H. (2004)
Umm Alqura Gazette, issue No. 3990 dated 15/03/1425 H. (04/05/2005)
Umm Alqura Gazette, issue No. 4170 dated 30/09/1428 H. (2007)
Weiss, Bernard, 'Interpretation in Islamic Law: The Theory of Ijtihad', *American Journal of Comparative Law*, 26 (1977–1978), pp. 199–212
White, Robin C.A., 'Expropriation of the Libyan Oil Concessions: Two Conflicting International Arbitrations', *International and Comparative Law Quarterly*, 30 (1981), pp. 1–19
Wohidulislam, Muhammad, 'Dissolution of Contract in Islamic Law', *Arab Law Quarterly*, 13 (1998), pp. 336–68
World Trade Organization, 'Report of the Working Party on the Accession of the Kingdom of Saudi Arabia to the World Trade Organization' (WT/ACC/SAU/61, 1 November 2005)
Zahraa, Mahdi, 'The Legal Capacity of Women in Islamic Law', *Arab Law Quarterly*, 11 (1996), pp. 245–63
Zahraa, Mahdi, 'Negotiating Contracts in Islamic and Middle Eastern Law', *Arab Law Quarterly*, 13 (1998), pp. 265–77

Electronic References

HeinOnline, <www.heinonline.org> [accessed 17 July 2009]
Ibn Hisham, *Seerat Ibn Hisham* (Ministry of Islamic Affairs, Saudi Arabia), <www.al-islam.com> [accessed 21 May 2009]
Jstore, <www.jstore.org> [accessed 11 July 2009]
King Fahd Complex for the Printing of the Holy Quran, <www.qurancomplex.org> [accessed 12 July 2009]
LexisNexis, <www.lexisnexis.co.uk> [accessed 26 April 2009]
Ministry of Commerce and Industry, Saudi Arabia, <www.commerce.gov.sa> [accessed 27 January 2009]
Ministry of Finance, Saudi Arabia, <www.mof.gov.sa> [accessed 1 April 2009]
Ministry of Islamic Affairs, Saudi Arabia, <www.al-islam.com> [accessed 12 June 2009]

Ministry of Justice, Saudi Arabia, <www.moj.gov.sa> [accessed 5 July 2009]
Ministry of Petroleum and Mineral wealth, Saudi Arabia, <www.mopm.gov.sa> [accessed 26 November 2008]
Saudi Arabian Oil Company, <www.saudiaramco.com> [accessed 18 September 2008]
Saudi Aramco, <www.aramco.com> [accessed 18 April 2008]
Saudi Lawyers, <www.mohamoon-ksa.com> [accessed 11 June 2009]
The Federal Bureau of Investigation (FBI), USA, <www.fbi.gov> [accessed 26 February 2009]
The GCC Commercial Arbitration Centre, <www.gcac.biz/en> [accessed 30 April 2008]
The International Centre for Settlement of Investment Disputes (ICSID), <www.worldbank.org/icsid> [accessed 26 April 2009]
The International Chamber of Commerce, <www.iccwbo.org> [accessed 14 July 2009]
The Legal Database of the Gulf Cooperation Council, <www.gcc-legal.org> [accessed 5 January 2009]
The Saudi Arabia General Investment Agency (SAGIA), <www.sagia.gov.sa> [accessed 14 June 2009]
The Saudi Arabian Monetary Agency, <www.sama.gov.sa> [accessed 8 June 2009]
The Supreme Constitutional Court, Egypt, <www.hccourt.gov.eg> [accessed 14 July 2008]
The US Department of State, USA, <www.state.gov> [accessed 1 May 2009]
Westlaw, <www.westlaw.co.uk> [accessed 15 July 2009]
World Trade Organization (WTO), <www.wto.org> [accessed 11 October 2008]

Index

For Product Safety Concerns and Information please contact our EU representative GPSR@taylorandfrancis.com
Taylor & Francis Verlag GmbH, Kaufingerstraße 24, 80331 München, Germany

www.ingramcontent.com/pod-product-compliance
Ingram Content Group UK Ltd.
Pitfield, Milton Keynes, MK11 3LW, UK
UKHW020008200926
475702UK00015B/2539

* 9 7 8 1 1 3 8 2 7 7 0 6 9 *